OVER HERE, OVER THERE

☆   ☆   ☆

OVER HERE,

The Andrews Sisters and the

OVER THERE

USO Stars in World War II

☆   ☆   ☆

Maxene Andrews and Bill Gilbert

ZEBRA BOOKS
KENSINGTON PUBLISHING CORP.

Some material obtained from USO Historical Archives
World USO
601 Indiana Ave., NW
Washington, DC 20004

Brief quotations from HOME AWAY FROM HOME by Julia M.H. Carson. Copyright, 1946 by Julia M.H. Carson. Copyright renewed © 1974 by Julia M.H. Carson. HarperCollins Publishers.

ZEBRA BOOKS are published by

Kensington Publishing Corp.
475 Park Avenue South
New York, NY 10016

Copyright © 1993 by Maxene Andrews and Bill Gilbert

Library of Congress Catalog Number: 93-077351
ISBN 0-8217-4117-9

First Printing: June, 1993
Printed in the United States of America

To Patty and LaVerne With Love

And

To the GI Audiences of Each of America's Wars

CONTENTS

AUTHORS' NOTE

When we began talking more than a year ago about writing this book, we were convinced of two things: it is a story that should be told for the present generations and preserved for future ones, and fifty years later seemed to be exactly the right time to do it.

This book represents our best efforts to tell the reader about this unique chapter in American history and in the history of show business, told by the entertainers who lived those four years themselves. In our thank-you's, the reader will see the long list of those who shared their experiences with us, enabling us to tell the story in first-person, we-were-there accounts.

World War II was a time when Americans everywhere answered their country's call, to a degree never achieved since and in a unified response that we sustained for almost four years, from the attack on Pearl Harbor until the peace treaty was signed by General MacArthur. Each of us was asked to contribute to what we soon called "the war effort," and we responded in the best way we knew how. Fifteen million of our young men and women served in the armed forces. Those who couldn't for one reason or another found other ways to serve, from acting as air raid wardens to playing baseball to boost the morale of our troops and those on the home front.

Those involved in show business made an enormous contribution of their own, as these pages will document, right from the
beginning of things, and even *before* the start. Bob Hope took
the cast of his radio show to March Field in May 1941, and Billy
Rose began presenting his first "draftee shows" at military bases
in that same month.

In those months *before* the attack on Pearl Harbor, the
brightest stars in Hollywood, the biggest names in the recording
industry, and performers, writers, directors, producers, and
technicians throughout the entertainment field were becoming
involved in the national effort to prepare America for war. When
the unthinkable happened, these people and thousands of others
began writing one of the proudest chapters in the history of the
American people.

This is that story, told in many cases in their own words by
those who served so proudly, willingly, and exhaustively—from
the USO and its leader, Abe Lastfogel, to lesser known performers. Not every member of a USO troupe here or overseas was a
household name. Two of the biggest heroes of all the USO
performers were people most of us never heard of—a dancer
named Gertrude Briefer and an artist named Don Barclay. Her
tap shoes and his pencil and sketch pad were among our mighti-
est weapons.

This book is a history of those times and the men and women
in show business who were a part of them, but it is more than
that. It is also the story of the way we were from 1941 to 1945,
as a nation and as individual Americans, of the awful challenges
we faced, the way our lives changed and how we coped.

This book is also one more thing. It is a tribute—to every
member of the entertainment profession in World War II and to
the American people, over here and over there, in their audiences.

—Maxene Andrews and Bill Gilbert
March 1993

THANK YOU

In writing this history, we conducted extensive research and spoke to many of the performers who entertained our servicemen and women during World War II both at home and overseas. For their memories, we are indebted to:

June Allyson
Jimmie Baker
Milton Berle
Jo Bernier
Kathryn Grayson
Anne Jeffreys
Frances Langford
John Maschio
Ann Miller
George Montgomery
Constance Moore
Patricia Morrison
Fayard Nicholas

Virginia O'Brien
Lou Wills
Margaret Whiting

In addition, others in show business, the USO, and as sources of our research and other essential work deserve our thanks. One person deserves mention before anyone else—Lynda Wells—for her coordination, research, and her considerable knowledge of American popular music and every other phase of show business. Without Lynda, this book would not have happened.

Others whom we are proud and happy to mention include the USO staff, especially Sherry Singer, Kevin McCarthy, Lane Sutton, Sue Brown, and its historian, Teri Tynes; Bob Gregoire, Jean Orme, and Beatrice Ambrose for their historical materials; Lillian Gilbert for her administrative services; Dave Gilbert for his editorial assistance; John Maschio for his information on the Hollywood Victory Caravan; Isabelle Stevenson for her background on New York's Stage Door Canteen; Peter Edwards of Atlas Video of Washington, D.C. and writer/historian Dr. Scott Ellsworth for information from their video cassette series, *V For Victory*; Marcia Ely, producer of the cable television special, *Stars and Stripes* and Eddie Brandt's Saturday Matinee; and Philip Azzollini and Timothy Hunter for information from their extensive collection of articles and other materials about the Andrews Sisters. We'd also like to thank Marc Courtland and Larry Eichler.

Special credit goes to Wallace Exman, our editor at Zebra Books of New York, Laura Shatzkin, Zebra's publicity director, and our agent, Russell Galen, a vice president of the Scott Meredith Literary Agency in New York, for his guidance in our behalf.

—Maxene Andrews and Bill Gilbert

CHAPTER ONE

Pearl Harbor and Cincinnati

There'll be blue birds over
The white cliffs of Dover
Tomorrow when the world is free.
There'll be love and laughter
And peace ever after
Tomorrow, just you wait and see.

Every singer or group began receiving requests to sing *"The White Cliffs of Dover"* immediately after Glenn Miller recorded it in November of 1941. Even servicemen requested it. Jimmie Baker, the leader of one of the Army orchestras in Europe during the war, said it was his band's most requested number. Ray Eberle sang the vocal on the hit record, and Tex Beneke played a solo in the middle on his tenor sax, but their sounds weren't the only reasons the song became a smash.

There was something else: the words and the times. The United States wasn't in the fight yet, but World War II was already more than two years old, and Americans could see what was coming next. Our country was going to be in the war sooner or later—probably sooner. The two Americans, Nat Burton and Walter Kent, who wrote the song, struck a chord deep inside all of us—apprehensive Americans, as well as weary Britishers whose homeland was pounded every day during the London Blitz by Hitler's bombers who had made Dover's famous white cliffs lining the English Channel one of their primary landmarks. Dover, the "Doorway to England," was a small town in southeastern England whose citizens hurried to bomb shelters often several times a day during the Blitz, as Hitler's *Luftwaffe*, sent flights of one hundred and more bombers and fighters over the English Channel to destroy London and everything else in sight.

In 1991, fifty years after LaVerne, Patty, and I first sang that song in those dark days, I made a personal appearance in Clearwater, Florida, and sang many of the World War II songs. Minutes after I finished, a World War II veteran came up to me and said, "I don't know if you think this is a compliment, but to me and my buddies, the Andrews Sisters are synonymous with World War II."

I told him it was one of the nicest compliments we ever had.

All Americans old enough to remember those four special years are proud of what they did to help our country win the worst war in the history of the world. It was a unique time, maybe the four most special years in American history, from the first fears, drama, and grief to what President Franklin Roosevelt correctly predicted to be "the inevitable triumph."

They were years of hardship. The daily papers—and there were so many more of them then—carried a "casualty list" on the front page of the young men reported that day as killed, wounded, or missing in action. All of us recognized a name on that list from time to time. My first shock of the war came when I spotted the name of my first big teenage crush, a boy in Mound, Minnesota, twenty-two miles from Minneapolis, where our family lived. We spent our summers in Mound, where two of our uncles owned a store. When I was thirteen, I met this seventeen-year-old boy who was unquestionably the handsomest man on the face of the earth. He was the first man—he was still a kid, really—from our area to be killed in the war.

Even the families who were spared such awful news suffered the pangs of long separations as husbands, fathers, sons, and boyfriends—not to mention two hundred thousand women—left home "for the duration and six months" to serve in the armed forces. When they did, a new kind of American flag was hung in our living-room windows—a blue star against a white satin background for every member of the family who had gone off to war. The families who later received the grimmest news of all replaced the flag with a new one showing a gold star for the loved one who had given the last full measure of his devotion to his country.

There was something else about those years—a sense of national togetherness that Americans haven't felt for a long time since. Those who call it "America's last popular war" have good reason. Public support for our part in it was almost unanimous, despite irritations and inconveniences like gasoline rationing that limited most drivers to three gallons a week, and the rationing of so many other items like meats and coffee, and the sugar to put in it. Each person was rationed to no more than two and a half pounds of meat per week.

There was an even longer list of items that weren't rationed but were so scarce that they seemed nonexistent, things like nylon stockings. You couldn't buy them anywhere—except maybe on the black market—because they were needed for military clothing and parachutes. Many women began using leg makeup and some drew a penciled line down the back of each leg to look like the "seam" in the "stocking."

The Andrews Sisters couldn't get nylons any more often than anyone else, so we appeared on stage with that makeup on our legs. But we refused to draw the seam down the back, convincing ourselves we looked as if we were wearing seamless hose.

Patty probably would have drawn seams if LaVerne and I had let her, and she might have made them intentionally crooked. Patty was the fun one of the group, the clown who kept us laughing during those endless periods of backstage boredom between shows when we were doing five and six shows a day.

Patty was wonderful. She helped not only LaVerne and me but the rest of the acts in our show and the members of our orchestra keep our sanity. I don't know who helped *her*, but she sure helped *us*.

☆

There were other sides of life on the home front that were scarier—air raid drills, and darkened cities at night, when outdoor lights and neon signs were turned off for the duration. That restriction included the ball of lights above New York's Times Square, which wasn't turned on again until New Year's Eve of 1944, when we knew our victory was only a matter of time.

But if there was a dark side to those trying years, there was a bright side, too—a sense of national unity, *real* togetherness, a feeling so strong, so exhilarating and so unifying that it did more than help the country to survive. It helped us to win the war.

The Andrews Sisters were right in the thick of all this, for the same reason that hundreds of other entertainers were—because we *wanted* to be. We wanted to visit every USO club and military base and GI hospital we could find, both in the States and overseas. If we were on tour doing four and five shows a day, seven days a week, fifty weeks each year in cities all across the United States, we still found time to visit the servicemen and -women. And when Patty, Laverne, and I went overseas for the USO, we often added four and five impromptu private shows to our schedule every day, for any two or three soldiers who might ask us.

The Andrews Sisters weren't the only entertainers who felt that way. Performers of every kind did all they could—singers, dancers, musicians playing both popular and classical music, comedians, actors and actresses and athletes. Jimmy Stewart and Douglas Fairbanks, Jr., were two of the first stars to become active in encouraging Hollywood's involvement in the national defense effort. There were ballet dancers, too, and mimics and jugglers, and artists who sketched the faces of wounded GIs in hospitals far from home that would be sent back home to the folks.

My sisters and I didn't just go when asked. We went when we weren't asked, too. We always told the people handling our schedule in the next city to find some soldiers, sailors, and Marines who would like to see and hear the Andrews Sisters in person. Our colleagues did the same: our friend and recording colleague Bing Crosby; Bob Hope; Danny Kaye; Mickey Rooney; Burns and Allen; Glenn Miller; Duke Ellington, and scores of others from every field of the arts.

When that World War II veteran in Florida told me he couldn't help thinking of the Andrews Sisters every time he thought of the war, he was paying tribute to all these men and women, not just the three of us. This is the story of all of us who entertained our GIs all over America and overseas through the USO, in civilian clothes as "soldiers in greasepaint"—the wartime title that was a source of pride to us all.

This is a uniquely American story, one that started for the Andrews Sisters on a cold December Sunday in Cincinnati, Ohio, when I noticed something different when LaVerne, Patty, and I arrived at the Shubert Theater. We had been packing them in throughout our engagement there, and the management told us we were attracting such large audiences every afternoon and night that we were about to break the theater's attendance record for a single engagement.

I believed it. Every day when we arrived, there was a long line of people standing on the sidewalk in front of the box office to buy tickets for our first show. It didn't make any difference how cold it was—and in Cincinnati, it gets plenty cold!—or how much snow we might get, people were lined up for blocks. But on that Sunday in 1941, the sidewalk was empty.

From a vantage point of fifty years, it's clear to see that the absence of a line in front of the theater that day was symbolic. We went inside and started down the center aisle toward the stage. But instead of seeing the lights up as usual and people busily preparing for another day's performances, the theater was dark. As we walked farther down the aisle, we could see that the doorman and the stagehands were gathered in a small cluster on the stage, huddled around a small table model radio. There was only a bare light bulb illuminating that one small spot at center stage. When we came within hearing distance, a radio announcer told Laverne, Patty, and me what the workers on the stage already knew: Pearl Harbor, a place we'd never heard of, had been attacked.

I looked at the doorman and asked the question that millions of other Americans were asking each other that day: "Where's Pearl Harbor?"

He said he wasn't sure, but that the voice on the radio was saying we were finally in the war.

Suddenly the empty sidewalk outside the theater symbolized a stark reality: The world was different now and would be for the rest of our lives.

It wasn't long before we were singing a song our parents had sung earlier: "Over There." George M. Cohan wrote it as an inspirational song for Americans in World War I, and now, twenty-three years after what was supposed to be the war to end all wars, we were in another world war and rallying our spirits all over again with Cohan's message: "We won't come back till it's over, over there."

☆

A day so tragic, dramatic, and even bizarre, with its grave consequences for every American life, was beyond anyone's wildest imagination in 1932 when the Andrews Sisters debuted as a professional singing act in Minneapolis, Minnesota. We weren't the first popular girls' singing trio of our day. The Boswell Sisters were a hit act in the early days of radio in the 1920's and became favorites of ours when we were kids.

We loved them and their music and began imitating their singing style around the house. LaVerne had a wonderful memory for music. She'd listen to a song by the Boswell Sisters and work it out for our own three-part harmony. Patty sang the lead, I sang a higher soprano, and LaVerne took the alto part.

When we began appearing at various small social events in Minneapolis, word about the three local singing sisters got around quickly. Our first professional contract was with a big "unit show," a program with one orchestra and a variety of acts. Unit shows were vaudeville's last gasp, and that particular unit proved it. We must have closed every RKO theater in the Midwest.

We went hungry at times, like anyone else starting out in show business. Mama and Papa traveled with us, helping to save money by cooking meals in our hotel room and doing our laundry. The *Richmond News Leader* in Virginia ran a feature article describing those early days and our eventual success with "Bei Mir Bist Du Schoen." The paper said we had been "an obscure trio on Starvation Street in vaudeville and radio. They believed in each other and in the song and soon they were in the four-figure income bracket."

I complicated the act every once in a while because of my love for dogs. I've always had a dog traveling with me. Today she's a tiny Yorkshire terrier weighing two and a half pounds and named Murphy Brown, but in our first years of performing every dog I owned was named Peter in honor of Papa.

When we were playing in Boston, Peter the cocker spaniel, got into some rat poison and died. For several days after that, every time I opened my mouth to sing, all I could think of was

poor Peter and I would burst into tears. It didn't do a thing for
our act. If I had done it much longer, I think my sisters would
have ordered me back to Minneapolis and continued the act as
a duet.

But we were on our way. We learned the responsibilities and
the disciplines of life in the theater—show up early, work hard
for your audience, and never peek through the curtain.

We worked hard at it every day, rehearsing our own Andrews
Sisters style and sound. Today I look back at those early years
and realize that, in one of those coincidences that dot the pages
of history, the Andrews Sisters were developing a new sound for
vocal groups at the same time and in much the same way that
Glenn Miller was developing a new sound for a new era—"Big
Bands".

We worked on perfecting it every spare moment we had,
mostly in the back seat of my father's 1929 Buick. When we
began traveling, my father closed his Greek restaurant in Minneapolis and our parents began to chaperon us across America.
They did it throughout our career, first in the '29 Buick, then in
a '31 Packard, and later back to Buicks for a 1939 model that
transported us for the balance of our prewar years.

We never got to drive, either. Papa was Old World Greek
and as chauvinistic as most men in those years: women weren't
allowed to do anything. The Andrews Sisters, three innocent and
naive girls from the Midwest with a Greek father and a Norwe-
gian mother, knew our place.

After we left the struggling vaudeville unit, we appeared in
every club and theater, large or small, that was willing to book
us for a few dollars a night. In the years of the Great Depression
you couldn't get picky. We sang anything the audience wanted
to hear, doing three shows, piling back into the family car and
heading for the next town.

Travel by car took a lot longer than it does today.

People drove slower, and there weren't any divided highways. If you got stuck behind a truck going up a mountain, there wasn't a thing you could do except grin and bear it. And highways around cities? Nobody even imagined such a thing. You had to drive right through the middle of every city, town, and village along the way.

We didn't have tape decks or four-speaker stereo systems to entertain us during the long automobile trips, and while only a few cars had radios, that was one luxury we enjoyed. We listened to a lot of music in that car, and thanks to the two most popular radio comedians, Jack Benny and Fred Allen, we got plenty of laughs to relieve our boredom. Jack's program, sponsored by Jell-O, was voted America's favorite radio program of 1937. Our favorite night "serial" was *Bambi*, starring Helen Hayes and brought to us by Sanka coffee. Fred Astaire's *Packard Hour*, another favorite, was voted the outstanding new program of the year, in the annual poll of 252 newspaper radio editors conducted by the *New York World-Telegram*.

The programs were followed by the news on the hour, and more and more of it was coming from Europe. Many were saying Hitler was going to start another world war, and he was making all of us believers of that fact with his belligerent speeches and massive buildup of his fighting forces.

As early as 1937, the English were not taking any chances. The British Air Ministry revealed plans to propose an aerial fleet of "kite balloons" as one of the front lines of defense around London. The plan was to float the balloons at heights from ten to twenty thousand feet around the outskirts of the city. They looked like the Goodyear blimp except for the long steel cables that dangled below them. This "aerial net," according to an article in *Life* magazine, "will supposedly be strong enough to shear off the wings of any plane that runs into it."

Just to be sure, the English also stepped up their production of more conventional air power. By the end of 1937, in what *Life* called a "frantic building of planes," England would have sixty-five hundred fighters and bombers waiting and ready.

In 1937, we recorded "Bei Mir Bist Du Schoen," a Yiddish folk song which we sang in English. Its title means "By Me You Are Beautiful." It became a smash hit in 1938, for Decca Records as people flocked to buy copies for their 78-rpm "Victrolas."

For Jews, there was bittersweet irony in the success of that song. It was a source of happiness to Jews in America, especially those who spoke Yiddish, in their newfound comfort with their fellow Americans, but the irony was that at the same time, their counterparts in Europe were suffering agony and even death at the hands of their Nazi aggressors.

☆

For the Andrews Sisters, the timing of "Bei Mir" couldn't have been better. Americans spent an estimated ninety million dollars to listen to dance bands in 1938 alone. That was the year Benny Goodman and his band delivered their sold-out performance at Carnegie Hall that is still a classic, the first concert ever performed there by a popular band. A "Carnival of Swing" was presented at Randall's Island in New York, with twenty-five big bands playing for six hours. That was a sellout, too.

The continued success of our first big hit, which went to the number-one spot on one of the most popular Saturday night radio shows, *Your Hit Parade,* led to another opportunity and another hit. The song was "Oh Johnny, Oh Johnny, Oh!," and for that tune it was the second time around.

The song had been a big hit during World War I after Abe Olman and Ed Rose wrote it in 1916. We recorded it in 1939, and so did a popular vocalist named Wee Bonnie Baker, with her cooing, almost suggestive style of singing. "Oh Johnny" became a big hit for the Andrews Sisters, and for Bonnie, too.

"Beer Barrel Polka" also came our way that year and provided us with another hit and another kind of song for us. Polkas fit our style of singing perfectly because of our upbeat, almost aggressive way of belting out our repertoire. By the time we recorded it, "Beer Barrel Polka" had been around for five years—around Czechoslovakia. Two Czechs wrote a song in 1934 called "Skoda Lasky," and it became a big hit in their own country and in Germany. In 1939, Wladimir Timm, one of the collaborators on the song, changed its title to "Beer Barrel Polka," Lew Brown gave it a new set of lyrics, and the song took off all over again, this time in the United States, first on a recording for RCA Victor by Will Glahi and his orchestra.

While the song was enjoying success for a second time, its composer had dropped out of sight. Jaromir Vejvoda, according to a newspaper article from 1939, is "lost somewhere in the upheaval that engulfs Europe. He may be unaware that more than one million recordings of his polka have been sold in the United States alone. It's even more probable that he hasn't heard the simple English lyric."

A rising young band leader in Chicago, whose eleven-piece orchestra was attracting attention at the Aragon and Trianon ballrooms, had a hit with the song, too. He had dropped the original name for his musicians, the "Hotsy Totsy Boys," and recorded the song under the new name for his organization, the Lawrence Welk orchestra. Although we weren't the only ones who made that song a hit, we were the only ones who recorded two different versions and had a hit both times. In 1942, with a new set of words and backed by Buddy Rich and his orchestra, we recorded the song as "Here Comes the Navy" for our eighth movie, *How's About It?*

At the same time that "Beer Barrel Polka" was enjoying enormous popularity, something else was happening that would change popular music. Glenn Miller and his group of talented arrangers began playing music aimed for America's young people who wanted to dance, and in 1938 and '39 that was most of us. He added a new vocalist/saxophonist, Tex Beneke, and re-corded "Moonlight Serenade" which became so popular Glenn made it his theme song. As the thirties turned into the forties, the same young men who were destined to be called to arms and the young women they would leave behind, held each other and danced to Glenn's music, and dreamed of the future.

Glenn Miller wasn't the only orchestra we danced to. There was a new one, Les Brown and His Band of Renown, plus Gene Krupa and Artie Shaw, and one that had been around a while and was still popular, Ozzie Nelson, with his wife, the former Harriet Hilliard, as his vocalist.

The New York World's Fair was starting in 1939 with its famous combination of a round building called a perisphere and the pencillike structure with a pointed top called a trylon. People were flocking to the Fair from all over the country. Some of them were driving the new 1940 model cars, and the magazine ads about them made it clear we were making exciting advancements in the American standard of living. De Soto ran a full-page ad on the first page of *Time* magazine in its issue of June 10 of that year telling us that its 1940 model was powered by a 100-horsepower engine, plus thirty-nine new features including a gear shift on the steering wheel, "out of knees' way," instead of on the floor. And if all that wasn't exciting enough, the 1940 De Soto cost twenty dollars *less* than the '39 model. Its "de luxe coupe" cost $845. The "de luxe sedan" was more, of course—$905. De Soto made sure to mention that both prices included bumpers, tail lights, and windshield wipers.

With the beginning of the new decade in 1940, the Andrews Sisters began a new style of music, or, more accurately, reintro-duced a very old style from the Deep South—boogie woogie, with its eight beats to each bar of music. Two songwriters, Don Raye and Hughie Prince, wrote some of our most popular "boogie" tunes in the first few years of the 1940s, including "Rhum-Boogie," "Scrub Me, Mama, with a Boogie Beat," "Beat Me, Daddy, Eight to the Bar," and "Boogie Woogie Bugle Boy of Company B."

The Big Band era was now in full force, and more and more bands were being formed to meet the growing popularity of the new sound and the swing that accompanied it. Vaughn Monroe and Claude Thornhill joined the pop music field with their new orchestras. Charlie Barnett, who formed his own band in 1934, was becoming a big favorite, as was Tommy Dorsey, with the help of a new vocalist, a kid from Hoboken, New Jersey, named Frank Sinatra. The mushrooming popularity of the big bands was another big break for the Andrews Sisters because it presented us with an opportunity coveted by any singer or singers at that time—the chance to sing with Glenn Miller.

Chesterfield cigarettes signed Glenn for a weekly fifteen-minute radio show in 1940. The sponsors weren't convinced that Glenn and his new sound would go over big with the radio audience, so they took two steps to protect themselves: they limited the contract to thirteen weeks, and because our songs were doing so well on *Your Hit Parade*, they brought us in to appear with Glenn and his band as sort of an insurance policy.

No one in show business is surprised by that kind of paranoia. Sponsors, and the advertising agencies that represent them, live in fear of failure, always seeking to protect themselves with some kind of additional security. That's why we were on Glenn's *Chesterfield Show*. We knew it, but we didn't care. We knew how successful Glenn was becoming, even if they didn't. But the sponsors found out soon enough. The show was immediately expanded from weekly to three times a week. *The New York Times* made a big story out of it on January 7, 1940:

MILLER NOW FEATURED ON CHESTERFIELD

The article reported that Glenn was well on his way, and we were, too. "Answering an avalanche of requests from dance fans," it said, "Chesterfield cigarettes will sponsor Glenn Miller's orchestra and the Andrews Sisters three times weekly, instead of once a week as originally announced." It added: "Glenn Miller's orchestra is called America's favorite dance band, leading all others in record sales and making box office history in personal appearances. The Andrews Sisters are said to be the most popular singing trio that ever came down the pike, both on records and on the variety stage. Chesterfield has definitely scored a coup in bringing these stars together for the radio audience."

We sang with Glenn's orchestra every Tuesday, Wednesday, and Thursday night at ten o'clock eastern standard time throughout those first thirteen weeks. The listener response was sensational, and Glenn was signed for another year, while we went back to the personal appearance tour we were already under contract for and which we actually preferred. But during those weeks we came to know Glenn as a thorough professional, a quiet man who went to extremes to make sure his band performed to its maximum potential and that every member of it conducted himself in a one hundred percent professional manner.

That even applied when he played music he didn't particularly care for. Though Glenn never really liked Dixieland music, he pushed himself and his band to play it the way it should be played. The result: Dixieland music by the Glenn Miller band sounded as good as the best Dixieland bands in the country.

We saw another example of his insistence on conducting one's self in a professional manner at all times, and this time the unfortunate target wasn't a member of his band. It was our arranger, Vic Schoen. As Vic was entering the studio one day, he pulled out a pack of Lucky Strikes and lit up a cigarette. Glenn was walking in right behind him. He caught up with Vic and said, in firm and unmistakable tones, "If you have to smoke, don't you *ever* let me catch you smoking anything but a Chesterfield as long as you're associated with this program."

CHAPTER TWO

The Best of Times . . .

America was still a year and a half from becoming involved in the war, but we were already concerned about those nations whose people were suffering and dying at the hands of the invading German and Japanese armies. The Japanese were the aggressors in a war against the Chinese, but the concern for most Americans was what Hitler was doing in Europe. As early as 1937, only four years after Hitler came to power, there were scrap drives in the United States to help England prepare for war. At one freight yard in New York, four thousand freight cars were loaded with old automobile brake drums and awaited shipment to England. It was part of what was being called "the munitions race" in Europe.

When the Red Cross appealed for financial help in 1940, an all-star lineup from show business responded with a special benefit program. We were proud to join the others in performing on Hollywood's Bronson Avenue—which was renamed the Avenue of Mercy for the occasion—at its intersection with Sunset Boulevard, in front of the Warner Brothers sound stage.

LaVerne, Patty, and I sang as part of a two-hour radio show which was broadcast simultaneously over every Los Angeles station, plus NBC and CBS, from nine to eleven on a Saturday night. The mayor, Fletcher Bowron, proclaimed the day "Radio Red Cross Day." Dorothy Lamour, Olivia de Havilland, Patricia Morrison, and other celebrities worked as volunteers in selling tickets on the air in advance of the show, hoping to top our goal of twenty-five thousand dollars.

The lineup was a Hollywood's Who's-Who: Shirley Temple, Gene Autry, and Orson Welles were some of the headliners. For Shirley, it was an extra special occasion. She had recently announced her retirement from the movies, at age sixteen, but was making a temporary comeback to help the Red Cross. Charles Laughton was there, too, along with Don Ameche, Kenny Baker, Lum and Abner, Jimmy Cagney, and Edward G. Robinson.

Irving Berlin and Kate Smith teamed up to do their part to motivate Americans. Kate was planning a radio special for Armistice Day, the holiday on November 11, 1938, marking the end of World War I, which we now observe as Veterans Day. She told Irving she was looking for something patriotic, a song that would inspire America. Irving remembered a song he had written during World War I for his all-soldier show, "Yip Yip Yaphank." He hadn't used the song in that production because he didn't think it fit well, so he literally put it into a trunk. It stayed there until he dug it out twenty years later. Irving called the song "God Bless America." The radio audience greeted the new song with great enthusiasm, but no one recorded it for almost two more years, until Kate herself, in August 1940. By November it was "Song Number Five," as the announcer used to say, on *Your Hit Parade.*

☆

In show business, the first measure of success is whether you're working. In 1940, we definitely *were* working. We recorded one of our biggest hits ever, "In Apple Blossom Time," for Decca Records in New York on November 14. It has become our signature tune over the years, one of the songs most associated with the Andrews Sisters. My audiences still won't let me make an appearance without singing it. We recorded twenty-four other songs that year, all with Vic Schoen and his orchestra. Some of our other big hits were "I Love You Much Too Much" and two boogie tunes, "Beat Me, Daddy, Eight to the Bar" and "Scrub Me, Mama, With a Boogie Beat." All that plus personal appearances and those thirteen weeks on the radio with Glenn. But we were having fun, and some of our show business colleagues were letting us know we were beginning to make it big by showing up at our performances. When we opened at the Casa Manana in Culver City, California, on June 7, the audience included one of the biggest-name orchestra leaders of the previous twenty years, Paul Whiteman, who was filming his new movie, *Strike Up the Band.* He caught our eleven o'clock show that night. On the same evening, we sang in front of Bing Crosby's orchestra leader, John Scott Trotter, Phil Harris and Dennis Day from the *Jack Benny Show,* character actor Andy Devine, and one of the popular comedy acts, the Ritz Brothers. For the Andrews Sisters, it was a night to remember.

☆

As 1941 began, we had things on our minds other than our career. The war clouds were growing darker as Hitler's armies continued to race across Europe, conquering everything in their way. Under Roosevelt's urgings, America began its own defense buildup. Henry Ford told a reporter: "If it became necessary, Ford Motor Company could, under our own supervision and without meddling by government agencies, swing into production of a thousand planes a day." When William Knudsen of General Motors was asked if his company could do the same thing, his reply was more reserved. He said, "I guess we could, if we laid plans for it."

One of the effects of the war was that the school systems in Greece were suffering from a lack of educational materials. Because of our Greek heritage the three of us began sending school supplies to Papa's native land to help the children continue their educations. Mama's side was affected, too. She had relatives in Norway who were living under Nazi occupation. As the days and weeks unfolded, it was soon clear that 1941 would be a year crowded with major events for all of us. It was an especially eventful year for me, although almost nobody knew it. I got married on July 28, in Elkton, Maryland, which was then famous for its quickie marriages. You could drive into town and get married right away, which is what Lou Levy and I did. It was a musical marriage. Lou, who became one of the most successful music publishers in the country, had found "Bei Mir Bist Du Schoen" for us and had been our manager for several years.

I confided the big news in Patty, but we kept the whole thing secret for almost two years before telling LaVerne and our parents. Why Patty? Because she could keep a secret better than anyone. We didn't tell the rest of the family until May of 1943, after which we were free to leave on a belated honeymoon to Mexico.

It was the best of times for all of us, especially the three young sisters who had grabbed the brass ring with "Bei Mir Bist Du Schoen" and were ecstatic about the future that we were sure lay in front of us. We had every reason to assume that this was the way it was going to be. But then came that Sunday in December of 1941 in Cincinnati.

☆

We were a changing nation in the last years before Pearl Harbor, slugging our way out of the Depression and raising our standard of living at the same time. By December 7, 1941, eighty percent of the homes in the United States had electricity, and sixty-one percent had telephones. Three of our biggest heroes were in the sports world—Joe DiMaggio, who hit safely in fifty-six straight games in 1941 for the champion New York Yankees; Ted Williams, whose .406 batting average remains the last .400 season for any major leaguer; and Joe Louis, who defended his heavyweight boxing championship seven times that year and was the toast of the country as the popular "Brown Bomber."

Time magazine's favorite man wasn't any of them, though. It was Gary Cooper, the star of the new hit movie, *Sergeant York*, the patriotic film about a Tennessee farm boy, Alvin York, who became a hero twenty-three years in the past by singlehandedly killing more than twenty German soldiers in World War I, wounding several others, and capturing 132 prisoners, all at the same time, in a one-man military victory.

It was one of two big hits that year for Coop. The other was the starring role in Ernest Hemingway's *For Whom the Bell Tolls. Time* called Coop "the most popular man in the nation." His two hits that year were impressive, but Humphrey Bogart topped him. He had three—*High Sierra, The Maltese Falcon,* and *Casablanca.* In the musicals, which we sisters paid more attention to, one of the big hits of the year was *You'll Never Get Rich,* starring Fred Astaire and Rita Hayworth.

The future didn't seem that promising for the Andrews Sisters early in the year, after the editors of the *Harvard Lampoon,* the national humor magazine, said we gave the "most frightening" performance of 1940. They must have liked our movies as much as I did. The editors lampooned others, saying that Victor Mature, who became one of Hollywood's most successful leading men, was "least likely to succeed."

The Andrews Sisters and Victor had reason for hope, though. After all, this was the same magazine that selected Ann Sheridan, one of Hollywood's most glamorous stars of the 1940's and '50s, as the winner of its "least likely to succeed" award the year before. Ann had the perfect comeback. "I already have," she responded to their low rating, then revealed her pay checks to prove it.

Then the Andrews Sisters recorded a song with which we are still identified, "Boogie Woogie Bugle Boy of Company B." The *Harvard Lampoon* never called us "frightening" again, and the editors were not heard from when we fired up the country with our hit song:

> *He was a famous trumpet man from out Chicago way.*
> *He had a boogie style that no one else could play.*
> *He was the top man at his craft,*
> *But then his number came up and he was gone with the draft.*
> *He's in the Army now, a-blowin' reveille.*
> *He's the boogie-woogie bugle boy of Company B.*

The song made it all the way to sixth place on the charts, and it become a smash hit for Bette Midler when she revived it more than thirty years later, in 1973. We recorded it for Decca with Vic Schoen and his orchestra after singing it in our second movie, *Buck Privates*, with a new comedy team that was keeping America in stitches, Bud Abbott and Lou Costello. Boogie was heard for the first time on a national scale in the mid-1930's after working its way north to Chicago, and by 1941 it was one of the most popular forms of music, usually as a piano solo. The big bands started playing it as the 'thirties ended, so again our timing was perfect. Don Raye and Hughie Prince wrote not one boogie piece but *two* for the film.

Buck Privates also included "In Apple Blossom Time" after it became such a big hit only a few months earlier, another fun boogie-woogie tune, "Bounce Me, Brother, With a Solid Four," and a song called "You're a Lucky Fellow, Mr. Smith."

In 1991, fifty years after we recorded it on the Decca label, a New York choreographer, Paul Taylor, wrote a ballet based on the World War II songs of the Andrews Sisters. *Company B* drew rave reviews in '91 and '92 at the City Center and the World Financial Center in New York, the Kennedy Center in Washington, and the Dorothy Chandler Pavilion in Los Angeles.

> *They made him blow a bugle for his Uncle Sam.*
> *It really brought him down because he couldn't jam.*
> *The captain seemed to understand, because the next day*
> *The cap went out and drafted a band,*
> *So now the company jumps when he plays reveille.*
> *He's the boogie-woogie bugle boy of Company B.*

We made three movies with Abbott and Costello in 1941. After *Buck Privates* we filmed *Hold That Ghost* and *In The Navy.* And we recorded no fewer than thirty-four more songs with Vic and his band. Some of them have long since been forgotten, and maybe that's just as well in some cases, but the list includes a surprising number that are still well known: "For All We Know," "Daddy," "Sonny Boy," "We're In The Navy," "Elmer's Tune," and "Why Don't We Do This More Often?"

We also found time to make two appearances in the summer of '41 on a new radio show from Chicago sponsored by the Holland Furnace Company and starring Benny Goodman and his band. In October, two months before Pearl Harbor, we went to New York and recorded a song with Vic that was to be instrumental in promoting the sale of war bonds throughout the course of the war—"Any Bonds Today?" The song eventually was recorded by many artists, from Bing Crosby to Bugs Bunny.

We were singing the other hits of 1941, too, including "Deep in the Heart of Texas" and "Chattanooga Choo-Choo." June Hershey and Don Swander wrote "Deep in the Heart of Texas," and it became a hand-clapping fun hit for Alvino Ray and his orchestra in '41 and for our friend Bing Crosby in '42, just before we began to record with Bing. Its popularity proved so great and so durable that it was sung in almost a dozen movies between 1942 and 1957.

"Chattanooga Choo-Choo" was introduced by one of our other friends, Glenn Miller, in the movie musical, *Sun Valley Serenade*. Mack Gordon wrote the lyrics, and Harry Warren composed the music. Tex Beneke, Glenn's new star, sang the vocal, accompanied by Marion Hutton and the Modernaires. The record sold more than a million copies, the first record to top a million since Gene Austin's "My Blue Heaven" fifteen years earlier, and other artists, including us, also recorded it. RCA Victor presented Glenn with a gold-plated copy of the record. Later, the Record Industry Association of America picked up the idea and began its practice of awarding gold records to an artist whose record sells a million copies.

Even as America prepared for war in 1940 and '41, there was no unanimous support for it. Many people, including some leaders in Congress and editorial writers, described the war in Europe that Hitler began with his invasion of Poland on September 1, 1939, as "that phony little war." Two-thirds of Americans interviewed in a poll just after the war's outbreak said America should stay out of what they considered a conflict that should be limited to the European continent.

The war "over there" spread rapidly and Hitler extended his military operations by bombing England every day and every night during "the London Blitz" and invading the Soviet Union. With relations between the U.S. and Japan deteriorating at an alarming rate, President Franklin Roosevelt took to the radio, our newest instrument of mass communication.

FDR became our first mass media President, proving himself a skilled performer in speaking to the public in a voice that was both firm and reassuring. In addition to mobilizing public opinion to support the possibility of all-out world war, Roosevelt also managed what had been considered the presidential impossibility of getting himself elected to a third term.

With his masterful use of the media and with events careening out of control on the far shores of both oceans, the public attitude showed a decided swing toward supporting Roosevelt's "mobilization program." By December 1941, near the end of the first year of FDR's third term, two-thirds of Americans polled said they supported the program.

One American who *didn't* was an American hero of the time, Colonel Charles A. Lindbergh—"Lucky Lindy"—who became the first person to fly alone across the Atlantic nonstop when he piloted his *Spirit of St. Louis* from New York to Paris in 1927. He immediately won top billing with Babe Ruth as one of America's two most popular celebrities, but when the war in Europe started, Lindbergh began speaking out against our participation and his popularity slipped.

After President Roosevelt delivered a major foreign policy address in June of 1940, Lindbergh lashed out at what he called FDR's "chatter about invasion." The next issue of *Life* magazine carried seven letters to the editor concerning Lindbergh's remarks, five of them criticizing him for "urging us to go to sleep."

A Methodist pastor in Pecos, Texas, said Lindbergh was "serving Nazi interests" with his calls for isolationism. A woman in San Diego asked: "Is Mr. Lindbergh so callous and thick-skinned that the tales of horror, rapine, murder, and ruthlessness coming from all the ravished countries of Europe mean nothing to him?"

That one-third of American adults were still opposed to our entry into the war as late as December 1941 was due in part to a normal difference of opinion, but there was another reason as well: organized opposition. A group calling itself the "America First Committee" was established in September of 1940 and became the powerful "isolationist" organization dedicated to opposing any American involvement in the war overseas. It claimed to have eight hundred thousand members who, in forceful terms and flag-waving rallies, said that America should remain neutral.

The German-American League boasted of two hundred thousand members and held a rally at Madison Square Garden in New York City. The League, headquartered in Detroit, conducted meetings that featured rousing speeches and fight songs—plus beer and pretzels. It also operated summer camps for kids and adult members of the League, including one on Long Island called "Camp Siegfried." The German word could mean anything from peace and protection to power and victory.

Another organization, the Committee to Defend America by Aiding the Allies, was trying to promote a similar view. The organization said America could, and *should,* stay out of the war by sending aid to the embattled countries in Europe.

Just as it changed everything else in our lives, Pearl Harbor changed the percentages of public support for our military buildup and America's role in the war. Support for what was suddenly "World War II" surged dramatically within hours of the attack and became virtually unanimous overnight.

The Andrews family gathered around the radio in our hotel room in Cincinnati the day after the attack on Pearl Harbor and heard Roosevelt describe December 7, 1941, as "a date that will live in infamy." When he asked Congress in the same speech for a Declaration of War—against not only Japan but her partners in their "axis" alliance, Germany and Italy, as well—there was only one dissenting vote in the House, cast by Jeanette Rankin of Montana, the only member of Congress to vote against our entry into each world war. In the Senate, the vote was unanimously in favor.

Four days after the attack, the America First Committee was disbanded.

☆

Cincinnati was like every other city, town, and village in America the night of December 7. The atmosphere was tense and somber. With twenty-four hundred soldiers, sailors, and marines killed at Pearl Harbor, every American felt there had been an overwhelming tragedy in the family—the American family.

We attracted an audience of six people or so for our early show that day at the Shubert. By evening, when we always packed them in, we only drew a few dozen in a theater of two or three thousand seats. For the rest of our engagement, we played to an almost empty house.

The shock was as overpowering as the grief. We knew war was expected, but no one really expected it was coming in a matter of days. On the contrary, *Life* magazine summarized events of the week before by telling its readers, "No one worried . . . Americans felt confident, rightly or wrongly, that the Japs were pushovers."

But newspaper readers in Los Angeles saw an omen in the newspaper twenty-four hours before the attack. In the horoscope column of its editions of Saturday, December 6, the *Evening Herald Express* said:

"Sunday's horoscope is noteworthy because of its strange, sudden, and wholly unpredictable and inexplicable occurrences, affecting all phases of life."

CHAPTER THREE

The Way We Were, And The Way We Changed

Let's remember Pearl Harbor
As we go to meet the foe.
Let's remember Pearl Harbor
As we did the Alamo.
We will always remember
How they died for liberty.
Let's remember Pearl Harbor
And go on to victory.

Sammy Kaye had one of the most popular orchestras when we entered the fighting, and Sammy teamed up with Don Reid immediately after Pearl Harbor to write the first rousing new song of the war. They recorded it only ten days after the attack.

Sammy's style of music was aimed at ballroom dancing, almost everyone's preferred form of dance, and he became known for the band's slogan, "Swing and sway with Sammy Kaye." The arrangement for his battle cry with Don carried a hint of a military march, but we danced to it anyhow—and the Andrews Sisters joined all other Americans in singing it.

The song jumped to the number three spot on *Your Hit Parade* almost immediately. For LaVerne, Patty, and me, it quickly became one of our most requested numbers. Even with the passing of all these years, I don't think it's overstating the case to say that Sammy and Don helped to keep aflame America's sense of outrage after the attack. The Japanese leaders had committed the fatal mistake of making America angry. They didn't need a couple of songwriters to come along and get us even more fired up. But that's what happened. In the midst of death and destruction, something as simple as a song helped to keep the American fighting spirit aroused. And it wouldn't be the last time.

☆

Although "Remember Pearl Harbor" played a significant role in helping us through the early part of the war, it was not the first contribution by show business to the national emergency. Some of the most prominent names in the entertainment industry were at work long before Pearl Harbor preparing for the day that most of us were sure would come.

Eight months before the attack, on April 17, 1941, a meeting was held in Washington that would establish a new undertaking, the United Services Organization—the USO. There was a growing sense of urgency that something needed to be done to bolster and maintain the morale of America's servicemen and women. Six major national organizations pledged themselves to become partners in the USO: the Y.M.C.A. and the Y.W.C.A.; the National Catholic Community Service; the National Jewish Welfare Board; the Salvation Army; and the National Travelers Aid Association. Delegates at the meeting agreed that the USO would be financed by the American people through voluntary contributions and not by government funds.

The organization's work was placed under the general direction of the Army and the Navy, its budgets subject to approval by the American government, which agreed to construct three hundred buildings around the country as USO facilities.

Only twelve days later, one of the great impresarios of show business, Billy Rose, announced that he would begin presenting what he called "draftee shows" for the young men called into the

Service and assigned to military bases around the country. The first show was scheduled for May 15 in Lakehurst, New Jersey. The last would be held on July 1 "when summer maneuvers started."

The shows were produced by two of the most famous members of the legitimate stage, George S. Kaufman and Robert E. Sherwood, who headed the Army and Navy Committee on Recreation and Welfare. And the biggest names on stage enthusiastically pledged that they would perform—free: Al Jolson, Eddie Cantor, Bill "Bojangles" Robinson, George M. Cohan, Georgie Jessel, George Burns and Gracie Allen, vaudevillian Ken Murray, and two of the most popular singers of the time, Jane Froman and Tony Martin.

In his announcement, Rose said the stars would perform from the back of flatbed trucks donated by General Motors as mobile twenty-four-foot stages, each with a piano and complete with floodlights and microphones. The *New York Daily News* reported that the "theaters" would be "open air, stand-up-and-watch-it. Every Hollywood studio has offered to lend its biggest and brightest stars between picture commitments."

Billy Rose was never one to leave anything to chance, so he staged what press reports called an "experimental show" earlier in May, outdoors on a boxing platform at Fort Belvoir, Virginia, a Washington suburb. The star was one of vaudeville's greatest names, Ed Wynn, who billed himself as "The Perfect Fool" and was the father of one of the best actors of our generation, Keenan Wynn. A second dry run was held at Fort Dix, New Jersey. Representatives from the War Department and the Navy saw both shows and endorsed the idea of continuing the program. Before and after the "summer maneuvers" of 1941, shows were staged in places like Pine Camp in Watertown, New York; Camp Lee in Petersburg, Virginia; Norfolk Naval Air Station; Camp Claiborne in Alexandria, Louisiana; Jefferson Barracks, located then in St. Louis; and Puget Sound, Washington. The delighted

GI audiences paid twenty cents for tickets. Where there was a state or local tax, the cost was twenty-two cents.

By the end of that last summer of peace, the total number of GIs attending these shows exceeded 3,200,000. The demand was so great, and their value in bolstering morale was so effective, that the USO established a new arm—USO Camp Shows, Inc.— in October. The War and Navy departments designated Camp Shows as "Official Entertainer" for the men and women in our armed forces.

By the time the war ended four years later, USO Camp Shows had presented 293,738 performances in 208,178 separate visits to a combined audience of 161,000,000 servicemen and women in the United States and overseas. During the war, the operation became the biggest production in the history of show business.

One of the first USO troupes toured bases in the Caribbean in November and early December. A B-18 transport plane christened *The Flying Showboat* carried Ray Bolger, Stan Laurel and Oliver Hardy, Mitzi Mayfair, John Garfield, and several other entertainers on a thirteen-thousand-mile tour from Puerto Rico to British Guiana. In the new USO-Camp Shows program, the group was identified in bureaucratic government terminology as "Overseas Unit No. 1."

An official memorandum reported that the troupe's performance at Borinquen Field in Puerto Rico on November 2 was attended by five thousand GIs. LaVerne, Patty, and I never limited ourselves to our scheduled performances, and the entertainers in that troupe didn't, either. "Ray Bolger and Laurel and Hardy gave a special impromptu performance for the men in the stockade," the report added. "They gave these men cigarettes and soda they had purchased. This thoughtfulness on their part was highly praised."

Reports to USO headquarters gave rave reviews from stateside audiences, too, reflecting both the attitude and language of those years: "The Bremerton Navy Yard date was swell . . . Razzle Dazzle opened last night in St. Louis to wonderful response. . . . Boys almost broke the front of theater down trying to get in for the first show. . . . Entire show beautiful and clean. . . . Audience reaction on both shows was splendid."

The report from Camp Lee added a warning from Harry Kalcheim of the camp's Advisory Booking Committee: "Think it should be explained that should there be a balance in the USO funds after the present crisis is over, this money will be placed in some army recreation fund. We ran into a couple of soldiers at the camp who seemed to feel the USO might be making a profit out of the shows. During the last war, the Y.M.C.A. and Salvation Army had some unpleasant and uncalled-for publicity due to charging [for] certain items furnished the soldiers."

Frederick Sears, manager of the company presenting *Follow The Crowd* at Camp Claiborne, complained about some of the conditions facing his "girls" after they were told they could not stay at the guest houses in the camps where they performed. He spotlighted one of the new problems associated with America's military buildup.

"That is quite a blow to the girls," Sears reported to his USO superiors, "as hotel rates are very high and hard to get into, as these towns near the camps are booming and everyone is jacking up rates."

His report was dated December 6, 1941.

The success of Overseas Unit No. 1 proved, in the words of a USO report near the end of the war, that "it was not only feasible but advisable that entertainment should follow our armed forces wherever they went."

As a result, four new units were dispatched immediately to Newfoundland and other locations in the Arctic. Al Jolson and Joe E. Brown headed for Alaska while other large units were sent to Panama. Two weeks after Pearl Harbor, fifteen entertainers boarded an airplane from New York and flew to the South

Pacific. Two months after that, ten more performers flew to the Middle East. Within five months, thirty-eight units had been sent to Bermuda, Iceland, Newfoundland, Great Britain, Panama, and Australia.

Entertainers were being recruited for every kind of personal appearance imaginable. LaVerne, Patty, and I were visiting camps and military hospitals in every city where we played, and other entertainers were doing the same. One of our hospital visits became something of a sentimental journey. It happened back home in Minneapolis when we were visiting the Snelling Veterans Hospital. All three of us were touched when some veterans of World War I and even a few of the Spanish-American War remembered that I sang for them when I was only four years old.

It made me think, not entirely with joy, that I might be one of the few entertainers of my generation who had sung for veterans of America's wars as far back as 1898. For all I know, there could have been some veterans of the Civil War who were residents in that hospital when I sang there as a toddler in the early 1920's. However, I deny emphatically that there is any reason to believe I ever performed for veterans of the Revolutionary War!

Another poignant appearance for us came early in the war when we went down to the docks during an appearance in Seattle and sang for the boys as their ship pulled away into the Pacific, headed for combat.

At the request of military officials supervising the departure at this "port of embarkation"—another term we learned in a hurry as soon as we entered the war—we sang "Don't Sit Under the Apple Tree," one of our most popular hits:

> Don't sit under the apple tree
> With anyone else but me,
> Anyone else but me,
> Anyone else but me.

No, no, no,
Don't sit under the apple tree
With anyone else but me
Till I come marching home.

Don't go walking down Lovers' Lane
With anyone else but me,
Anyone else but me,
Anyone else but me.
No, No, No,
Don't go walking down Lovers' Lane
With anyone else but me
Till I come marching home.

The scene is still vivid in my memory. We stood down on the pier, looking up at all those young men leaning over the ship's rails, waving and yelling and screaming. Any time that scene was reenacted, and it was happening countless times every day in groups large and small all over the country in 1942, one thought nagged at you: How many of the young men shipping out wouldn't come back?

I can still see the mothers and sweethearts standing on that dock and singing along with us as the ship sailed away to war. It might sound corny to some people today, but in 1942 the young Americans on those ships—and those of us on the docks with tears in our eyes—knew they were going away to fight in the worst war in the history of the world.

"Don't Sit Under the Apple Tree" was just the right song for those early months of World War II, especially after Charlie Tobias and Lew Brown changed the last line of their original lyric. The first version ended with an expression of a young man's undying love for the light of his life, but in 1942, they changed the line to sound like a departing GI asking his girl to be true to him while he's gone. Sam H. Stept wrote the music almost ten years earlier, in the mid-1930's, and called his melody "Anywhere the Bluebird Goes." Lew and Charlie added the words in 1939 for a Broadway musical called *Yokel Boy*.

LaVerne, Patty, and I sang the 1942 version with Harry James and his band in a movie, *Private Buckaroo*, with Abbott and Costello. Then we recorded it for Decca, and it became one of the first big hits of the war, right after "Remember Pearl Harbor." Glenn Miller recorded it, too, with Tex Beneke, Marion Hutton, and The Modernaires, and Kay Kyser also recorded a version. All three arrangements became hits, one of the few times in the recording business that three artists had major hits of the same song at the same time.

We were glad for Glenn's success because we were still friends with him, going back to the *Chesterfield Show* in 1940. And we were glad for Tex Beneke, too. We knew Glenn was working Tex hard, making him a better singer, and the result was continuing success for the whole Miller organization. Glenn used to demand that his musicians have neat haircuts, a shine on their shoes, and an overall clean-cut personal appearance. As for his coaching, Glenn's big project with Tex was to make him pronounce his words clearly when singing.

"We had to sing 'Don't sit under the *apple* tree'," Tex said years later, "not the *yapple* tree." That was Glenn Miller, and his striving for perfection was one reason he achieved a level of greatness in the music field that remains unmatched a half-century later.

LaVerne, Patty, and I made three movies with Abbott and Costello, and because of Lou, they were easily the most fun of the seventeen films the Andrews Sisters made. He was a delight, and one of the hardest workers imaginable. Lou wanted to succeed more than anyone I think I've ever known, and not just in comedy. He always wanted to move beyond comedy into serious acting roles, but his fate was to remain a comedy actor—albeit a good one.

We also appeared in three forgettable movie productions: *Give Out, Sister, What's Cookin'*, and *How's About It?* You get an idea of just how bad they were from the comments of William Boehnel, movie critic for the *New York World Telegram*. He called *What's Cookin'* "some of the dreariest cinema highjinks I have seen in a long time. . . . What's depressing is not that this is the same old plot over again, but rather that it has been done with practically no imagination or enthusiasm."

While these movies weren't film classics, they did carry a big plus for us. They enabled us to continue singing with two more big bands, Woody Herman and Buddy Rich. Woody and his band backed us when we sang two big wartime numbers, "Amen" and "Pack Up Your Troubles" in *What's Cookin'*, and Buddy backed us in *How's About It?* as we sang "East of the Rockies," "Here Comes The Navy," "The Elevator Song," "Take It and Git" and "Don't Mind the Rain."

Big bands and their leaders were America's newest superstars, and Hollywood knew it. As a result, producers were signing up more and more bands to appear in their films, especially after Glenn Miller's appearances in *Sun Valley Serenade* and *Orchestra Wives* became big box office.

In addition to the appearances by Woody, Buddy and Harry in our movies, Kay Kyser and his "College of Musical Knowledge" made two movies in 1942, and so did Skinnay Ennis and his orchestra. Other big bands made their film debuts: Xavier Cugat, Jimmy Dorsey, Tommy Dorsey, Sammy Kaye, Freddy Martin, Ray Noble, Ozzie Nelson, to name a few. One feature film, *Syncopation*, had seven big bands in the same movie— Harry James, Benny Goodman, Charlie Barnet, Gene Krupa, Joe Venuti, Alvino Rey, Jack Henney—in a swingin', stompin' jam session.

For the Andrews Sisters, singing with the big-name bands was always a kick, as our recordings continued their success and climbed their way up to the top of the chart on *Your Hit Parade*.

By the middle of 1942, we added another hit, a song still sung today even though the movie, *Give Out, Sisters,* with Dan Dailey and William Frawley, has long since been forgotten. The tune: "Pennsylvania Polka."

The big bands provided an important morale boost to Americans all across the home front, and on board ships and in fox holes in every corner of what people were calling our "war-torn world." Their contribution to our national spirit, and especially to the young men and women in uniform, may have been largely overlooked over the years, but that doesn't change history. It is a matter of fact that our young people were able to keep their chins up and their wits about them in part because of the pleasure they found during their off-duty hours in singing the songs of the big bands and dancing to their beat.

We were proud and excited to be a part of it. Our fans seemed to be climbing all over themselves, sometimes literally, to make us a success. On a tour in mid-1942, we set attendance records at theaters in eighteen cities across the United States from the Paramount in New York to the Golden Gate Theater in San Francisco.

For the big bands, the war was already producing both good news and bad news. The good news was that their popularity zoomed. The bad news was that the military draft was breaking up the bands. The "manpower shortage" worsened with each year of the war. A year after Pearl Harbor, Les Brown lost all but four musicians from his band in only four months. The Delta Rhythm Boys, who harmonized their way to success with "Dry Bones," were forced to break up their group when one member was drafted and another decided to take a civil service job.

Marshall Cram, who played the trombone for the Harry James orchestra, quit the band because he was about to be drafted. Benny Goodman ran into one problem after another with the draft. After losing his trumpet player, Ray Linn, to the service, he signed Brody Schroff, who was married and the father of a four-month-old child. That didn't impress his draft board, and he was reclassified 1-A, so he joined the Merchant Marine band at Catalina Island. Benny had another problem. One of his stars, drummer Louie Bellson, was sweating out his draft notice, too.

Even Kay Kyser was available, as far as the Selective Service was concerned. His draft board rejected Kay's request for a deferment, even though he had taken his band, one of the most popular in the country, to more than three hundred Army, Navy, and Marine bases by the first half of 1943 and presented 1,121 shows for the servicemen and women.

The rejection sent shock waves throughout the music business. If someone who had contributed so much to the morale of our military personnel could be drafted, the reasoning went, so could anybody else. That presented all kinds of implications, none of them good, for the entertainment avenues available during the rest of the war for our service personnel and the civilians on the home front. Even getting the music and the entertainers heard on the radio was becoming a problem. The engineers from radio stations and networks were also entering the armed forces. But a solution was available, thanks to our allies in England. Within a few months of the start of the war in 1939, 417 of England's 1,300 radio engineers were drawn into military service. An immediate, critical need developed, compounded by the urgency of getting emergency information to the citizens of England on a moment's notice. The solution: Develop a new source, composed of underage kids, overage adults—and women.

Sir Noel Ashbridge, chief engineer for the British Broadcasting Corporation, was one of those who led the crash program. "Before the war, no women engineers were engaged," he said in 1943, "but recruiting women and training them for technical work has now proven an undoubted success."

The British started an engineering school in May of 1941. By

1943, over five hundred women were working as engineers in radio control rooms, studios, and at transmitting stations. BBC's chief engineer said that, "BBC found the results of its training school most encouraging. Particularly, the use of women as operators has been a definite success. They make rapid progress and are most painstaking in grasping the highly intricate business."

The war was posing serious new threats in every facet of show business. *Billboard,* which told you on its masthead that it was "the world's foremost amusement weekly," ran several stories the week after the attack on Pearl Harbor reporting the war's first effect on our industry:

"First week of this country at war hit the band biz with a number of cancellations and a sudden drop-off of bookings in all major band management offices. But all booking execs voiced the opinion here today that the situation is temporary, and looked forward to an almost immediate boom."

The paper also pointed out one of the other, unanticipated effects: "Most of the cancellations sprang from the government's immediate taking over of all armories for military training."

CHAPTER FOUR

The Big Bands—In the Army Now

Ironically, new big bands were being formed in the Army itself. One of them was headed by Jimmie Baker, a college student before the war and an Emmy-winning producer for ABC-TV now.

Jimmie was drafted from the campus of Oklahoma State University—it was Oklahoma A&M then—in July of 1942. He was majoring in radio and stage production and leading his own student dance band when he was called up. The Army sent him to another part of Oklahoma, to its infantry post at Fort Sill.

"I was scared," he says today. "I had never had a gun in my hand in my life, and I didn't know what I was going to do, so I went over to the office of the Commanding Officer and told the CO my background. He said he'd look into what I could do in the Army."

With the Army's typical closed-mouth attitude, Jimmie was transferred to St. Petersburg, Florida, where the Air Corps was operating a new basic training camp. "They had no barracks there, or anything," he remembers. "They just took over every hotel they could find in St. Petersburg." Jimmie received an unusual wartime assignment: Form a dance band.

"I was sent there for the 11th Army Air Force Band, and that's where I put together my first dance band, The Men of the Air." He had other qualifications in the music field. He was the drum major of the Oklahoma A&M band and was rated by *Metronome* magazine as "the highest-stepping drum major in the United States."

Soon after he arrived in Florida, he hit on the perfect way to carry out his assignment. "Since that was a basic training center," he chuckles today, "I was able to grab off all the good musicians as they came through there. I had a friend in Personnel, and he'd shortstop any musician who was reporting for basic training."

To carry out his new duties, Jimmie was awarded the three stripes of a buck sergeant. Better than that, as the leader of the band, he outranked those musicians in his orchestra who held grades above him. He "fronted" the band, playing the role of the one who stands out front and faces the audience or the dance floor as the leader of the orchestra.

After a year in St. Petersburg, he was transferred to an Air Corps base in Gulfport, Mississippi. His band played every weekend at the Gulf Coast Military Academy and at a respected two-year girls' college and finishing school, Gulf Park. To this day, Jimmie remembers the atmosphere during his dances at Gulf Park.

"They had chaperons for the girls," he told me. No "fraternizing" with members of the band was allowed. School officials also told their students that close dancing with those flyboys from Gulfport Field was forbidden. That meant no contact. The chaperons had to be able to place a hand between the boy and the girl to make sure they were maintaining a proper distance.

"The chaperons would walk around the dance floor checking on the couples," Jimmie remembers. "If a couple got too close, the girl would feel a tap on her shoulder." In such cases, the chaperons told the couples to put a little air between them. The school officials didn't waste words. They simply said: "Part." And the soldier and his dance partner complied.

☆

The people in show business were displaying the firmest kind of resolve to help keep America's chin up. In another front-page story, *Billboard* reported from Washington: "Altho the present war is now greater than any other in history, showmen thruout the nation are hopeful. It may become a curtailed or restricted show business, but most important is the fact that there will remain a show business thruout the war."

Even the juke box business would be affected, but *Billboard* was predicting a positive change. A story out of Chicago said: "Outlook for the coin machine industry is that both operators and distributors of coin-operated equipment will enjoy boom business while manufacturers turn to defense work. Demand of locations for music machines will increase and operators will be able to choose their spots carefully, since production of new machines will be cut to 25 percent February 1."

The changes kept on coming as America hurried to pick itself up off the floor. Night clubs, theaters, and restaurants tried everything they could think of to avoid a sharp drop in business. Within days after Pearl Harbor, the Rainbow Room on the sixty-fifth floor of New York City's RCA Building, "the highest night club in the world," was preparing a publicity campaign to tell patrons that the steel-and-stone skyscraper was "safer than your own home." Night clubs and theaters began installing radios for patrons who wanted to keep up with the flood of news bulletins and the news-packed nightly reports from here and overseas broadcast by Edward R. Murrow, Gabriel Heatter, H. V. Kaltenborn, Lowell Thomas, and Walter Winchell.

Billboard speculated that the government "will probably

encourage decentralization of amusements so as to avoid providing enemy planes with mass targets." Business began falling off immediately. "A lot of jobs," *Billboard* said, "have already been lost due to the war's outbreak. Private entertainment bookers report cancellations of scores of affairs because various groups believe this is no time for a good time and, furthermore, because increased working hours will make it tougher for many people to attend parties."

Censorship was rearing its wartime head, even on a voluntary basis, according to *Billboard:* "Theaters and clubs are meeting the war temper of patrons by censoring their shows also. The Lowe Circuit inserted a clause in its contracts forbidding war jokes . . ."

Japanese performers were losing work because bookers and agents would not hire them. On the other hand, patriotic songs and gags were instantly popular, and we were seeing more acts with American flags being waved proudly, always to enthusiastic applause.

Some performers, including many of the musicians in the big bands, were losing work because they could not travel. Members of the bands and other performers had to stay in their hometowns by order of their local draft boards, to be on hand for an immediate call to military duty.

In Seattle, where blackouts were already taking place every evening, matinees suddenly drew the big crowds, while evening audiences were smaller because people wanted to stay indoors or had to work.

Show business, like every business, jumped into the war with both feet. In its December 20 issue, *Billboard* ran an ad across the bottom of its pages:

LET'S GO, AMERICA!!
This will be the theme of next week's issue of The Billboard. It

will tell you, as a member of the Amusement Industry, what you can do to help your country win this war.

Mama and Papa always made sure we never let our success go to our heads, and others did, too, sometimes without meaning to. Like the trip we made back home to Minneapolis in 1942, when the Sunday *Tribune* did a big spread on the hometown girls who were making good.

The layout featured four pictures of us and an article which said: "No one has ever accused these three of being good-looking, yet in a few years they have recorded their way to the top of America's juke box royalty." The story talked about the eight million records we had sold and said, "Wherever hot music addicts huddle around a juke box, their name is spoken with awe."

But the reporter also wrote that I was "a tomboy and something of a soprano." *Something?* The paper said Patty was "blond and merry" after she told the reporter she was happy "because I got no brains." As for LaVerne, our hometown paper said she was "dark and a baritone. She worries about getting places on time." She had reason to. LaVerne was the one who was always late.

With publicity like that, we thought we just about broke even on that interview.

Right after finishing *Give Out, Sisters,* we had two more recording sessions in New York with Vic Schoen, one on July 17 and the other five days later. In all we recorded seven songs: "Kalamazoo," "The Humming Bird," "Strip Polka," "East of the Rockies," "Mr. Five By Five," "Massachusetts," and "Here Comes The Navy."

Then, to the shock of the nation, we had a strike in the music industry. The American Federation of Musicians was headed by a strong-willed president, James Caesar Petrillo, and when negotiations with the record companies were unsuccessful, Petrillo imposed a ban on any new recordings by union musicians. It began on August 1, 1942, and lasted for Decca Records and us until September 1943.

It was a critical blow to everyone in the recording industry. It came at a time when we were turning out records at a rapid rate. We wanted to capitalize on our growing popularity, and we were following Lou Levy's advice that things were changing in show business, and popular recordings had a much shorter life span.

He used to tell us that when the Boswell Sisters and Al Jolson and some of the other early recording stars were at their peak, a tune would stay popular a year or more. "But not anymore," he told us. "Today, after a hundred and twenty days, a song is dying. You have to keep finding them and introducing them."

The strike was a big break for singers and groups who wanted to sing without accompaniment. A group called The Song Spinners cut a record of a song by Mack David and Vee Lawnhurst about a boy who got too many zeroes on his school tests but became a hero when he started bagging another kind of Zero— Japan's most famous kind of warplane.

The two song writers called their man and their song "Johnny Zero," and it became a huge hit. The flip side did, too. The Song Spinners sang a tune by two of America's most respected and successful song writers in war or peace, Harold Adamson and Jimmy McHugh. It told the story of a plane crew's confidence that it would make it back to the base even though the plane had lost an engine. The "crew members" sang that they would make it safely because they were "comin' in on a wing and a prayer."

Our first record after the strike was with Bing, backed by Vic Schoen's band. It was called "Pistol Packin' Mama." The song didn't have anything to do with the war. It came from a story about a woman who owned a honky-tonk joint and whose husband operated a whiskey still in the mountains of Kentucky. A songwriter, Al Dexter, met the woman in his travels and learned that she carried a pistol for protection from both the moonshiners and the "revenooers." She told Dexter that at night, she'd go looking for her husband in the hills, hollering his name into the dark. "Lay that pistol down, Ma, or I ain't comin'," she said he'd call back. The woman asked Dexter to write a song about it. He did, but that's not the end of the story. He wasn't convinced that the song had much potential, so he recorded it as the "B" side—the "flip" side—of a record with another of his songs, one called "Rosalita," on the "A" side. "Pistol Packin' Mama" sold over a million records for us.

During that entire strike period, the Andrews Sisters did not make one commercial recording. The only recording we did was on the "V-disks," large records produced by Armed Forces radio for broadcast to our troops through AFRS and the camp radio station. And, we appeared on many shows produced by the Armed Forces Radio Service and broadcast to our troops across the United States and all over the world. We made two appearances on one of the most popular Armed Forces Radio Service shows, *Command Performance,* including its Christmas show for the troops all over the world.

It was ironic that fear, the only emotion we had to worry about according to President Roosevelt's first inaugural address in 1933, was now a national concern again. Rumors were constant, especially on the two coasts. You heard that Germans were on their way to bomb New York, or Japanese planes were headed for Los Angeles and San Francisco. Or the enemy had just landed on our shores.

We didn't need any rumors to worry us. America had plenty to worry about anyhow. We were losing badly in the Pacific, with the Japanese army pushing us back, off Wake Island, then Bataan, then Corregidor, until finally our Pacific commander, General Douglas MacArthur, had to withdraw to Australia under orders from Roosevelt to plan how we could begin a comeback in the South Pacific.

In Europe and Africa, things were no better. England was still being pounded by the bombers of Göring's Luftwaffe, Stalin's Russian troops were trying to hold the gates of Moscow against Hitler's fanatic determination to conquer the Soviet Union, and the tanks of Field Marshal Erwin Rommel's Panzer Division rolled over the sands of North Africa in defiant conquest.

The lives Americans were leading on the home front were drastically different. *Everything* seemed to be rationed, and what wasn't rationed wasn't available anyhow. Most people had an "A" gasoline sticker that allowed them three gallons of gasoline a week. There was a national "victory speed" limit of thirty-five miles an hour. In the case of thousands of Americans, gas rationing and the unavailability of tires prompted them to put the cars up on cinder blocks. New cars? Forget it. Detroit quickly converted its manufacturing plants to be suitable for the production of planes, tanks, and ships. The only car coming off the assembly lines was a new model—the military jeep.

Back in the thirties, automobile dealers gave kids a free cup of ice cream if they wanted to come in and look at the new cars so they would rush home and tell their parents to buy one, but that was something else that stopped with the war. After the 1942 models rolled into America's showrooms, no new cars were manufactured until the 1946 model year, and the kids went without that source of free ice cream for the duration.

If you were lucky enough to get enough gas for your car, you still needed tires, and they were even harder to find than gas. The government initiated the Idle Tire Purchase Plan. Every car owner who had more than five tires was required to sell anything over that amount to the government at prices that varied according to the tread on the tire and its overall condition. A brand-new tire would bring you the top prize: $19.63. If you had a recap that you paid $6.50 for, the government would pay you ten dollars. And a used tire with sufficient mileage remaining on its tread would bring you $8.20.

The government wasn't fooling. The Office of Price Administration cracked down in 1942 and began to revoke the "B" and "C" ration stickers displayed on the windshields of motorists who said they qualified for more than three gallons of gas a week because of their occupations. In November, OPA found too many of those stickers on cars in the parking lot of Long Island's Belmont race track. Officials determined that thirty-eight automobile owners were using "supplemental" gas rations—gas possibly bought on the "black market"—and promptly revoked their stickers and collected their ration books.

Food became a major concern, and the subject of intensive government campaigns encouraging Americans to grow their own. The Secretary of Agriculture, Claude Wickard, called for citizens to grow vegetables in "victory gardens" so the crops from the nation's farmers could be reserved for feeding our armed forces. As early as November 1942, the change in America's food-growing practices was becoming apparent. As more and more Americans responded to Secretary Wickard's appeals and grew their own potatoes, tomatoes, corn, peas, beans, and radishes that autumn, school kids were dismissed from school for weeks at a time in rural areas to harvest the crops that their big brothers and fathers used to take to market or bring into the barn.

The same applied to the animals. Almost half of the 100 million swine slaughtered that year went to feed the military and civilian populations not just in the United States but in the countries of our Allies, too. *Life* magazine described the changing picture in its November 9 issue that year:

"The Middle West is now the breadbasket of the United Nations; its great reservoir of food must be conserved so that it will nourish our fighters and our allies. The war has brought this strange paradox to the Middle West: In a land that swarms with fat pigs and cattle, it is sometimes difficult to buy bacon and milk."

Coffee became one of the most sought-after items on the home front, in a country that often seems to fuel its national engine on the brew from that bean. Americans drank an average of twenty pounds of coffee a year, more even than Brazilians, before the war, but we would have to satisfy ourselves with half that amount. Coffee was rationed on November 29, 1942, because German submarines, Hitler's "U-Boats," were sinking freighters bound for the U.S. with their loads of coffee from Brazil.

Newspapers and magazines responded to the crisis by publishing tips on the differences in amounts required for each of the three brewing methods—boiled, percolated, and drip—and how to preserve your precious supply by brewing "stretched coffee." We were told to use level tablespoons instead of heaping ones, scour the pot thoroughly after each use, and store coffee in a cool place. You could stretch your supply by "double dripping," giving you thirty percent more coffee, or adding chicory, a French technique that would give you one-third more.

American humor helped us to survive that aspect of life on the home front. Restaurants posted signs informing customers that they could be served only one cup of coffee, but in Hollywood, a cafe owner painted a sign on a mirror behind the counter that caught everyone's attention:

> *Plenty of Coffee*
> First Cup—5 Cents
> Second Cup—$100.00

CHAPTER FIVE

The Challenge of Getting There

LaVerne, Patty, and I could do without the coffee, but the gasoline problem was a different matter. We were on the road fifty weeks every year throughout the war. You needed a government "priority," papers saying your trip was essential for the war effort, to ride a train. Flying was out of the question. That left the automobile as our only way of traveling from one engagement to the next. If we couldn't get gas for our family car so that Papa and Mama could drive us to the next town, the Andrews Sisters would have to find a new line of work.

Our schedulers tried to book us in towns no more than five hundred miles apart. The people at Universal Studios, where we filmed our movies, always provided us with enough gasoline ration stamps for our road trips, if we practiced the most severe kind of conservation.

We assumed that Universal was able to get the stamps by convincing the local Ration Board—every city and town had one—that our travel was essential for the war effort. It was considered a legitimate reason in many cases. Actors and other entertainers were even given draft deferments for the same reason in the early part of the war.

Papa was able to finesse his way through each challenge and conserve enough gas to get us and our '39 Buick to the next city on our tour. But we had to be smart about it. When we arrived, we tried to leave the car parked until the end of our engagement except for driving to a gas station for our weekly ration of gas. We walked from our hotel to the theater whenever it was possible or took a taxi. Anything to save gas.

The other challenge was to get to our engagements on time. The closest call we ever had came when we finished one of our runs at the Paramount Theater in New York City. After our last show, we had to jump in the Buick and head west toward Cleveland, Ohio, for a rehearsal at nine o'clock the next morning with Johnny Long and his orchestra at a time when Johnny was enjoying peak popularity because of the success of one of his biggest hits, "Shantytown." We made it, but only because Papa was able to weave his way across New York, New Jersey, Pennsylvania, and Ohio and take certain liberties with that national "victory speed" of thirty-five miles an hour all night long while LaVerne, Patty, and I slept in the backseat.

☆

Every time we visited the GIs, it did as much for our morale as it did for theirs. Their enthusiasm over our performance was matched by the respect they showed us, both here and when we were sent overseas for the USO.

Every contact we had with our servicemen and women convinced us about the quality of our people in uniform. They showed us every courtesy, and they never tried to make advances to any of us. We were never considered sex symbols anyhow. We had the girl-next-door image, and that suited us just fine. When we were beginning to sing around Minneapolis at the start of the 1930's, our mother told us, choosing her words the way only a mother can: "Never let it bother you that you're not beautiful. You all have"—then she'd pause—"*wonderful* personalities." With that kind of diplomacy, she could have been Roosevelt's Secretary of State.

Groucho Marx seemed to agree with Mama about our "beauty." We were traveling on the same train with Groucho when he told one of the members of his group: "I thought they made all their trips by broom."

☆

A letter published in *Life* from an American Navy pilot to some friends in Toronto just after the Battle of Midway in 1942, was convincing evidence of the quality of our fighting men and the women in uniform who were supporting them behind the scenes and behind the lines, the same people who were in our audiences:

> Many of my friends are now dead. To a man, each died with a nonchalance that each would have denied was courage. . . . If anything great or good has been born of this war, it should not be valued in the colonies we may win, nor in the pages that histories will attempt to write, but rather in the youth of our country who were never trained for war, and who almost never believed in war, but who have, from some hidden source, brought forth a gallantry which is homespun it is so real . . .
>
> Out here, between the spaceless sea and sky, American youth has found itself, and given of itself, so that a homespun spark may catch, burst into flame, and burn high. . . . My luck cannot last much longer. But the flame goes on, and only that is important.

It seemed as if everyone on the home front was doing everything possible to help America in the first year of the war. It was a tense and tragic time, but it was an exhilarating time, too—

with all of us pulling together toward the victory that Americans believed would come one day in the uncertain future.

The Andrews Sisters felt the same way, maybe even more than most. Our parents, in their early fifties, were super patriots who supported the war and FDR with enthusiasm. That rubbed off on LaVerne, Patty, and me, and we were able to project our Americanism to our audiences. Our feeling was that we had beaten the Depression, and now we were going to beat the enemies. Americans could beat anything and anybody, and if you didn't believe it, the Andrews Sisters would make a believer out of you.

Patty, LaVerne, and I wore our patriotism on our sleeves in the khaki clothing that became popular, especially for us in our wartime movies. The response to our own enthusiasm became so great that the Air Corps crews began naming their fighter planes and bombers after our song titles. All types of planes—C-47's, B-25's, B-17's—had some of our titles painted on their noses, especially "Pistol Packin' Mama" and "Shoo-Shoo, Baby."

A former governor of New Jersey, Harold Hoffman, wrote a song called "We're All In It Now" while he was a major in the first year of the war, teaming up with songwriters Paul Cunningham and Leonard Whitcup. It was introduced at a Saints and Sinners luncheon, then Vaughn Monroe introduced it to the public in a radio broadcast from the Hotel Commodore in New York City. It might not be remembered as one of the World War II classics, but its lyrics, saying that all of us, regardless of our occupations, were "in it now," accurately described the attitude—"that fightin' spirit"—of the American public in 1942.

Men who were veterans of World War I were overage for this one, so they volunteered for service as members of the local draft board, or volunteered for wartime service as Civilian Defense wardens, wearing the white helmets and arm bands with the red and blue C.D. triangle and patrolling the streets to ensure complete darkness during the many "blackouts" and air raid drills. Americans bought "blackout curtains" of dark green or black material so the lights wouldn't be visible on the outside, but during the drills we sat in pitch-black darkness, even with the blackout curtains.

No outdoor lights were turned on, period. The marquee lights were out at every theater we played during the war. They stayed out until the war was over. Usually the air raid drills were announced ahead of time, but occasionally the sirens wailed their mournful sound without advance notice. On those nights, the darkness was only half of what was scaring you. The other half was the genuine fear that this one might be real.

Women served in all sorts of voluntary roles. They worked as nurse's aides at hospitals. They prepared bundles of clothing for overseas as part of the "Bundles for Britain" campaign to help the English people survive Hitler's bombing raids. They conducted blood donor drives to ensure a sufficient supply for our wounded servicemen and "scrap drives" to recycle used metals, fats, paper, and everything else that could be manufactured again in a different form as essential equipment for fighting the war.

Women also contributed to a new development, and left their homes, six million strong, to work in defense manufacturing plants to help manufacture the arms, ammunition, and vehicles that would help us win the war. On the same assembly lines where their husbands, brothers, and fathers turned out Fords and Chevrolets before 1941, women were now mass-producing B-17 bombers, Sherman tanks, and giant aircraft carriers—and in numbers that far exceeded each year's goal. In the process, they became the vanguard of the women's movement that reached national prominence in the 1960's and '70's and continues today.

Even the kids jumped in with the enthusiasm of young

patriots. The government's War Manpower Commission asked
the nation's high schools in 1942 to organize their students into
their own Victory Corps, saying the establishment of such a
program would "give them the opportunity to take a definite
place in the national war effort through a voluntary enrollment
plan."

America's high school students and their faculty members
responded by organizing the student body into one battalion
composed of companies, platoons, and squads. Every member
spent an hour each day in military drills and calisthenics. A
full-scale curriculum offered the students courses in metal work,
blueprint reading, airplane riveting, and drafting. Some of the
boys learned Morse code with an eye toward future military
service. Girls in sewing classes made overseas caps for both the
boys and the girls to wear as part of their Victory Corps uniforms. And girls as well as boys were able to take courses in
welding as preparation for working in defense production plants
after graduating from high school.

Part of their school day included leaving the classroom to work
in factories and on farms, as well as in stores, restaurants, and in
other industries which were now finding it difficult to recruit
employees. Other students worked as janitors or cooks, helped the
adults in the scrap drives, or conducted drives of their own.

America's ten million high school students had firm convictions about what the country was doing and should do in the
future. *Fortune* magazine conducted a survey of a cross section
of students in November of 1942. With the war approaching the
end of its first year, and none of us knowing how many years
away peace was, the students expressed their opinions on the
critical issues of that critical time in these numbers:

91 percent said the U.S. should keep on fighting
82 percent said we should play an active role in the postwar
world

69 percent said military training should be compulsory after
the war
78 percent said the government should provide jobs for
everyone

More than ever our entertainers were doing their part all over the globe, and their audiences were giving them the greatest applause of their careers, something the Andrews Sisters were experiencing "over here" before the USO approved our request to go "over there" as part of its Camp Shows tour. For every performer, known and unknown—and many of them were not big names—the GIs were the best audiences of our lives.

The written reports that were sent back to USO headquarters proved it over and over again. When singer Lanny Ross played Jefferson Barracks, Missouri, Second Lieutenant Robert J. McIntosh reported: "Send us concerts of this type more often. I think it would be swell if you could send us a program at least once a week instead of once a month."

A captain in the Infantry, William F. Upton, Jr., had similar raves for Kay Kyser's appearance at Camp Edwards, Massachusetts. Upton reported: "Words fail to properly express this office's appreciation to USO Camp Shows for making entertainment of such an excellent caliber available to the men of Camp Edwards."

Earl "Fatha" Hines, the immortal jazz pianist, drew the same high praise for an appearance at the USO club in Lawton, Oklahoma, on May 28, 1942. The program director, Meredith Mathews, commented on the "magnificent concert and his grand band . . . soldiers hanging from the windows."

Earl's audiences became even more enthusiastic when he moved on to Fort Bragg on June 14. Lieutenant Ed Flynn reported to the USO on the unusual double bill featuring jazz's Hines and classical pianist Arthur Rubinstein. The show attracted fifteen thousand cheering, whistling GIs who "tore up the seats in wild acclaim in the Hines-Rubinstein battle of swing vs. classics. Rubinstein superb concert. Hines solid as a rock."

The Hines band spent most of 1942 touring military bases. Its performances have since been called a preview of "bebop" jazz that was to come in the postwar era. Earl's shows included at least two other jazz greats, Dizzy Gillespie and Charlie Parker. One of his vocalists was Billy Eckstine, who formed his own band and after the war became one of the biggest singers.

The men and women of the Army, Navy, Marines, and Coast Guard weren't the only ones who were grateful. We performers were, too. Bunny Berrigan, whose trumpet solo of "I Can't Get Started Over You" became a classic as soon as he recorded it before the war, took the time to write a report to the USO himself after playing before an audience of sailors at the Norfolk Naval Air Station: "I enjoyed playing this engagement for the boys in service very much. I am always willing to do my part in entertaining the men in service whenever possible."

Orchestra Leader Enoch Light gave a performance at New Cumberland, Pennsylvania, on June 12 and then sent a check to the USO with this note: "I have taken care of all expenses that were necessary to incur, and I ask that you accept this as a very small offering on my part toward your very wonderful cause."

The report from Mitchel Field, New York, was that Guy Lombardo's show was "excellently received from beginning to end. Guy Lombardo cooperated one hundred percent." Next door in New Jersey, forty-five hundred soldiers at Fort Monmouth sat in the rain to laugh at comedian Danny Kaye's antics.

One of the headline acts was the tap dance team called the Nicholas Brothers, Fayard and Harold. They were the sons of show business parents. Until Fayard was drafted in 1943, they toured the camps and USO clubs, performing with Bob Hope, Dick Powell when he was still a singer, the comedy team of Laurel and Hardy, George Jessel, Mary Martin, and the Jack Benny troupe with Eddie "Rochester" Anderson, Irish tenor

Dennis Day, and Phil Harris and his orchestra. Some of their government travels took them to Mexico on tours arranged by the State Department to help keep Mexico a strong ally during the war.

Fayard calls their style of dancing "classical tap." "We're so different from other tap dancers," he says today. "We don't just concentrate on our feet. We concentrate on the whole body. We use our hands a lot, gracefully. We use class and grace and style. We move all over the stage, very gracefully. . . . We don't just stand in one spot."

They were performing classical tap as far back as the war. The response from their GI audiences: "They loved it. Later on we found out everybody loved it—all over the world." Fayard remembers that Bob Hope was easily the most popular of all the entertainers with the GIs. The cover of *Time* magazine for its issue of September 20, 1943, confirms Fayard's rating. The cover features a picture of a smiling, bug-eyed Hope with a caption underneath that describes him as "first in the hearts of the servicemen."

But the war broke up the Nicholas Brothers act and slowed down their careers in the same way it took years from the careers of other entertainers and professional athletes. When Fayard was drafted, and assigned to a processing center for men bound overseas, his brother Harold suddenly found himself forced to work as a single.

Fayard remembered certain fringe benefits accorded to entertainers in the Special Services division. "We didn't have to make roll call," he said, "and we didn't have to make reveille. We could come and go as we pleased. It was just like civilian life."

It was like civilian life in at least one other way, too. In many places, especially in the South, America was still largely a segregated society, and so were the armed forces. Fayard was assigned to an all-black outfit. And when he was in the audience for a show instead of on the stage, the entertainers who came to their camp were all black, too.

"We had white officers, and there were black officers, too. But the soldiers were all black."

Was there any resentment about that segregated society?

"There was always resentment. We hated discrimination and segregation and all those things. We always hated it."

But, unlike the seething atmosphere in many American cities and towns in 1943, where heightened racial tensions reached a climax, there were no race demonstrations or protests at his camp. And Fayard Nicholas had a five-word explanation for that: "We were in the Army."

Fayard and his fellow entertainers performed away from their camp, too, at USO canteens and other Army camps. And others came to their camp to entertain the entertainers. "Lena Horne came to our camp. My brother came. There were always entertainers coming to entertain *us.*"

Were they always black?

"Yes."

☆

Kathryn Grayson, one of the biggest movie stars of them all with a beauty in her face that matched the beauty of her trained, accomplished singing voice, remembers those days of segregation in the armed forces—and her own stubborn refusal to sing before audiences where black soldiers were not admitted.

She was in the early years of a career that has made her one of America's best singers and most prominent stars, appearing in such major hits as *Showboat* and *Kiss Me, Kate.*

As her career was moving into full swing, Kathryn appeared in one of the top ten movies of 1941, *Andy Hardy's Private Secretary*, with Mickey Rooney, and then, like the rest of us, began going out on camp tours and appearing at bond rallies and doing all the other things she could do to help the war effort.

Even before Pearl Harbor, she performed at a large rally to raise funds for Russian relief in Boston. As a part of her wartime service, she also agreed to star in two of the big morale-boosting patriotic films, *Thousands Cheer* and *Anchors Aweigh*.

Kathryn is from Winston-Salem, North Carolina, but that southern lady has a mind of her own on the subject of race relations. When asked about her most memorable experience in entertaining the troops, she answered, "I was probably the first to make them let me sing for the black people." She remembered the shock when she discovered that the audiences for her GI shows were frequently segregated, because the services themselves were. "I was so annoyed," she said. "I'm from the South, but I didn't believe in it then and I don't believe in it now. They were giving their lives for their country, and we were treating them like that."

She made it clear to the military brass that she wanted the black troops to be able to attend her performances along with white soldiers. "Everywhere I went, I insisted on it. Listen, if they could go out and give their lives for me, I could certainly sing my heart out for them." Did she meet official resistance in demanding that black troops be admitted to her performances? "No, I didn't. They didn't say anything about it. When I found out that there was segregation, I made it a point, and I didn't get any resistance from the higher-ups."

Her appearances with black troops are the part of her USO tours she remembers best. "I think that was the most memorable thing about the tours," she recalls. "I would sit down and we would all sing the spirituals and the hymns. We would all wind up crying. They were all homesick, and nobody had bothered to do anything for them."

Harry Truman felt the same as Kathryn about segregation in the armed forces. After he became President, he ordered the practice discontinued.

The race issue was bubbling below the surface both on the

home front and in the armed forces throughout the war years, and it became front-page news in both military and civilian life in the long, hot summer of 1943 when racial disturbances and even riots broke out in many American cities, large and small. The worst and most tragic was in Detroit, Michigan, where thirty-four people were killed and eight hundred injured. Five hundred people were arrested, and property damage was estimated at two million dollars. At a time when there was a nationwide emphasis on productivity, two million man-hours were lost. The riot was brought under control only after President Roosevelt ordered Army troops into the city.

Riots also occurred that summer in Beaumont, Texas, where martial law had to be declared. In Los Angeles, racial disturbances were the worst in a generation. Citizens in Mobile, Alabama, staged a "hate strike," and there were racial problems in Chester, a suburb of Philadelphia, and in the Harlem section of New York.

In Los Angeles, one scene of the racial unrest occurred, believe it or not, in the Hollywood Canteen. The Canteen, which was doing so much good in serving the morale of our military personnel, was established on the initiative of several stars, including Bette Davis and John Garfield, and with Local 47, the "white musicians union," and Local 767, the union for black musicians. Both locals were affiliated with the American Federation of Musicians. When the Canteen opened, members of Local 767 were given assurances that there would be no racial discrimination. Both white and black hostesses were on hand to dance with the servicemen and socialize with them.

Down Beat, one of the show business weeklies, reported in April 1943: "The girls were told that they did not *have* to dance with *anyone* in the Canteen against their wishes. Their only instructions were that they show courtesy in refusing an invitation to dance and to be particularly courteous in refusing invitations extended by soldiers of races other than their own."

Down Beat said problems began when white hostesses and white soldiers began to dance with black partners. "Certain persons," the article said, "evidently women acting as 'chaperons' of the hostesses, attempted to break up this practice, causing embarrassment for those concerned. An investigation conducted by *Down Beat* uncovered evidence that there is a faction within the Canteen administration, which, if not actually anti-Negro, is fearful of progressive attempts to overcome prejudice. This faction, led by a nonprofessional Beverly Hills woman who is very active in the affairs of the Canteen, attempted at the recent meeting to pass a rule forbidding 'mixed dancing.' " But the attempt failed when two of Hollywood's biggest stars, Bette Davis and John Garfield, threatened to resign from the Canteen's board and withdraw the support of the Screen Actors Guild.

The problem of race relations flared up repeatedly during the war. Kathryn Grayson learned that segregation was not limited to the armed forces. When she was one of the participating stars on a tour of entertainers to promote the third war bond drive—the most successful of the seven conducted during the war—she ran into it again, and this time it was applied against the stars.

"That was one of the things I didn't know when I did that tour," she says today. "Lena Horne and the other black performers had to go to separate hotels. I didn't know that, or I would have raised Cain. I loved Lena. She was a good friend of mine."

The troupe went all over the country. It was a Hollywood galaxy, featuring Kathryn, Greer Garson, Jimmy Cagney, Jose Iturbi, Paul Henreid, and a long list of others. In each city, the whites were assigned to one hotel, the blacks to another—this practice on a government tour as part of an important government program.

Kathryn ran into the problem a third time during the war, and this time it was a reminder that segregation existed in spots all over America, including the nation's capital. As she was working on her next picture, the MGM employees who opened the fan mail addressed to the stars began reading letters from one of MGM's own employees who was following her and threatening to kidnap her. The threat eventually evaporated, but until it did, two FBI agents were assigned to Kathryn and accompanied her everywhere, including on a business trip to Washington.

At the Mayflower Hotel, Kathryn was told that her maid, who was traveling with her, could not stay in her suite. Kathryn asked, "Well, where *is* she going to stay?"

When officials told her, Kathryn had a ready response: "Then I'll just take my things there."

She won again. "I think my maid was the first black woman ever to stay at the Mayflower."

In 1943, the USO announced that it had signed the Al Sears band for a tour of Army camps across the country as its first "Negro" unit. *Down Beat* said the band "rivals any of the white orchestras already set for similar tours." The paper said the Sears band was comparatively safe, at least temporarily, from the military draft calls that were depriving so many of America's bands of their musicians. Sears had one 4-F member, and most of the others were married with children, a marital status that protected young men from military service, though not permanently.

For Fayard Nicholas there was nothing new in appearing as a black entertainer before an all-black audience. He and Harold were performing at the Cotton Club uptown in New York's Harlem with Cab Calloway and Duke Ellington as early as 1932. He and his little brother—and they really *were* little, with Fayard the taller at five feet four inches—had gotten their start in show business with their parents in 1930, when Fayard was eleven, and Harold was seven.

By the start of the war they had appeared in night clubs, in ballets and on the stage and on radio, in addition to making several records. "We were in every type of show business except opera. We were even in the circus." They had even appeared in a variety of movies, including *Down Argentine Way, Stormy Weather, That's Dancin',* and *The Pirate,* where they danced with Gene Kelly, and two films with Glenn Miller—*Sun Valley Serenade* and *Orchestra Wives.*

The Nicholas Brothers played a part in introducing "Chattanooga Choo-Choo" in *Sun Valley Serenade* and "I've Got a Gal in Kalamazoo" in *Orchestra Wives.* History credits the Glenn Miller orchestra with Tex Beneke, Marion Hutton, and the Modernaires for introducing the songs in the films, but "we introduced them, too, because right after he and his singers and his musicians played them, we would follow them and also sing. So we helped to make those songs popular, too." When the Nicholas Brothers played the USO clubs and military bases, those were the two songs the GIs wanted the most. Their place in the history of American show business is now secure. In 1991, still dancing their classical tap after sixty years, they were chosen for the prestigious "Kennedy Center Honors" award in Washington.

CHAPTER SIX

Tyrone's Opinion of *Der Fuehrer*

It seemed that everyone in show business was serving our country, and not always in their usual roles as singers or entertainers. Ray Block, leader of the orchestra for a popular show called *Johnny Presents*, was an air raid warden for a five-mile area around his farm in Brewster, New York. Joan Edwards, one of the singing stars on *Your Hit Parade*, gave informal concerts at her home on Long Island. The price of admission: at least five pounds of scrap iron.

The long lineup of familiar performers who were lending their talents and time seemed to stretch forever—pianists Eddy Duchin and Alec Templeton, comedians Stubby Kaye, Billy DeWolfe, Bert Wheeler, Eddie Mayoff and Pinky Lee, singer Jeanette MacDonald, many song-and-dance vaudevillians such as Gus Van, and the big bands.

Oh, how they loved the big bands—Duke Ellington playing "Take the 'A' Train"; Russ Morgan in his old Pennsylvania coal miner's helmet playing and singing "Does Your Heart Ache for Me?"; Shep Fields and his "Rippling Rhythm"; Ted Weems, who became such a big hit right after the war with his whistling rendition of "Heartaches"; the Ink Spots singing "If I Didn't Care"; and Vaughn Monroe's rich vocal of "Racing with the Moon."

One of the early heroes among the USO entertainers was Virginia O'Brien, a popular singer who used a deadpan expression and a ramrod-stiff stature in delivering her song. She had attracted attention in a movie called *Hullabaloo* in 1940, a spoof on the Orson Welles radio drama, *War of the Worlds*, two years earlier. Virginia, stone-faced and moving only her shoulders and then only occasionally, stood frozen on the screen while singing "Carry Me Back to Old Virginny" and "I Dreamed of Jeannie with the Light Brown Hair."

After that act, she was on her way to stardom. She appeared with Judy Garland in *The Harvey Girls*, and with Red Skelton, Lucille Ball, Gene Kelly, and Tommy Dorsey in *DuBarry Was a Lady*, where she sang "Life Upon the Wicked Stage."

Her friendship with Lucille Ball helped her to overcome one of the two fears she had at that time. The first was a fear of flying, which Virginia later conquered when she married a pilot and found herself flying with him as a matter of necessity. At the start of the war, though, that fear was still with her, and when Bob Hope asked her to accompany him on his first overseas tour, she declined, asking him how she was going to get there.

She contributed in a major way, however, by appearing at military posts and hospitals throughout California, beginning with the first USO show staged there, at Fort Ord in the San Francisco Bay Area. She had plenty of stellar company—Marlene Dietrich, Claudette Colbert, Dick Powell, Joan Blondell, the Ritz Brothers, Carole Landis, George Burns, Gracie Allen, and Jack Benny.

When she appeared with Lucille Ball at a hospital in the Bay Area, Lucy helped her to overcome her second fear—that of hospitals. The USO performers entertained the troops at a show outdoors, and when it came time to move inside and tour the wards to entertain those soldiers who were bedridden, Virginia asked to be excused.

She told Lucy she simply couldn't stand hospitals.

"Virginia, you *have* to do it," Lucy told her.

Virginia knew Lucy was right. She couldn't go on being afraid of hospitals for the rest of her life, and she knew she couldn't let down the GIs who were making such sacrifices for their country. She took a deep breath, went inside with Lucy and the others, and performed with them.

Then she arranged a tour for herself, lasting six weeks—to nothing but military hospitals.

Lou Wills may have been the youngest of the USO entertainers. He was only fourteen when the war started, but already he was performing on stage and in a Broadway show as a comedy dancer and acrobat. By the time of Pearl Harbor, he was getting his education at the Archibald Lodge, a school for children in the theater, while appearing on Broadway. He was in *Best Foot Forward*, the first show choreographed by Gene Kelly, then *Something For the Boys*, and later in *Laughing Room Only*, a dizzying, whirlwind vaudeville show of sight gags, pratfalls, and slapstick comedy produced by the team of Olsen and Johnson— Olie Olsen and Chick Johnson.

In the early days of the war, he was appearing in *Something For the Boys* when its producers decided they wanted to start doing something for the GIs. They teamed up with Ed Sullivan, then a famous New York columnist and not yet the TV personality he was to become in the postwar years. Sullivan helped make the arrangements—and met Lou. Lou started calling the much older Sullivan "Uncle Ed," and from that time on, for the rest of his life, Sullivan referred to Lou as "my nephew."

The troupers from *Something For the Boys* performed all up

and down the East Coast. To express their gratitude, officials at the military locations often sent a supply of some of the local products to the performers. Lou quickly learned that not all of these modest expressions were appropriate—such as the time he played Norfolk with the Olsen and Johnson company, and a week later a delivery man dropped off a honey-baked Virginia ham at the family home in Yonkers, New York. Lou's family was Jewish, and his father, who subscribed to the strict Orthodox philosophy of his religion, could only laugh at the unintended humor of delivering a forbidden meat to an Orthodox Jewish household. "Isn't this wonderful?" he said to his wife. "Our Jewish son goes down to Virginia and performs for our boys in uniform, and they give him a ham."

On another weekend, Lou and his colleagues played a Marine base in North Carolina. A week or so later, another package arrived in Yonkers—five cartons of cigarettes. "I never heard of any of the brands," Lou says. "There weren't any Chesterfields or Lucky Strikes or Camels. And they were awful, the worst cigarettes anybody ever smoked."

Lou remembers Ed Sullivan's tireless work in taking troupes up and down the East Coast every weekend. "We'd leave New York on Saturday night, after our show, and get to our base or hospital at two or three in the morning. Then we'd put on a show at a hospital at nine or ten, an afternoon show at a base and a full evening show, then fly back to New York on Monday morning. We'd play on Broadway all week long and head out again the next Saturday night and do the same thing."

When we talked to him about his USO shows, Lou said: "Ed Sullivan did more for bringing entertainment to the bases, camps, and hospitals than anyone I know. He dragged people everywhere—taking trains, taking buses, taking planes. We'd get into a base at two o'clock Sunday morning, and at eight he'd be getting everybody up and saying, 'C'mon. The hospital's ready for us any time after nine. Let's go. Let's do a show.' "

All of the entertainers performed under conditions that were makeshift at best. Lou remembers tap dancing on an eight-by-ten floor board put down on the deck of a submarine—and trying not to slide into the Atlantic Ocean.

"We were playing the sub base in New London," he says, "and that boat's going up and down in the water, and I'm sliding around the deck, and even falling. It was like trying to dance on the back of a porpoise."

Some of the weekend cast he was part of included some big names, but many of them were less famous. Betty Garrett, one of the popular singers, is in almost every picture Lou has of those years. Dodie Goodman, who gained fame after the war in her frequent appearances with Jack Paar on the *Tonight* show, was in the group, too, wearing an upswept hairdo. Later in the war Olsen and Johnson themselves performed for the men and women in uniform, at a time when they were the most famous madcap comedy team in America.

The troupes Lou traveled with were notable for their variety—singers, dancers, comedians, novelty acts, even a drummer named Jack Powell who used a set of props that looked like a kitchen. He would play his drumsticks on every "instrument" in his "kitchen." "That guy played those drum sticks on chairs, tables, pots and pans, dishes, coffee cups, glasses. He was an amazing act," Lou says.

A handsome singer named Bill Johnson was one of the performers. In the lingo of New York entertainers, Lou used to call him "you good-looking bum." Others thought he was good-looking, too—and healthy looking. They wondered, sometimes to his face, why he wasn't in uniform like almost everybody else.

He was 4-F, but he never said why. The reason: He had a hole in his heart. But he maintained the same rugged schedule the rest of the troupers did, knowing he was taking a serious risk, but also knowing that war is a time when many people take risks. He never took offense at the questions about his civilian status.

He sang his heart out for the GIs, almost literally, and never asked for any favors because of his physical condition. He endured the same hardships as everyone else in his troupe—never enough sleep, meals on an irregular schedule or not at all, frequent changes in temperature, and an exhausting schedule—and died shortly after the war.

The troupe included a performer with the stage name of Lord Buckley, who used to pick six GIs out of the audience, stand behind them on the stage, and tell them to move their mouths when he tapped them, without speaking any words. Then he told the audience that he was going to do the talking for all six of them.

The GIs would be standing there looking as if they were having an enjoyable conversation, but they weren't saying a word. From behind, Lord Buckley was speaking in six voices—different in every way—as the audience collapsed in laughter.

Those USO weekends were a learning experience for Lou, and Lord Buckley was the source of one of Lou's early lessons. On a bus ride to a weekend military stop, Lou smelled something strange. He asked the passenger in the seat next to him what that funny smell was.

"Don't you know?"

"No. What is it?"

"Marijuana."

"Lord Buckley would sit in the back of the bus on our way from the airport and smoke pot," Lou says, "and start to preach and chant, 'The Lord sent me down here. He told me that if we all smoke the same thing we'll be flying high and we can fly over this war and we'll all be happy.' He was hilarious, especially with that pot in him."

When his skin began breaking out with large red bumps, Lou went to the family doctor in Yonkers and learned something else—he was allergic to the smoke from Lord Buckley.

The teenage Lou began to ask himself the same question that

people of every age ask in time of war: Why? Why do men feel they have to fight wars?

"We'd visit hospital wards," he remembers, "and I'd see all those wounded men, especially the ones they called the 'basket cases,' the guys with their arms and legs shot off and just lying there in a basket, completely helpless, and I wondered why. To this day, I still ask why."

Like many other USO entertainers, Lou formed lifelong friendships during his wartime experiences. One of them was with Betty Garrett. They remain close friends today. And in a tap dance class that Lou teaches in Hollywood every Wednesday night, one of his star pupils is Betty Garrett.

Today Lou says flatly, and fondly, "I was in nine shows on Broadway. I've performed on opening nights at night clubs, I was in vaudeville and movies, I've helped to open hotels in Vegas and Florida, but those GI audiences were the best of all."

While the rest of us were busy playing at the camps and USO clubs in the United States, other troupes were touring the Pacific, the Caribbean, and the Arctic. The first troupe visited the European Theater of Operations. Four women—Kay Francis, Martha Raye, Mitzi Mayfair, and Carole Landis—blazed that trail, leaving New York for England on August 24. After several weeks there, they went on to North Africa for several more weeks.

On this side of the Atlantic, the first USO troupe to perform in Panama arrived there later in the year, composed of a popular actress and model, Jinx Falkenburg, the zany comedy team of the Ritz Brothers, and a radio singer, Barbara Lamarr.

The troupe spent three weeks in the Panama Canal Zone. They performed in thirty-eight shows at twenty-five Army and Navy bases. Some were large, permanent military installations, but other spots where they performed were little more than small clearings in the midst of thick jungles.

Like all of us, Jinx, Barbara, and the Ritz Brothers had no idea of where they were going when their plane took off from LaGuardia Airport. Military secrecy was as tight for us performers as it was anywhere else during the war, so we were never told where we were going until we were in the air. It was obvious to anyone who saw Jinx when she arrived in Panama that she hadn't been told anything. She landed in that tropical climate wearing a long-sleeved woolen dress and carrying a fur coat!

Their first show gave the performers the same elated feeling that all of us felt in front of GI audiences. It was in a gymnasium, and Jinx said later: "It was the most terrific experience I have ever had in my whole career."

When the troupe returned to the U.S., Jinx wrote an article about the tour for *Life*. "Wherever we played, we were forced to forget everything we had ever learned about stage appearance," she reported. "Always the stages were small and sometimes the dressing rooms were behind the audience instead of behind the stage."

☆

The inconvenient conditions under which they entertained the troops never bothered the USO performers. Jo Bernier, one of my best friends for over fifty years, has a long line of "war stories" of her own. We met after Patty, LaVerne, and I recorded "Bei Mir Bist Du Schoen." She was just getting her career started, too, as a ballet tap dancer whose maiden name was Andrews. She had a lot of fun with that, because she couldn't resist the temptation to tell people she was "the fourth Andrews sister."

Jo must have set some kind of record with her USO service. It included eight months in Alaska, six more months in Europe, right behind the front lines, then another tour to Europe for almost another year. She was there when the war in Europe ended.

Somewhere along the line, she also found time to spend six months playing one-night stands at military posts and hospitals up and down the East Coast of the United States, from Maine to Florida and back.

In Alaska, she and the other members of her troupe lived in tents or quonset huts, trying to stay warm in the Alaskan winter by feeding wood into a stove that was so hot you couldn't get within three feet of it, though you froze if you were *four* feet away.

She saw only a hint of daylight during her winter in Alaska, two hours of a dusklike sky. In the spring months, the sun took up its twenty-four-hours-a-day position. When Jo came home to Brookline, Massachusetts, for a brief rest before heading off to Europe, she told a reporter for her hometown paper that she was having trouble getting used to dancing, or even walking, on hard surfaces after eight months in Alaska. The paper ran a feature story on the hometown girl who was making good for her country, under a less-than-heroic headline that said:

Brookline Dancer's Feet Hurt After Alaskan Mud

They traveled by dogsled to remote posts and once gave a show at a location where only four soldiers were stationed. There was no music or props. The USO entertainers danced to the songs being sung by their private audience. Then the four "girls" in the USO troupe cooked dinner for the four GIs.

Their troupe consisted of Jo Andrews, Nancy Healy, Margie Liszt, and Julie Lane. After sailing on November 5, they endured the harsh Alaskan winter through Thanksgiving and Christmas, spent Easter there, too, and didn't leave until summer was approaching. Together they covered ten thousand miles by air and performed in 830 shows, including eight a day at many stops, for men who hadn't seen a woman for as long as eighteen months. Jo remembers that they had to be escorted by guards through throngs of lonely GIs. When they ate, the soldiers would just stand around and stare at them.

"They had a hard time believing we were really four American girls," Jo says. "The ones in front would reach out their hands to touch our faces and then yell to the guys behind them, 'Hey—they're real!' They wanted desperately to touch us, but when they did it was with real respect, almost an attitude of reverence."

The GIs used to beg the four girls from home for any kind of souvenir—an empty powder box, a used perfume bottle, *anything*. Every morning during a stop at Adak, the troupers would find stacks of "love letters" outside their barracks door.

At many of their shows, GIs actually hung from the rafters. "I'd heard that expression," Jo says, "but that was the first time I ever saw it really happen."

When they left Alaska, they wore yellow ribbons, pinned on them by Lieutenant General Simon Cuckner, who was in charge of Alaskan operations.

The commanding officer of the Naval Auxiliary Air Facilities in Atka may have expressed the appreciation of the GI audiences better than anyone. On July 16, 1943, he wrote to Jo: "It is, needless to say, and yet harder to explain, what the smell of perfume, the glimpse of shapely legs, the twist of a lovely torso, and the ring of feminine laughter does to man. The big man, little man, fat man, skinny man, the young and the old, it makes no difference—it affects them all."

He went on. "They are then putty in the hands of the possessor of such charms. They want to be her protector, they want to fight for her safety, they want to fight hard to win this war, so that soon they may return to their dear ones back there. Your very presence here has done this to the fighting men of this island."

Before one of her European tours, Jo Andrews signed the standard contract with USO Camp Shows, which included these stipulations:

(9) You agree to eliminate from your act any spoken material or theatrical business which may be deemed objectionable by Camp Shows, Inc., or their representatives. Camp Shows, Inc., reserves the right to cancel this agreement immediately in the event that you refuse to comply with its written request for such eliminations.

(10) You agree that neither you nor any of your employees will give any indecent, immoral or offensive performance, nor conduct yourself or themselves in a manner offensive to public decency or morality . . .

In Europe, Jo heard the sounds of war—the German bombs during the London Blitz, the "buzz bombs" as Hitler frantically tried to prolong the war four years later with his new "secret weapons" near the end of the war, the wailing sirens when the German bombers were approaching, and the bursts of the heavy mortar weapons just beyond the front lines, near where she was performing.

Jo was in the thick of the combat zones, so close to the fighting during one of her European tours that she got to fire a mortar shell at the enemy. One of the soldiers let her pull the trigger.

☆

Applause and laughter were never so loud, or so easy to get, as when you were playing before GI audiences. They wrote a gag into the routine for that troupe in which Jinx Falkenburg would ask the Ritz Brothers, "Hey—can one of you tell me where a girl can get a date around here?"

Bedlam followed—every time. The guys would jump out of

their chairs or up off the ground and holler up to the stage, "Hey, Jinx! Here I am! Over here!"

One of the Ritz Brothers would ask her, "Jinx, look at all those faces. How do they make you feel?"

Jinx: "Like Little Red Riding Hood."

Ritz Brother: "Yeah, they *do* look like a pack of wolves, don't they?"

"It didn't make any difference what you said," Jinx said later.

That's how appreciative the GI audiences were—and it was also how anxious all of us were to laugh. Every GI audience that LaVerne, Patty and I played for was enthusiastic and appreciative. Just to feel that you were doing your part by entertaining the service personnel was reward enough, but the men and women in the GI audiences made our reward even greater.

Comedian Eddie Bracken remembered the enthusiasm of the GI audiences when he appeared in a TV special about the role of Hollywood's entertainers in the war. In *Stars and Stripes* on the American Movie Classics cable network, Eddie said, "If you wanted your morale picked up, all you had to do was walk across the stage and you would have gotten the biggest hand, the yelling would have been absolutely tremendous, the whistles fantastic. You had to cross that stage thinking, 'God put me on the face of the earth for this.' "

Even my little dog, Tyrone, discovered how to get an easy laugh during the war. Despite our constant traveling, Lou and I found time to establish a home in the Hollywood Hills, and a ranch on Cold Water Canyon in the San Fernando Valley near Hollywood. As a dog lover all my life, I was in my glory. I owned a kennel on the ranch, and had seventy-five dogs—boxers, Dobermans, and cocker spaniels. During one break off the road, I helped to deliver thirty-five boxer puppies. With all my canine friends, plus two hundred chickens, two calves, and four cows, I couldn't have been happier.

The farm animals were a wartime necessity. There was a shortage of dairy products, so Lou and I decided to produce our own milk, cream, and butter. It was also a help for Mama and Papa, who loved cream and butter but weren't able to find any in the stores. Through an interview with the *Minneapolis Star Journal*, I told our old friends and neighbors back home, "Now our parents get three quarts of cream a week, the dogs get the skimmed milk, we have a barnyard, and everybody's happy."

At the same time, Patty, LaVerne, and I bought our parents a home on an acre of ground in Brentwood, and my sisters moved in with them. They lived on the same street as Gary Cooper, Tyrone Power, Caesar Romero, Eddie Bracken, Nelson Eddy, and Deanna Durbin. Those celebrity neighbors used to run into one another when they walked their dogs in the evenings. LaVerne told us she thought their Doberman pinscher was in love with Deanna Durbin's cocker spaniel.

Lou, who was being called "the fourth Andrews Sister" in the press almost as often as Jo Andrews because of his success in managing us and selecting the songs for our recordings, surprised me one day with a tiny black cocker spaniel, sitting in a loving cup. I named him Tyrone, something that Tyrone Power, one of the leading matinee idols of that time, might not have appreciated.

We were playing the Hippodrome Theater in Baltimore during the war, and Tyrone, as always, was with me. I took him on every trip we ever made for the entire fifteen years of his life. But I never made him part of our act. He was an incredibly obedient dog and he seemed to understand what people said to him. At rehearsals, if I told him, "Go sit in the brass section," he'd head past the strings and the reeds and go right into the brass section. If I told him, "Go sit with the drummer," that's what he'd do. During our shows, he'd sit obediently and patiently offstage, waiting in the wings for me to come off.

Except for that night in Baltimore. Tyrone got tired of waiting, or of our act, and walked onto the stage. After we finished our number and before we went into our next one, the three of us just stood there looking at him—and he sat there, head cocked and tail wagging, looking at us.

Finally, Patty put her hands on her hips and said to Tyrone for the first time in his life, "Now what would you do if *Der Fuehrer* walked in here right now?"

That little thing got right up from where he was sitting in the middle of the stage, walked to the front, straight to the floor microphone, lifted his leg, and wet the base of the mike. The applause was deafening.

CHAPTER SEVEN

Praise the Lord, and Its Tragic Irony

Praise the Lord, we're on a mighty mission,
All aboard! We aren't a goin' fishin'.
Praise the Lord and pass the ammunition,
And we'll all stay free.

The "manpower shortage," an expression we were hearing more often, was hitting every industry hard. Entertainers, ball players—young men from every walk of life were either being drafted or enlisted because they wanted to do their part. That's how wide and deep the public support was for this war.

The band business was no exception. In the first year or so of the war, some of the biggest names of the "Big Band era" were in military uniform. Glenn Miller joined the Army Air Forces as a captain and later a major, but the Navy seemed to make out the best of all the branches, getting Artie Shaw, Orrin Tucker, Eddy Duchin, Claude Thornhill, Clyde McCoy, and Tex Beneke. Phil Harris and Ted Weems joined the Merchant Marine, and Rudy Valley went into the Coast Guard.

The Merry Macs, a popular quartet that included three brothers, had the first big hit of "Praise the Lord and Pass the Ammunition" in 1942, followed by Kay Kayser's arrangement of the song in 1943. Frank Loesser, who later wrote such smash Broadway musicals as *Guys and Dolls* and *The Most Happy*

Fella, wrote both the words and the music for this song, and the American people began singing its upbeat message late in the fall of '42. It immediately became one of the most motivational numbers of World War II.

The song's origin remains the subject of disagreement even today. Most accounts agree that the song's title comes from a rallying cry voiced by a Navy chaplain at Pearl Harbor during his sermon that Sunday morning of the attack, but the identity of the chaplain is disputed. Some accounts identify him as Howell Forgy of New Orleans, others as William Maguire.

The song became such an enormous hit that the Office of War Information, which exercised the strongest kind of wartime government control over America's radio stations, finally appealed to the stations not to play it more often than once every four hours so audiences wouldn't tire of it. The government could have saved itself the worry and the trouble of appealing to the radio stations. I never heard anybody say they got tired of hearing it. And the audiences we sang for never got tired of asking us to sing it.

In one of the many bitter ironies of war, one of the brothers in the Merry Macs, Joe McMichael, was killed in the service two years later.

LaVerne, Patty, and I began doing everything we could think of to help the guys and gals who were in the service. We were running out to camps and hospitals between shows in every city on our tours, and then we started doing something else: In each city, we would take three servicemen to dinner every night. If we had to eat with someone else for business or family reasons, we left the cost of three dinners at the restaurant with orders that the next three servicemen through the door be served as our guests.

We also began making frequent visits to the Hollywood Canteen, along with other show business celebrities. Virginia O'Brien remembers that she appeared there every Friday night, because that was "MGM Night." She served food to the GIs and sang for them. She would have danced with them, too, but she was too shy, so she stuck to serving and singing.

The Hollywood Canteen was an MGM galaxy on those Friday nights, with Virginia one member of a cast that included Hedy Lamarr, Clark Gable, Spencer Tracy, Judy Garland, Ray Bolger, and Mickey Rooney.

When we were in New York City to play the Paramount Theater and later the Roxy at Seventh Avenue and Fiftieth Street, we always made as many appearances as possible at the Stage Door Canteen. It was on Forty-Fourth Street, between Broadway and Eighth Avenue. A wall plaque donated by *The New York Times* still marks the spot.

The founding of the Stage Door Canteen in New York was set in motion even before the war, when a group of prominent women in the theater, including director Antoinette Perry, for whom the Tony Award is named, and actresses Vera Ellen and Gertrude Lawrence, formed the American Theatre Wing of the British War Relief Society. In January 1940, the women, joined by Helen Hayes, Lynn Fontanne, Katharine Cornell, Tallulah Bankhead and others, raised funds and knitted clothing for French and British refugees and brought orphaned children of English actors to the United States.

With America's entry into the war, the group renamed itself the American Theatre Wing War Service. Its expanding membership included Lee Shubert, Billy Rose, Raymond Massey and Moss Hart. The American Theatre Wing's current president, Isabelle Stevenson, told us her organization opened the Stage Door Canteens in New York, Boston, Philadelphia, Cleveland, Newark, San Francisco, Washington, and London. A ninth canteen was added in 1945 in Paris after that city was liberated from Nazi occupation.

Servicemen danced with the likes of Marlene Dietrich and Ethel Merman, were served food by Vincent Price and Oscar

Hammerstein and Alfred Lunt and were entertained by Celeste Holm and Benny Goodman. One of the "junior hostesses" in New York was a young actress, Lauren Bacall. As a current brochure of the American Theatre Wing points out, "Ironically, servicewomen were not permitted in the canteens in America because the Wing could not permit any romance in the canteens."

The Stage Door Canteen was so successful that it prompted Bette Davis to team up with entertainment journalist Radie Harris to found the Hollywood Canteen with the help of other movie stars including John Garfield. By 1946, the Wing's volunteers had produced one thousand five hundred auditorium programs, three hundred fifty legitimate plays and over six thousand seven hundred ward performances. Over one thousand two hundred volunteers a month went to camps and hospitals during the war, including 25 hospitals in the New York area.

No one simply *performed* at the canteens. You sang or danced or told jokes or played a musical instrument, whatever your specialty was, but you also waited on tables, danced with the guys or gals, and provided a friendly or sympathetic ear whenever the occasion arose in conversation, which was often.

The whole country was dotted with USO canteens. They were in every town, either in their own buildings, or in church social halls, train stations, and even bus depots. Comedian Ed Wynn used to joke about the one in Washington, saying the members of Congress ate with the GIs there. As a result, he concluded that "those poor fellas must be starving, because you know how long it takes Congress to pass anything."

When Fred Waring introduced us at the Stage Door Canteen, he said, "You know, some of you may think I'm pretty smart because of the success the Pennsylvanians have had. But I'm pretty dumb. I had three girls audition for our group three years in a row, and each time I told them no. Twice I even told them to go home. If I had hired them, I could have had the Andrews Sisters for seventy-five dollars a week."

He was telling the truth. He told us our voices were too husky, and we were too young to develop his kind of "sound" for his shows. Each of those rejections was a blow to us. We were three cocky kids, and we thought we could compete with anybody, including his own group, The Smoothies.

I was thrilled when Fred told the audience at the Stage Door Canteen that he had rejected us not once but three times. Each of his turndowns took something out of me. I was supposed to be the business brains of the Andrews Sisters, and I worried more about our careers than Patty and LaVerne did. Every time he turned us down after we auditioned, Fred's decision told me that maybe we really weren't that good, that maybe we weren't going to make it all the way to the top. But when Fred said what he did at the Stage Door Canteen that night, he was telling us that we had made it all the way to the top after all.

We sang "Bei Mir Bist Du Schoen" with Fred's Pennsylvanians that night. Everywhere we went in those years, that song was a must. If we didn't include it in our act, we had to sing it as one of our encore numbers. We used to tell each other that apparently the whole world was Jewish, because people seemed to think their chances of getting us to sing it for them would be better if they said—and they did, almost every time—"I'm Jewish, and that's my favorite song."

That night at the Stage Door Canteen was the only time the Andrews Sisters ever sang with Fred Waring and His Pennsylvanians.

Russ Milton, the manager of the Stage Door Canteen, had a "don't-play list" of songs that he wanted performers to avoid. The emphasis at all the canteens was on fun, helping the servicemen and women to get their minds off the war. Russ didn't want any war songs included in the program, even those that were popular.

He discouraged anyone from singing or playing "We Did It Before," "Dear Mom," "Remember Pearl Harbor," "My Buddy," "When the Lights Go On Again," "White Cliffs of Dover," and even "God Bless America."

Irving Berlin described the yearnings of the GI patrons at the USO canteens in a song he wrote for the biggest musical of the war, *This Is the Army*. The show was a tremendous hit on Broadway in 1942 and a highly successful movie—in Technicolor, one of the big treats in any movie then—in '43. The Broadway musical was an all-soldier show. The Hollywood film featured the well-known stars of the time, including a future senator and a future President, George Murphy and Ronald Reagan.

As he did with "God Bless America," and his other inspirational songs about life in the U.S.A., Irving Berlin captured the mood of the times perfectly, writing *The Stage Door Canteen*, about its atmosphere and what it meant to the soldiers, sailors, and Marines who visited there while awaiting overseas duty or on the way back. Every GI headed for that USO club when he hit New York, for its free food and free coffee and the company of entertainers famous and not-so-famous who performed for them, served them their meals, washed their dishes, and sat with them and talked—and listened. The place became so popular and so famous that CBS began broadcasting a half-hour radio show from there every Thursday night at nine-thirty, sponsored by the American Theater Wing and the Corn Products Refining Company.

The sponsors took out a full-page ad in some of the show business weeklies in April of 1943 saluting all the performers who were entertaining there any time any of us were in New York. Because of our own visits there, and only five years after our first hit, imagine how thrilled we were to see ourselves thanked in that ad along with such show business giants as Burns and Allen, Eddie Cantor, Milton Berle, Ralph Edwards, Morton

Downey, Joan Fontaine, Jane Froman, Lillian Gish, Benny Goodman, Victor Borge, Bob Hope, Yehudi Menuhin, George Jessel, Al Jolson, Jeanette MacDonald, Chico Marx, Smith and Dale, Mary Martin, Lauritz Melchior, Ethel Merman, Zero Mostel, Bill "Bojangles" Robinson, Alec Templeton, Sophie Tucker, Ethel Waters, and Orson Welles.

The canteens in Hollywood, New York, and all those other cities brought out the best in the people there, as well as in the entertainers. All those stars, those who weren't stars, those who gave so many hours to sit and talk and dance with the GIs, and those behind the scenes in the kitchen and elsewhere deserved medals of their own.

The word about the New York Stage Door Canteen got around, helped in part by the Navy signal men who blinked this rave review when ships passed each other on the Atlantic and Pacific: "No liquor, but damned good."

Nineteen forty-two was a year as difficult as we had feared. Thousands of our "boys," who were now men, were being killed overseas, and thousands more were leaving their homes every month for basic training in the Army or boot camp for the Navy and Marines. The Japanese simply overran our forces in the Pacific in the first half of the year, capturing everything in sight and inflicting humiliating and tragic losses on our Army and Marine units.

A shocking bombing raid over Tokyo, Yokohama, Kobe, and Osaka, by a flight of sixteen B-25 bombers from the carrier *Hornet* led by Lieutenant Colonel Jimmy Doolittle was one of our few bright spots. The raid, on the anniversary of the midnight ride of Paul Revere, was flown by eighty crew members after secret training. It did little military damage to Japan's four cities, but it did wonders for the American morale, while also causing grave concern among Japan's leaders. It was the first time an enemy had attacked the Japanese homeland and escaped. In that one swift strike, they learned that our bombers could reach their cities—and their most sacred shrine, the emperor's imperial palace in Tokyo, the capital city. And worst of all in terms of the Japanese culture, the nation's leaders had lost face.

The Japanese captured Manila in the Philippines on the second day of the year. The peninsula of Bataan fell, then the island of Corregidor. The Japanese landed on American soil, our island of Attu in the Aleutians off the coast of Alaska, and occupied another island, Kiska, not knowing it would be their farthest penetration westward.

But something else happened at that same time, in the first half of June—an event that would ultimately bring about Japan's defeat. Many of us didn't realize it at the time. The shooting and bombings and torpedo firings would drag on for another three years, but in the first half of June 1942, Japan's fate was sealed. While the Japanese were rejoicing over their landing in the Aleutians, they suffered their first decisive naval defeat, and it spelled doom for them.

It was called the Battle of Midway. In that engagement near the island of Midway in the central Pacific, we met the enemy head-on, the same enemy that boasted of having the most powerful Navy and Air Force in the world and tried to demonstrate it with the attack on Pearl Harbor. But in five minutes on June 4, two squadrons of dive bombers from our carriers, the *Hornet* and the *Enterprise,* caught four Japanese carriers and a heavy cruiser by surprise. The enemy lost three of the carriers, and the battle ended in a decisive victory for the United States against what had been the most powerful fighting force in the Pacific.

What made Midway even more decisive, with an impact that determined the course of the rest of the war, was a victory in intelligence and cryptography that the Japanese never learned about.

The victory: We broke their radio code.

The result: We knew everything they were going to do—before they did it—at Midway and for the rest of the war.

The achievement was remarkable in itself, and when related to its influence over rest of the Pacific War, it becomes miraculous. Like so many other achievements of great magnitude, it unfolded in a series of connected developments.

After the Doolittle raid on Tokyo, the commander of our naval fleet in the Pacific, Admiral Chester Nimitz, dispatched a message from Pearl Harbor to Admiral William "Bull" Halsey at sea:

"RETURN TO PEARL. . . . IT APPEARS THE JAPS PLAN ANOTHER OFFENSIVE IN THE NEAR FUTURE . . . MAYBE IN THE CENTRAL PACIFIC. THE PLACE IS NOT DETERMINED, BUT IS DESIGNATED 'AF.'

A young decoder for the U.S. Navy, Joseph Rochefort, stationed at Pearl, had been monitoring Japanese communications in the basement of the 14th Naval District headquarters, in a room with no windows called Station Hypo. He fought his war in a smoking jacket and bedroom slippers as he and his staff worked behind guarded doors to decipher the radio traffic and Morse code crackling back and forth between the Japanese military command in Tokyo and its Army and Navy units in the Pacific.

Rochefort was sure he knew what "AF" was. He was convinced it stood for Midway Island. If he was right, it would mean he had broken the enemy's radio code. To find out, Station Hypo sent a message to U.S. forces on Midway over a secure telegraph hookup instructing them to send a message back by radio that they were running out of water. Rochefort knew that the Japanese monitored all American radio transmissions and might react to the information, thereby tipping their hand.

The message came back, and the enemy took the bait.

Shortly after the fake American message reached Pearl, the Japanese sent a message by code to their fleet in the central Pacific saying that "AF" had reported a shortage of water. Now the Americans had their proof. They had broken the enemy's code. The first payoff came when Station Hypo intercepted a message, decoded it, and learned that the Japanese were going to attack American forces at "AF"—Midway—on June 4.

The enemy threw an armada at the U.S. forces—eighty-six ships including six aircraft carriers, eleven battleships, sixteen cruisers, and fifty-three destroyers. To oppose that fighting force, the Americans had twenty-seven ships consisting of three carriers, seven cruisers, and seventeen destroyers.

In those five minutes on June 4, starting at 10:25 A.M. and ending at 10:30, three enemy carriers were ripped apart by explosions. A fourth carrier and a heavy cruiser were sunk later as the battle lasted three days. The final toll was 332 Japanese planes lost and 2,500 men killed. The U.S. lost one destroyer, plus the carrier *Yorktown*, 147 planes, and 307 men.

For the rest of 1942, the war news was grim, but at least we were winning once in a while. Our Marines invaded Guadalcanal in the Solomon Islands in August. That was another boost to our national morale because it was the first American land offensive of the war.

The Japanese countered by sinking four Allied cruisers and threatening to seal off our men on Guadalcanal. Then they landed reinforcements and challenged our forces in a savage battle for control of the island. Bitter and unrelenting jungle warfare followed that lasted until the Japanese evacuated on February 9, 1943. In what might have been the most tragic loss of the war, five brothers of the same family—the Sullivans of Waterloo, Iowa—were lost at sea when one of our cruisers, the *U.S.S. Juneau*, was sunk.

Our young men began fighting on a second front even while we were still trying to hang on in the Pacific and begin to fight our way back. Operation Torch, under the command of General Dwight Eisenhower, was launched on November 8 with the landing of American troops in North Africa to aid the British in their fight against Hitler's tanks commanded by Rommel. Now we were fighting the Germans in combat, too.

Margaret Whiting remembers performing for the troops of Operation Torch the day before they shipped out. Just after returning from her one-woman show, *Personally Margaret Whiting,* in London early in 1993, she told us of an emotional performance before what may have been the largest GI audience of the war—one hundred thousand soldiers.

On Pearl Harbor Day, she arrived by train in Los Angeles, fired only four weeks after getting her first big break, a spot on *Your Hit Parade,* because she had trouble singing with the beat. It wasn't the kind of start you'd expect for a young singer following her father, Richard Whiting, into the music profession after he wrote a long list of hits including "Till We Meet Again," "Japanese Sand Man," "Breezing Along With the Breeze," "Hooray for Hollywood," "Too Marvelous For Words," "My Ideal," and "Funny That Way."

When her aunt, Margaret Young, a singer in vaudeville and on records, began appearing before the servicemen and women, she took young Margaret Whiting along. "That's when I became a performer more than just a girl singer," she said.

"The thing I remember best was being sent to an Army post in Arizona between Phoenix and Tucson. We entertained one hundred thousand men who were going over to fight Rommel's troops in the Sahara. I knew they were being sent overseas the next day. I sang in a pouring rain. It was very dramatic." She sang "Dream", a sentimental number that begins, "Dream when you're feeling blue." She remembers that the reaction was "thunderous, full of emotion."

She had to struggle to get through the song, but she found the strength to finish. "That taught me a great deal about per-

forming," she says now. "I really learned my craft during the
war." Just how well she learned it is reflected in the hit songs
that soon followed: "Moonlight in Vermont," "Silver Wings in
the Moonlight," "My Ideal," and a long list of others.

She traces that success directly to her wartime performances.
"I was a kid, and I was learning," she said. "It was the training
that I got in front of those audiences, working with stars like the
Andrews Sisters, Judy Garland, Red Skelton, and all the big
names." The experience of that enormous audience, with Margaret knowing that the soldiers were going off to war the next day,
has had a lasting impact on her. She tells the story every time she
performs.

In Europe, American military men and women were helping
the British in their fight against Hitler's bombers and preparing
for the eventual invasion of Europe. The USO troupers were
doing their part, and in the process, we were acquiring new,
unsung heroes.

☆

Kay Francis, Martha Raye, Carole Landis, and Mitzi Mayfair
were touring together, the same four who made the first European tour in June. They were back at it as winter began, and
everyone seemed better for their presence.

Variety, the weekly show business newspaper, called the
four of them the "Feminine Theatrical Task Force" and said,
"Shuffle them any way you want and you must come up with a
heroine of sorts."

They were gone well over a month on this second tour, doing
as many as three shows a day, six days a week for a total of
thirty-six dates. "The girls," *Variety* reported, "usually make an
appearance at some military hospital, not to perform but to
mingle with and cheer the boys who were incapacitated."

At one point, Kay was confined to bed with a heavy cold and
Mitzi had a strained back. Both landed in a military hospital, but

Carole and Martha continued meeting the commitments for the four of them. Carole was in bed for several days, and although Mitzi left the hospital, she had to return for a week after developing an infection. The itinerary for the group never changed, and no show was canceled.

☆

At night the four traveled fifty miles or more on country roads in blackouts to reach their next military post. *Variety* pointed out: "In London itself, because of the traffic lights, driving in the blackouts isn't so bad, but on the country roads, where the girls have been doing most of their travelling, it's like finding your way through a barrel of tar."

They gave a command performance before the Queen of England and princesses Elizabeth and Margaret. Also in the audience was Abe Lastfogel, the general manager of the respected William Morris Talent Agency in New York before the war, who in these years became the head of the USO Camp Shows. He was seated next to a British Army chaplain, D. N. Menchy.

Abe learned later that British officials were concerned about some of the humor in the show, fearing it might be slightly off color and therefore an embarrassment to Her Majesty, the Queen. Several days later, Lastfogel received a letter from the obviously relieved chaplain. "I have never been at an entertainment that was so well presented and in the best of taste," he reported.

The four women began their marathon tour on October 31. When they finished almost two months later, on December 27, they had set a record for the longest consecutive tour by volunteer performers at off-shore bases. *Variety*'s Joe Schoenfeld called it "one of the great chapters in the saga of American show business in the war effort."

☆

One of the popular singers of the time, Patricia Morrison, remembers another tour to England that year, with Al Jolson, actress Merle Oberon, and singer Allan Jenkins, the secrecy surrounding their departure from New York, and the exhilaration and dangers of being in the thick of things overseas during a world war. As always, the USO performers were not told ahead of time where they were going. They were quartered at a hotel in New York, awakened in the dark at 3:00 A.M. and driven to their waiting plane.

"It was a 'flying boat,' " she says, recalling the large planes equipped with pontoons for landing on water. "We flew all the way across the Atlantic Ocean at only three hundred feet." That tactic was to avoid being spotted by German planes, but the performers didn't feel all that secure, especially after being told that their whole flight was being tracked by the German submarines—U-Boats—in the waters below.

The group performed at military bases and hospitals all across England. Like all the rest of us, Pat was thrilled to be a part of America's war effort, and, also like the rest of us, she looks back on those years as a highlight of her life and her career.

"It was a strange but wonderful time. There was this terrible war going on, with all the suffering, and yet there was a terrific feeling that we were all together and working for the same thing. I wanted to do it. I had to do it."

She remembers the same thing as the rest of us about the conduct of the American servicemen and women. "They were always polite," she said. "They used to want to touch your hand or kiss you on the cheek, but that's all." At some of the bases, she was lucky enough to be assigned a hut as her living quarters. Though a guard was stationed outside her door, she never needed one.

She, like most of the rest of us, declined the invitations she received for dinner at the officers' club. "Sometimes I'd tell people I'd meet them after dinner," she said, "but I ate all my meals with the enlisted men."

Pat remembers Jolson's performances for the soldiers. He was always an inexhaustible singer and showman. He seemed to want his shows to go on forever, and he was that same way when he performed as a member of the USO troupes. "You couldn't get him off," Pat remembers. "He loved it as much as the GIs did."

Jolson's exuberance and willingness to work hard at his craft caused some awkward moments during those overseas tours because of the makeshift arrangements—like having no stage at times, singing, as LaVerne, Patty and I did, too—on the back of a flatbed truck or just in the middle of a field.

"I was singing one afternoon," said Pat, whose most popular number with the troops was "Embraceable You," "and I could hear Al off to the side warming up, singing his scales. That's what you do when you're off to yourself in the wings of a theater, too far away to bother the performer who's on stage, but Jolie was going to practice his scales, and if somebody was on stage at the time, that would be too bad, even if he was only a few feet away."

All of us remember something else about Al. He was always there when the troops needed him. Maybe it was because he was a compulsive performer, or maybe it was just because he was a patriotic American, or maybe it was both. But it may well be that Al Jolson died in the service of his country.

In the fall of 1950, only five years after his unending service in World War II and at the peak of his popularity with the highly successful Larry Parks films, *The Jolson Story* and *Jolson Sings Again*, Al was one of the first performers to travel to Korea in the opening months of the war there. We were losing badly, but Al went anyway. He performed for our troops there, under dangerous conditions, then flew back to the States, to San Francisco. Shortly after his return, he was found dead in his hotel room. Who knows? Maybe he wore himself out in Korea.

Pat Morrison's experience typified the strangeness of a combination of emotions we all experienced. "We were taken on a picnic outside London one afternoon before our evening shows," she remembers, "and we were lying there on the ground in this beautiful, idyllic country setting, with green grass and trees and cows and flowers and delicious food and good wine and looking up at a beautiful blue sky when we noticed white trails across the sky. Our host explained that they were trails from the English and German planes directly overhead." There the USO troupers were, surrounded by peace and the beauty of nature, and watching the start of an aerial duel—they were called dogfights—right above them. There was peace on their little patch of earth, but war in the sky.

Pat remembers the biggest scare they encountered on that tour. It happened on a country road in the dark of night as they drove from London to their next stop. Hitler was continuing his aerial bombardment of London, and as they were driving in the dark, German fighter planes overhead suddenly dropped flares, illuminating the English countryside in a bright light all around them.

Our enemies were always aware that killing some of America's star entertainers or sports heroes would be a brilliant psychological victory, and in wartime, psychological victories have a strong influence on efforts to produce military ones. Certainly, killing an entertainer of the star quality of Al Jolson would have given the Germans rich material for the Third Reich's propaganda machine operated for Hitler by Joseph Goebbels.

The group was aware of this, and when the flares exploded into brilliant light overhead, the performers knew that either the planes were trying to strafe anything they saw—or somebody had talked, and the enemy had gotten word of their night travel.

"They were hoping to strafe us with their machine guns,"

Pat says, "so we jumped out of the car and hid under the branches of a big tree for hours. It was a very scary experience."

As we talked, we remembered one of the biggest stories of that kind in the war, the death of one of the great marquee names, Leslie Howard, who starred with Olivia de Havilland in *Gone With the Wind* in 1939, the year the war started. By the time that film was produced, Howard had already established himself with his performances on the American stage and in the movies *The Scarlet Pimpernel, Romeo and Juliet, Pygmalion,* and *Intermezzo.*

He left a wife, a daughter, and a son. Patricia remembered the story behind the story. "The English used a 'double,' a lookalike, for Winston Churchill, their Prime Minister, during the war. The story went around that Leslie had the tragic misfortune of being on the same plane with Churchill's double when the Germans shot it down, thinking they were killing Churchill. Instead they killed his double and one of the most acclaimed actors of that time."

Fifty years after her wartime service, Patricia Morrison was appearing in *The King and I* in Stockton, California. While she was there, she visited a veterans' hospital. At the bedside of one of the patients, he told her she visited him at a hospital in England during the war, after he had been wounded.

"While you were there," he told her, "somebody took a picture of me with you." He showed her the snapshot, a half-century later.

Some of the travel on USO tours in the States was as rough as that overseas. Ask Anne Jeffreys.

Anne, who is still a popular singer on tour and became a national TV favorite in the *Topper* series, was a rising young star from Goldsboro, North Carolina, via New York's Julliard School of Music, when she toured for the USO throughout the war. She began entertaining the troops at the time of her first movie, which united her with her first love—Nelson Eddy, the handsome tenor with the golden voice who was the idol of millions of American girls during the war.

Anne appeared with Nelson Eddy and Jeanette MacDonald in *I Married an Angel* at a time when the two were the most popular duet in America, and it was only fair that she be given that opportunity. After all, Nelson broke her heart when she was only twelve years old back home in Goldsboro.

"I was visiting my sister when I heard on the radio that Nelson had just gotten married," Anne laughs today. "I went out into the apple orchard in the backyard and climbed up a tree and sat there and cried all afternoon. He didn't wait for me to grow up."

One of Anne's most exhausting trips during the war was when she appeared in a hundred towns in east Texas in thirty-four days with Gabby Hayes and Wild Bill Elliott, selling war bonds and entertaining GIs.

"They took us in two police cars," she says. "We played in Tyler, Kilgore, Honey Grove, Denison. We plowed our way through all of east Texas. We performed on flatbed trucks, school auditoriums, parks, out in an open field just off a highway, anywhere."

Anne learned something about Gabby Hayes that the Andrews Sisters learned later, when he was one of the regulars on our weekly radio show. Gabby always played this lovable old western cowpoke with irresistible charm, but the truth is that at times he could get on your nerves.

"He was forever complaining about how bad he felt," she says today, and I can confirm that. "He was always grumbling and complaining. And he was very opinionated. But I became very fond of him. I just took him for what he was. I made almost a dozen western movies with him."

Young Anne made other friends during the war years, too, including Jackie Gleason, Harpo Marx, and Orson Welles. Anne sang what the GIs requested, songs about the war and the girls they left behind—"I'll Be Home for Christmas," "I'll See You Again," "Somewhere I'll Find You," and "Stage Door Canteen." Gleason performed his comedy routines. Harpo, in his white frock and top hat, played beautiful, serious music on the harp, one of Anne's favorite musical instruments, and Orson Welles, an amateur magician, presented his magic act, even before an audience of GIs at San Simeon, the estate owned by William Randolph Hearst in northern California, where Welles starred in his 1941 film classic, *Citizen Kane.*

Anne makes the point today that the war that united the nation "also united Hollywood." Entertainers were thrown together in trying conditions and on long trips. They came to know each other well, and out of those years came many lasting friendships.

She says she found Gleason and Harpo to be contrasts in personality, Gleason the loud, fat, and occasionally obnoxious comedian, Harpo the quiet, almost introverted serious musician.

"Jackie and I later became good friends," Anne says, "but Harpo and I were friends right away. I would go into his dressing room while he was warming up before our performance and say, 'May I just sit here and listen?' His harp music always sounded so beautiful to me."

Anne found Harpo to be a "warm, withdrawn person," in stark contrast to the madcap comedy atmosphere surrounding him when he performed with Groucho and his brothers. "He was very articulate," she remembers, "and highly intelligent. Just the opposite of the zany character he played. He didn't speak much, even out of his character, but when he did we found he had a soft, rich baritone voice."

On one of her most memorable tours, she and Arthur Treacher and Charlie Ruggles visited thirty-four cities in the southwest part of the United States. One stop was Las Vegas, New Mexico. No, not Nevada. New Mexico.

They were traveling by train, and Anne found out that Arthur Treacher bore something of a resemblance to the movie roles he played as a British butler or a wealthy stuffed-shirt, something that Patty, LaVerne, and I discovered ourselves when we went on a USO tour in Italy with Arthur in 1945.

"On the train," Anne says, "he would tell me, 'Now, my deah—you go to your compahtment and you stay theah. Don't expect to dine with me. I prefer to dine alone.' So I stayed out of his way and spent my time with Charlie Ruggles," whom Anne found to be as comfortable as an old shoe.

But Anne got to know Arthur better after the war in several engagements, including their appearances in the road show of *Camelot* in the 1960's. They became good friends.

"We pulled into this absolutely desolate town," she said about one of her experiences with Arthur and Charlie, "to visit a hospital with wounded veterans the next day—the basket cases," GIs who had their arms or legs shot off in combat. The entertainers always found those stops the hardest to play simply because the sights were so heartbreaking. It didn't help Anne, Arthur, and Charlie when they saw their quarters for the night.

"The hotel looked like a Hollywood set for a western," Anne remembers. "To say it was broken down would be flattering. It looked like something from the 1800's—the *early* 1800's. It was wooden and dilapidated. The termites met you coming down the hall. The building was dark. The floors squeaked. My 'suite'— that's what the hotel called it—consisted of an ancient iron bed, no carpet, one wooden chair, and one bare light bulb hanging from the ceiling. I assume the bathroom was down the hall."

Anne was exhausted from the rigors of a thirty-four-city tour, so she went straight to bed, and then sat straight up again. "I started to itch," she says. "It got worse in a hurry, and before I knew it I was itching all over. So I reached up from my bed and turned on the one light bulb. There were bed bugs running everywhere—under the sheets, under the pillow, everywhere."

With no phone in the room to call the men, Anne spent the

rest of the night sitting in the wooden chair in the dark in the middle of the room, with her legs drawn up to her knees so the bed bugs wouldn't take a liking to her feet.

For Anne, like many other entertainers who were so young when the war started—including the Andrews Sisters—the war years were our time of maturing. We were learning, and some of what we learned surprised us. Like the time Anne was at Camp Pendleton preparing to sing in a show for the Marines. The members of the USO troupe were staying in a converted barracks, and as Anne tried without much success to wash her hands in the public washroom at the white porcelain fixture on the wall with water trickling down it, another female singer came in and burst into laughter at the sight.

Anne still laughs about it and says, "I was young and innocent. I had never seen a man's urinal before."

☆

She was another of the regular visitors at the Hollywood Canteen. She remembers dancing with the GIs, serving coffee and just keeping them company by talking to them. But her most memorable experience, and her most lasting, took place at a hospital in San Diego.

"Most of us sort of adopted a serviceman here or there," Anne says. Hers was a young GI from Boston, Bobby Noonan, a burn victim who had been wounded on a battleship in the Pacific. "He was swathed in bandages," Anne says, "with slits for his eyes." On the table next to him was his picture of what he looked like before he went overseas. "He was a *gorgeous* young man. When I saw that picture, I just broke down."

After the tears, though, something nice happened. The two became friends. "We corresponded for years and years."

CHAPTER EIGHT

Scares on the Home Front

Things were frightening on the home front, too. The Japanese shelled an oil refinery near Santa Barbara, California, in February of 1942, which didn't do a thing to help us overcome our case of jitters that started with the attack on Pearl Harbor. Along the East Coast and Gulf Coast, things were more frightening.

The German U-Boats were sinking tankers and freighters within eyesight of Americans in the beach communities of New York, New Jersey, Delaware, Maryland, Virginia, Florida, and the Gulf states. Before convoys were assigned to protect our shipping, five thousand men, many of them Americans, were killed at sea, and 397 ships were lost within eyesight of our beaches and front porches.

The panicky feeling expressed itself in many ways, one of which proved highly beneficial to our parents. A woman in the Brentwood section of Los Angeles was so scared that she sold her new home to us for our mother and father, for a fraction of what it cost her to build.

On June 27, 1942, J. Edgar Hoover, the director of the

Federal Bureau of Investigation, announced that his agents had arrested eight "highly trained" Nazi saboteurs who had alighted from German submarines on Long Island just outside New York City and on the east coast of Florida, near Jacksonville. They landed with bombs, TNT, fuses, and timing devices which they had buried in the sand.

The two groups, with four members in each, carried a total of $149,748.76 both for their expenses and for bribing key officials. When the FBI captured them, they were dressed in civilian clothes and carried forged draft cards and Social Security cards. The prisoners confessed that they had been ordered to blow up bridges and manufacturing plants and to create panic in large cities on the East Coast and throughout the Midwest. Their efforts were to last for two years in a special sabotage campaign.

Hoover said the eight men, all in their thirties, were members of the German American Bund, "Friends of New Germany." They had already identified four plants among their targets: Aluminum Corporation of America plants in Alocoa, Tennessee; Massina, New York; East St. Louis, Illinois, and Philadelphia. But the saboteurs were going for other big game, too: facilities of the Pennsylvania Railroad and the Chesapeake and Ohio Railroad in industrial areas, bridges, canals, locks, the New York City water supply system and the hydroelectric power plant at Niagara Falls.

The enemy agents were prosecuted by no less than the Attorney General himself, Francis Biddle, under the close interest of President Roosevelt. Two of them turned state's evidence, testified against their colleagues and were sentenced to life at hard labor. The other six were executed in the electric chair in the District of Columbia.

From the date of their arrest to their convictions, imprisonment and deaths, the total elapsed time was six weeks.

☆

As America neared the end of the first full year of the war, the wartime environment was evident everywhere on the home front. Posters encouraged workers to strive for perfect attendance in their jobs to help the war effort, other posters warned against loose talk that might help the enemy, and every time we went to the movies, Bugs Bunny, born only one year before the war, encouraged us to buy war bonds.

Even though we were still suffering defeats, and our victories carried sometimes staggering numbers of losses, morale continued high on the home front. We responded enthusiastically when Barry Wood and The Wood Nymphs gave us a new rallying cry in a song introduced by Eddie Cantor in his own musical, *Banjo Eyes* in 1941. It appeared again in a 1942 movie, *Sweetheart of the Fleet*, and gave us not only a motivational song but a new slogan:

> *We did it before and we can do it again,*
> *And we will do it again.*
> *We've got a heck of a job to do,*
> *But you can bet that we'll see it through.*
> *We did it before, and we can do it again,*
> *And we will do it again.*
> *We'll knock them over and then we'll get*
> *The guy in front of them.*
> *We did it before. We'll do it again.*

We were still being booked for tours lasting twenty and thirty weeks each, a week in each city, adding up to fifty weeks a year. Sometimes we were able to leave the Buick at home during the gas shortage and were booked onto our own Pullman railroad car. At other times, our train accommodations consisted of sitting on our suitcases in the middle of the aisle for hundreds of miles at a time.

When train travel was out of the question, we improvised

with automobiles. That's when things got trickier, because when we were on tour it wasn't a case of just the three Andrews Sisters. We had our own eighteen-member band in addition to other acts in the show, maybe a comic and a female dancer. Arranging transportation for twenty or twenty-five people traveling to twenty or thirty cities on a trip lasting six months or more was difficult enough during peacetime. In wartime, it was impossible—but we did it anyhow, remembering the slogan of the Navy Construction Battalions, the CB's: "The difficult we do immediately. The impossible takes a little longer."

Hotel reservations weren't any easier to get than anything else. We had one beginning comedian who joined our group as we started a new tour at the Palace Theater in Cleveland and proceeded to set some kind of a standard for ingenuity. Just before our train pulled out, we learned that the comic had just gotten married and wanted to bring his wife along. "Fine. Bring her along," I said. "It's another ticket, but bring her anyway."

As the train pulled us across the western part of the country, I asked our tour manager to bring in our new comedian, that we could use a few jokes.

Someone went looking for him, but the young man was never seen during that whole train ride across more than half of the country. We never did find out where he disappeared to, or whether he even was on the train. On our first morning in Cleveland, after an eight o'clock rehearsal, just as I was ready to hurry out of the dressing room to catch up with LaVerne and Patty, there was a knock on the door, and it was the comedian.

Of all things, he asked me if I could get him passes to some of the movie theaters in Cleveland. "My wife likes the movies," he said.

I got him passes to the three or four good theaters there, with no questions asked. But LaVerne, Patty, and I wondered what he was going to do with theater passes. He couldn't use them himself, because he would be playing five and six shows every afternoon and evening on the bill with us.

Under the terms of his contract with the tour manager, he was responsible for his meals and lodging. That was true of all the other performers, since they were not big names. Beginners were not able to command all of the fringe benefits that the stars could, so they had to settle for that kind of a contract with the tour's promoters. But they made up for it by paying each of the acts $750 a week, a very comfortable salary in those days.

We found out later that the comedian had devised a unique arrangement for making his $750 a week go even further. I ran into him one day during our Cleveland appearance and asked if he was enjoying the movie passes.

"No, but my wife is," he said. "She *really* likes the movies."

Then we learned about his system: He checked into a single room in our hotel, paying the lower rate. His wife slept in the room during the afternoon and evenings, while the comedian was performing with us at the Palace Theater. Then, when our last show ended and the comedian headed back to his hotel room, his wife would be at the movies. She'd stay there all night long.

Another beginner on one of our theater tours was a young guitarist, Les Paul, who with his wife, Mary Ford, became a star after the war by creating a "multiple sound" through the technique of recording his guitar music two and three times on the same record. Mary did the same thing with her singing voice. The effect was the sound of three guitars and three singers, all in harmony, although in reality it was only one guitar and one singer. It was an innovative technique and a sound that made Les Paul and Mary Ford one of the headline musical acts in the 1950's, with their smash hit of "How High the Moon" among others. Patti Page created the same effect with her vocals.

When he was breaking in with us, Les told us he'd had much better success with Fred Waring than we had. Les is a genius, pure and simple. He used to sit in his dressing room between shows on our tour and make guitars. When he bought his own home outside New York, he built several recording studios, doing all the electrical and acoustical work himself, without ever studying electrical engineering. It was all in his head.

So was his ability to play music without being able to read it. On a record date, Mr. Waring handed Les a piece of sheet music and told him, with that exacting discipline that made people like Fred Waring and Glenn Miller great, "Play this, just the way it's written here."

Les played something, but even today he's not sure he played any of the notes that were on that sheet. Fred came over to him at the finish and raved. "Man, you're wonderful! You played that music as if you wrote it yourself!"

Les said that told him something: Fred Waring couldn't read music, either.

A lot of us got by on guts plus whatever talent we had in those years. We didn't have the formal training and musical schooling of the concert artists, but as popular singers and musicians we had the ability to give the people what they wanted, making them think in many cases that we knew everything there was to know about music.

"You girls are wonderful." people used to tell us all during our peak years. "You must have perfect pitch." I didn't even know what perfect pitch was.

Another reason that people such as Fred Waring, Les Paul, and the Andrews Sisters became successful was that we obeyed an old golden rule in music: Stick to the melody.

That was especially true of all the artists who were recording for Decca Records. Decca's studios in New York City were a long, rectangular room. At the far end was a large picture of an Indian maiden, standing up and holding her hand in the air, as if signaling that she had a question. In the "dialogue balloon" she's asking: "Where's the melody?"

As you were recording at the opposite end, you couldn't help seeing that question. It was staring you in the face the entire time you were singing. At Decca, under Jack Kapp's insistence, you played and sang the melody, and never mind a whole lot of improvising, or you didn't record for Decca again.

I learned a lot about my country during World War II, and not just its geography. I learned about the American people, too, and the variety of their preferences. The response to our songs was different, because the people and their backgrounds were different.

A song that was well received in one town might not go over in another. Then we had to change our act and work in several new songs to take the place of those that weren't going over well. When we came away from the East Coast, we switched our routines to meet the taste and personality of our Midwestern audiences. When we left the Midwest, we switched our routines again to appeal to the people who made up our audiences on the West Coast.

When "Bei Mir Bist Du Schoen" came out, it took about a year to convince the people in California that it was a big hit, yet through all that time it was a smash in the East. It took a long time for that song to get around the country, and I don't think it ever was popular in the Midwest. But if you sang a polka in the Midwest—like the hits we had with "Beer Barrel Polka" and the "Pennsylvania Polka"—you were a smash. When you worked the South, you learned that the folks down there loved Dixieland and sentimental music.

It was frustrating for us because we were always faced with the need to change our act—our songs—on short notice after finding out that a certain song that had gone over so well in our last city all of a sudden was bombing with our new audiences.

In 1941, we recorded a song written by Bob Troup called "Daddy," and it became a big national hit almost immediately, for us and for Sammy Kaye, too. It was a toe-tapping number that caught America's fancy and showed up on *Your Hit Parade* in a hurry and stayed there for seventeen weeks, seven of those weeks as the number-one song in the country. But then our tour took us to Dayton, Ohio, and the people there hadn't heard it. When they did, they didn't like it.

The problem was compounded because of the size of our band. If we decided to switch to another number, sometimes we'd have to limit our accompaniment to a piano because we didn't have arrangements for the song that we were working into our act at the last minute as a substitute. It was only after the great migration to our cities in the years that followed World War II that the musical tastes of Americans became something closer to universal.

The experience was a wonderful insight into the makeup and tastes of people in different parts of our country. It taught me that all of us are the same, yet all of us are different. And in the middle of a war, we learned not to let our differences get in the way.

America's advertisers were in a patriotic mood, too, and appealed to it in their magazine ads. Bell Telephone's ads said materials to expand service "are needed for shooting" and urged citizens, "Please don't make long distance calls to centers of war activity unless they are vital. Leave the wires clear for war traffic."

An ad for Ray-O-Vac flashlight batteries reminded us that "leakproof sealed-in-steel construction safeguards your flashlight against corrosion . . . safeguards the vital supply of civilian flashlights on the home front."

Kellogg's Rice Krispies ads said that "our country needs more work from all, so heed the Breakfast Crispness Call."

Sunbeam Mixmaster's magazine ads showed a drawing of a woman telling readers: "The money Mixmaster saves helps buy our war bonds."

Kaywoodie Briar pipes, selling for ten dollars, advertised: "It is fitting that the pipe, symbol of peace, should meet and survive war with all its goodness intact, and unimpaired until peace comes again."

Ads for Dixie cups made a persuasive case for that product's contributions to our health and hygiene: "Dixies are helping to protect the health of American's warriors, workers, and civilians. The paper cup has truly become a wartime necessity."

Mimeograph duplicators displayed a full-page salute to the women in the Women's Army Auxiliary Corps, "The lady in Khaki":

"She's ready to serve her country with her head, heart, hand and soul. Because she is serving where she is, one more soldier can serve where the battle calls him. A nation salutes you, member of the WAAC."

The chocolate industry was heard from, too. Nestle's, "the world's greatest name in chocolate," took out a full-page magazine add with a headline that said boldly and proudly:

CHOCOLATE IS A *FIGHTING* FOOD!

The ad told us that "maximum nourishment with minimum bulk has been the objective of the U.S. Army in selecting the food for our fighting men. That is why the chocolate bar has come into its own on every fighting front of the war

. . . everybody's favorite on the fighting front . . . or on the home front . . ."

Pullman said its railroad cars completed over seven million trips by GIs in 1942 with an average distance of fifteen hundred miles. Pullman said a "carload of uniformed men climbs aboard a Pullman every two minutes and forty-five seconds!" The company made sure to mention in its ad that the release of this information had been approved by the U.S. Bureau of Censorship.

The ads from the folks at Mennen told us:

SAVE TIN—HELP WIN!
BUY SHAVE CREAM
IN GLASS JARS

The ad made one final selling point that was guaranteed to appeal to anyone on the home front: "You don't have to turn in an empty tube to your druggist."

At the movies, we were being entertained by Bing Crosby and Bob Hope in another one of their road pictures, *Road to Morocco*, again with Dorothy Lamour. The ads said: "Screwier than *Road to Singapore!* It's zanier than *Road to Zanzibar!*"

Fred Astaire and Rita Hayworth were dancing together again, this time in *You Were Never Lovelier*, to the music of Jerome Kern and Johnny Mercer. Cary Grant and Ginger Rogers were featured in *Once Upon A Honeymoon*.

Fred MacMurray, Paulette Goddard, and Susan Hayward were starring in *The Forest Rangers*, another Technicolor feature film, which included a song by Frank Loesser called "Jingle, Jangle, Jingle." The ads said it was a "witty ditty" about a cowboy and the girls he's riding away from as he gallops his horse into the setting sun. LaVerne, Patty, and I enjoyed singing all of Frank's songs, and that one was special fun because of its bouncy rhythm and pleasing harmony.

The ability of Americans to laugh, even in the depths of a world war, was proved again as the year ended. One of the songs we were singing during the war's second Christmas didn't have anything to do with the holiday. It was about Adolf Hitler, a man we loved to hate—along with Italy's Benito Mussolini and Japan's Emperor Hirohito.

The song was "Der Fuehrer's Face," and we had Walt Disney to thank for it. It was written by Oliver Wallace as the title tune for a 1942 Disney production and was an incredibly big hit for Spike Jones and his City Slickers.

The song came along at just the right point, the darkest time of the war for the United States when Hitler's forces dominated Europe and North Africa, and the western part of the Soviet Union. Then along comes this new song that ridiculed Hitler, even including a loud Bronx cheer right in his face.

It was just as much of a hit with our GIs overseas as it was at home. During the "All-Femme" troupe's tour of England in December, *Variety* said Martha Raye "introduced 'Der Fuehrer's Face' to England, and her robust Bronx cheer was a sensation."

CHAPTER NINE

Sacrifices

After struggling through 1942, we began to feel ourselves turning the corner in 1943. The news from overseas was getting better, although we still suffered terrible losses from time to time in bloody battles both in Europe and the Pacific. On the home front if wartime life wasn't any better, at least we were getting used to it.

Hitler's attempt to conquer Russia was falling apart as the year began. Stalin's army stopped the German offensive, and the entire Nazi Sixth Army, trapped in Stalingrad on Christmas Day, was destroyed in early January. Then the Russian Army broke through the German lines around Leningrad, ending the longest siege of the war, and the German army fled in full retreat. They surrendered on January 31 after losing more than two hundred thousand of the three hundred thousand members of the Sixth Army who began the offensive.

In North Africa, the English and American units chased Rommel's tanks across the desert until Eisenhower's forces linked up with Montgomery's Eighth Army in Tunisia. On May

12, Rommel flew back to Germany, leaving his "Afrika" Corps to surrender to the Allies.

The news from the Pacific produced a great victory for the Americans on April 18, the first anniversary of Doolittle's raid over Tokyo, when a Japanese airplane carrying Admiral Isoroku Yamamoto, commander in chief of the Japanese Combined Fleet since 1941, was shot down by American pilots from Guadalcanal.

It was another smashing victory for American intelligence. Yamamoto was on his way to the Solomon Islands, but our military forces knew about his flight beforehand. They were ordered to attack. Yamamoto, the architect for the attack on Pearl Harbor, was killed only eighteen months after the event that pulled us into the war.

We invaded Sicily on July 10, then Italy. After only two months, on September 8, the Italian Army surrendered unconditionally. Then Italy turned around and declared war on Germany on October 13. The Italian campaign dragged on into 1944 and produced some of the bloodiest fighting of the war, on battlegrounds called Salerno and Anzio.

On the other side of the world, a true-life story of heroism that helped to elect a President was unfolding. On August 1, a young Navy lieutenant, John F. Kennedy of Boston, saved eleven of his thirteen-man crew after their boat, the PT-109, was run down by a Japanese destroyer in the Pacific. Seventeen years later, Kennedy became one of three men whose heroism during World War II helped to elect them President. General Eisenhower's war record was instrumental in his election in 1952, and George Bush's combat duty as a Navy pilot helped him win election forty-three years after the war.

☆

Although we could see things beginning to turn our way, the fury of the fighting did not lessen, and in many cases grew worse—and so did the casualties and the fatigue of those who

The Andrews Sisters—Maxene, Patty and LaVerne (from left to right)—in a World War II publicity photo. —AP/Wide World Photo.

Arthur Treacher with the
Andrews Sisters during their
USO tour of Italy in 1945.

The Andrews Sisters visit with the GIs between shows in North
Africa.

Bob Hope entertains the troops at Munda air strip in New Guinea on October 31, 1944. —AP/Wide World Photo.

Veronica Lake and Air Corps orchestra "Men of the Air," conducted by Sergeant Jimmie Baker (on Veronica's left), in Paris in 1944.

Private Mickey Rooney gets a big laugh from the troops in Germany in early 1945.
—National Archives Photo.

Hollywood tough guy Edward G. Robinson at a USO show for an armored unit near
the front lines in France in August 1944—two months after D-Day.
—National Archives Photo.

Danny Kaye clowns on stage (above). The GIs (below) are members of the army of occupation in Japan a month after the surrender treaty was signed. The lettering on the front of the stage says. "Officers Keep Out—Enlisted Men's Country."
—National Archives Photo.

"Command Performance" was one of the popular shows on the new Armed Forces Radio Service. The Andrews Sisters endure Jimmy Durante's attempts to play the trumpet (above) and check a script (below) with Bob Hope, Eddie "Rochester" Anderson (left) and Dennis Day.

On another "Command Performance" show, the Andrews Sisters appeared with composer Meredith Willson (left) and two stars of *The Wizard of Oz* —Judy Garland and Frank Morgan.

A welder in a defense plant, one of the two million women factory workers who became the inspiration for "Rosie, The Riveter." —National Archives Photo.

Government posters, like this one and the one on the opposite page, warned against the dangers of loose talk that might be of value to "the enemy."

LOOSE LIPS

MIGHT
Sink Ships

THIS POSTER IS PUBLISHED BY THE HOUSE OF SEAGRAM AS PART
OF ITS CONTRIBUTION TO THE NATIONAL VICTORY EFFORT

Martha Tilton (at left in photo above) and Carole Landis (center) buy items at the quartermaster's store in New Guinea in July 1944 while on a USO tour with Jack Benny. Below, Martha waits with her mess kit in the enlisted men's "chow line" at a military hospital in Cape Gloucester, New Britain, on July 28, 1944.
—National Archives Photo.

Carole Landis jitterbugs with Private First Class Joseph B. McCoy of Rochester, N.Y., (upper left) during the Jack Benny USO show in New Guinea on July 15, 1944. The crowds were as close as they could get (upper right) and enormous (below).
—National Archives Photos.

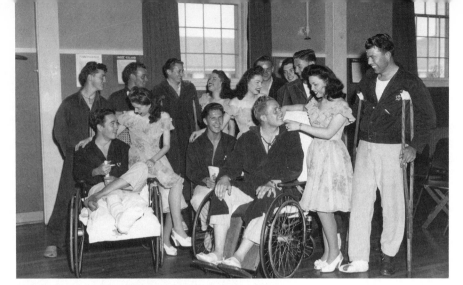

Entertainers visited military hospitals and camps at every opportunity. Above, a troupe of USO performers visits Moore General Hospital, North Carolina, in 1944. Members of the USO show "Hit The Deck" appear at the Army Infantry Replacement Center at Camp Wheeler, Georgia, January 25, 1943 (left). An injured pilot gets a visit from the Andrews Sisters (below).
—National Archives Photos.

The enlisted men join the chorus girls in the rousing finale to Olsen and Johnson's
"Hellzapoppin' " at Camp Claiborne, Louisiana, on January 27, 1943.
—National Archives Photo.

Duke Ellington was always a hit with the
troops. So was singer Jane Froman,
shown here with her husband, Don Ross,
still on crutches two years after the plane
crash in which she was seriously injured.

The Allies were closing in on Berlin early in 1945 when the Andrews Sisters recorded "There'll Be a Hot Time in the Town of Berlin" with Bing Crosby (left). Below, Bing sings for the GIs at the USO's Stage Door Canteen in London. —National Archives Photo.

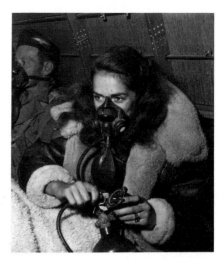

Flying on military planes was part of the everyday routine. At left, above, Hollywood
star Ann Sheridan (in sun glasses) and Major General Claire Chennault sign
autographs at Kunming Airport in China in 1944. Comedian Ben Blue and dancer
Mary Landa are at left. Actress Jinx Falkenberg (above right) adjusts her oxygen tank
on flight over the Himalaya Mountains to entertain the troops in China in 1944.
Below, left, opera star Lily Pons boards an Army transport plane for a flight from
China to India in 1945. Below, right, Marlene Dietrich and her USO troupe in front
of their C-47 in Greenland in 1944. Actor Edmund O'Brien in second from left.
—National Archives Photos.

The Andrews Sisters wow the GIs at the Hollywood Canteen (above) during the war, then are on hand to welcome the boys home when the Queen Mary docks in New York with 14,500 troops aboard on September 28, 1945.   —National Archives and AP/Wide World Photos.

survived. The entertainers were right there with the GIs in the combat zones, close enough to have to duck shells and earning their new nickname as "soldiers in greasepaint." Stories about them were beginning to surface.

A USO singer, Ella Logan, a well-known and highly popular Broadway star who had just finished appearing in *Finian's Rainbow*, was one of the heroes of the Italian campaign. Ella signed up for a tour of eight weeks and ended up playing for five straight months in various overseas locations. At the peak of the fighting in Italy, she was singing at an evening show in Naples. After her last number, she told her GI audience that she hoped she had brought them the spirit of their mothers, sweethearts, or wives.

All of a sudden a tall blond soldier came down the aisle. He was covered with mud, his helmet and guns were slung over his shoulder, and his face reflected too many days and nights of seeing too many friends die. With everyone in the audience watching him apprehensively, he walked up to the stage and listened as Ella continued speaking. Then he climbed up onto the stage, took the mike away from her and said, "I'd like to say something." Ella looked down at the floor, wondering what might be coming next. Everyone else was, too. "I've got to contradict you, Miss Logan," he went on. "You don't look like anyone's sweetheart. You don't look like anyone's wife. And God knows you don't look like anyone's mother."

Then he lifted her chin. She saw tears on his cheeks. He kissed her on the forehead and said, "You look like an angel." Then he turned around, climbed back down off the stage, and thumped out of the theater in his combat boots.

A USO publication released later in the war described the end of that story: "Every man in the audience had his handkerchief out, and Ella stood there in front of the mike, crying like a baby."

☆

A chaplain stationed in the Aleutian Islands, Jacob Rudin, wrote a letter to a friend about his experience at Dutch Harbor, where a warship was tied to the dock with no one allowed to go ashore as they waited to sail for Attu to attack the foothold that the Japanese had just established there.

"They had no recreation," Chaplain Rudin wrote about the American soldiers. "There has been nothing to do to break the monotony of the trip. Now they stand around idly, waiting for something to happen. And it does. By happy coincidence, there are two traveling units of USO Camp Shows in Dutch Harbor at that particular moment. One of them is an all-girl unit; the other is made up of two men and three girls. Since the men cannot come ashore to a show, then the show will come to the men. And in almost less time than it takes to tell it, an improvised stage is erected on the dock immediately in front of the ship, a loud-speaker is hooked up to a microphone, and the show is on."

The chaplain told his friend it was "a thrilling sight." He said every inch of space on the ship was jammed with men watching the show. They stood three or more deep along the rail and sat in lifeboats and on the life rafts. "I don't believe," his letter said, "that any troupers ever played to a more appreciative audience than did those USO entertainers to the amusement-starved soldiers."

As the show rolled on with songs, dances, jokes, and imitations, an officer approached the master of ceremonies and whispered something to him. The emcee turned to the audience and said, "I've just been told that your ship is to shove off right now. But with your permission, we'll carry on the show just as long as you are within sight and hearing. Okay?"

After the men shouted their approval, the show continued. A woman singer with an accordion approached the mike and sang several songs. The ship began to slip slowly from the dock.

"Then," Chaplain Rodin wrote, the vocalist "began, softly and warmly, to sing 'Aloha.' The voices of the men, joined with hers, drifted back across Dutch Harbor. The ship had turned. Only her stern showed to us ashore. But we could hear the men singing as they sailed for Attu. A transport of men had been made happy as they sailed away to war."

Jo Bernier, the ballet tap dancer who logged so much USO service in Alaska, the Aleutians, and in this country as Jo Andrews, can verify that story. She was a member of that "all-girl unit."

☆

The entertainers continued to win praise at home as well as overseas, and so did the USO Camp Shows. *PIC* magazine published a feature article in May of 1944. "No Hollywood adjectives are adequate to describe the great job being done by the show business for the war effort," it reported. The magazine praised the USO Camp Shows highly. "The tumult of whistles, cheers, and shouts of applause began in Camp Lee, Virginia, when the first show opened and it has since echoed around the world."

By that time in the war, Camp Shows had brought our servicemen and women around the world sixty-two Hollywood stars, 173 concert artists and seventy-five name bands. To illustrate its point, *PIC* ran a spread of ten pictures showing the entertainers on stage in combat areas and at USO Clubs here and overseas. Al Jolson was shown singing "April Showers" in Africa. Ray Bolger and Little Jack Little were strutting their stuff in New Guinea. W. C. Fields, with a cigar in his mouth, his flat straw hat on his head, and a cue ball in midair, was doing his vaudeville routine.

Orson Welles, the boy genius of Hollywood, was sawing Marlene Dietrich in half as part of his magic show. Sophie Tucker, "the last of the redhot mamas," was singing "The Bigger the Army and Navy." Jeanette MacDonald was in one of the pictures singing "I'll See You in My Dreams" to a wounded GI in a hospital bed with a bandage over his eyes. Dinah Shore was there, singing "I'll Walk Alone" to a GI audience, and we were in a picture with the Freddie Slack band singing a medley of our hits on a ship bound for Australia.

☆

Lou Wills, the teenager from Yonkers, was doing more than just performing his comedy dancing and acrobatics with Ed Sullivan and his troupes. He was flying the plane, too.

Lou didn't turn eighteen until the end of the war, so he was never drafted, but while the war was still going on, he wanted to be ready. He began to take flying lessons through the Civil Air Patrol. When his time came to enter the service, he was going to be a pilot.

Despite his tender years, Lou would sit in the cabin with the pilot and co-pilot and fly the C-47 cargo plane that flew the Sullivan troupe up and down the East Coast. He was logging enough hours to meet his objective of qualifying as a pilot of multi-engine aircraft—and enjoying a bonus at the same time: When he was forward in the cabin, he didn't have to be sitting in those cold, hard metal "bucket" seats, with a parachute that nobody knew how to use strapped on his back.

He still has an autographed picture from Ed Sullivan of the troupe standing in front of its C-47, signed with the message:

To Lou—And stay away from the controls, ya hear!
                    Your loving nephew, Ed Sullivan

Every USO entertainer can tell you his or her own war stories about close calls in flying all over the country and around the world to entertain the troops. Even though he was becoming a pilot, Lou remembers being scared stiff on several occasions.

One of those times, the troupe was flying out of New York

on its C-47 for a weekend flight to the Marine base at Cherry Point, North Carolina. It was winter, and Lou looked out the window and noticed what every pilot—and most passengers—live in fear of: ice on the wings. It made for an unnerving flight, but they landed safely.

On another trip, Lou was looking out the window of the plane as the plane headed down the East Coast again. The C-47's legendary bucket seats are in two rows, lined up and down each side of the plane. Passengers sit with their backs to the windows on one side of the plane and look out the windows across the aisle on the opposite side.

That's what Lou was doing when he saw something that puzzled him. "That's the strangest sight I've ever seen," he said out loud, to no one in particular.

The passenger next to him quickly said, "What?"

Lou said, "There's something black on the wing."

That passenger got up without saying another word, unhooked the static line connecting his chute to the line overhead, and walked straight up the middle of the plane to the cabin and said emphatically to the pilot and co-pilot, "The kid just saw some oil on the damn wing."

Then they heard a terrifying sound—that kapocketa-pocketa-kapocketa that can mean only one thing: You're losing an engine.

The entertainers became alarmed, and when they yelled into the cabin and asked what was going on, the pilot called back to them: "Oh, we're okay. We just blew an oil line to one of the engines. But don't worry about it. We'll be okay. We'll make it on only one engine."

Fortunately, they were only fifteen minutes from their destination. They landed without incident, but not without that scare.

☆

In her 1946 history of the USO during World War II, Julia Carson reported that twenty-eight USO entertainers gave their last full measure of devotion to their country during the war, mostly in plane crashes. Performers died when their planes went down in France, Alaska, and off the Italian coast. A C-47 cargo plane disappeared somewhere near the Philippine Islands. Other performers died from illnesses contracted while they were on their tours.

The worst, and most publicized, plane crash occurred on February 22, 1943, when a Yankee Clipper, one of the most popular and modern of the prewar commercial airliners, approached the lights of Lisbon while carrying seven USO entertainers. The plane crashed into the Tagus River near the end of its final approach. Two entertainers died—Tamara, a Russian singer, and Roy Rognan of the husband-and-wife dance team of Lorraine and Rognan. His wife, Jean Lorraine, was among the injured, along with one of the star singers of that time, Jane Froman, plus entertainers Gypsy Markoff and Grace Drysdale. The seventh member, a singer named Yvette, was not injured.

Jane Froman, like all of the injured in the accident, made a valiant and remarkable comeback. Although her right leg was almost torn off, her left ankle crushed, her right arm broken, her back dislocated, and her pelvis cracked, she resumed her career as a night club singer, propped up on a small portable platform.

Before she did, though, Jane encountered one of the harsh realities for all of us who were USO entertainers. The USO's accident insurance provided only a thousand dollars for medical expenses and fifty dollars a week as disability payments for a maximum of fifty-two weeks. According to an article in *Time* magazine a year later, Jane's accident cost her ninety thousand dollars.

Jean Lorraine, in addition to losing her husband, had seven teeth knocked out, hurt her back, and crushed her right leg. She had been a comedy dancer with her husband, but after the tragedy she became a singing comedienne. She changed her name to Lorraine Rognan to keep her husband's name alive. She was on crutches for seven and a half months, but she showed the same kind of bravery as the men in her audiences. She entertained at the Hollywood canteen while still on crutches, then went overseas again a year after the accident to fulfill her contract with the USO.

Her husband's death didn't meet the criteria spelled out in the literature, which said the life insurance was "valid in case of death from all causes except airplane accident or act of war." In what surely must have been one of the cruelest blows of all, *Time* magazine reported that Jean's accident cost her fourteen thousand dollars.

"Yvette" was Elsa Harris, a twenty-one-year-old from Birmingham, Alabama. Although she was reported to be uninjured, she suffered a delayed reaction and collapsed six months later. She had gone to England alone and organized and toured with "Snow White and Her 13 GIs." After recovering from her collapse, she continued to perform in benefits and hospital shows.

Grace Drysdale was a puppeteer and a banjo player from Boston in her late twenties. She suffered a broken leg and spent three months in a hospital, then went to England. There was one saving piece of luck for her in the terrible plane crash. Her trunk with her puppets was retrieved. She repaired their "injuries" while she recovered from her own in the hospital.

Gypsy Markoff was from Milwaukee, Wisconsin, the daughter of an Egyptian mother and a Bessarabian Gypsy father. Her parents took her all over the world, but they died when she was only twelve. Ironically, she made her New York debut as a pianist and accordionist at the Club Abbey at the age of fourteen with Tamara, who failed to survive the crash. Gypsy made a second concert debut in New York's Town Hall in the first week of April 1945 after recovering from multiple injuries and seven-

teen operations. *Time* said the crash cost her twenty-five thousand dollars.

☆

Others sacrificed their health, too, including Ann Miller. She
was one of the greatest dancers on stage anywhere—and still is.
She remembers one trip she made "for the boys," and one she
didn't.

She and her best friend, Linda Darnell, one of the leading
actresses of those years, were scheduled to make a Pacific USO
tour in the fall of 1942 when they received word that they
couldn't go. The reason: America was about to invade Guadalcanal.

"The whole thing blew up," Ann told us last year, "but we
got a citation anyhow, for wanting to go."

She remembers dancing everywhere—on the decks of battleships, at military bases, in hospitals, and at the Hollywood canteen. At the Canteen she didn't limit her activities to dancing.
"I did some shows down there, and then I went down and served
coffee and did things like that. There was no particular problem
with getting stars to go there. They had them by the pound."

Ann performed more times than she can remember all over
the country, but the shows in the South stick out in her memory.
She appeared at military bases throughout Georgia, Alabama,
and other states of the Deep South. "It was so hot, with the
perspiration just rolling off you from the humidity. And trying
to work on those USO stages outside. Most of the time it was just
so hot. It was very, very hard to do, but I did it because my heart
was in it to help the boys."

One of the songs Ann and all the rest of us were dancing to
was a jitterbug number called "Juke Box Saturday Night," a big
hit for Glenn Miller and the Modernaires because of its beat and
its lyrics. Al Stillman and Paul MacGrane wrote it for a musical
review, *Stars on Ice.* Its words were an accurate description of

the fun that millions of young people were having with their dates around a new kind of entertainment product that had become a prominent part of the American social scene in the 1930's and '40's:

Moppin' up soda pop rickeys
To our hearts delight,
Dancin' to swingeroo quickies,
Juke box Saturday night.

Goodman and Kyser and Miller
Help to make things bright
Mixin' hot licks with vanilla,
Juke box Saturday night.

The performances Ann remembers most were the forty-eight shows she did in one day at the Coral Gables Hotel in Florida, which had been converted into a hospital. She appeared there in front of an audience of "basket cases." She had the same horrified reaction that teenage Lou Wills did when he saw them for the first time on his weekend USO tours with Ed Sullivan.

Basket cases were one of the sights of war, and nobody found it easy to cope with the first sight of them. "They were lying all over the floor of the lobby on stretchers," Ann said. "I did forty-eight shows and then collapsed. They had to send me home in an Army plane. We went from ward to ward to ward, singing and dancing and trying to boost the morale of these men. It was just hell, but I did it, and then they had to send me home. I was very sick."

Ann was suffering from dehydration, stress, and fatigue. It took her two months to recover.

"I just fell apart," she told us, "and I think the shock of seeing those men with their arms and legs blown off—it was just frightening. But when you do it, you do it. You try to help them, try to sing and dance. You try to keep their spirits up. It's heartbreaking."

Milton Berle was another performer who compiled an impressive record of service, taking a year and a half off from his career at one point to entertain our servicemen and women all over America. He had been declared unqualified for military service anyhow because he had bad feet, and his record during World War II proved that certain people, including entertainers and the wartime baseball players, could do a whole lot more for our country by continuing their professional performances.

We never played with Milton during the war, but we performed with many other draft-age men at USO clubs, camps, and hospitals, and of all the thousands and thousands of GIs we sang for, not one ever displayed any resentment against the male performers on the bill with us. People like Milton Berle were doing as much to help us win the war as anyone else, and in the case of exceptional workers like Milton, they were doing more than most.

Milton played as many as forty shows a day in hospital wards, plus special shows he presented frequently. He was starring in *Ziegfeld Follies* on Broadway when the war started. He immediately packed up the whole cast and crew—and the scenery, too—piled everything and everybody onto trucks and drove out to Fort Dix, New Jersey, and put on the entire Broadway production right there for the GIs. Milton paid for the whole operation.

By 1943, this kind of war service by America's entertainers was winning praise from all sorts of individuals and publications in and out of show business. On March 3, *Variety* published an editorial headed, "Dedication to a Cause," praising the USO performers in a collective description of them:

> I am the spirit of all actors . . . . I am an acrobat, a singer, a
> comedian, a dancer and a tragedian. I am the ingenue, the

juvenile and the leading man. I am the modest performer and I am the star.

At this moment I am playing in a tin hut somewhere in Alaska . . . a camp in Australia . . . a makeshift theater in the Caribbean. I am slogging through mud in North Africa. I am in the Solomons, in Ireland, in England and in Iceland—wherever there's an American soldier, sailor or marine . . .

If I persuade a man to buy his limit in war bonds, if I inspire a worker to quicken his lathe, if I brighten the lot of a lonely soldier—then these are my contributions to an America at war . . .

For this work I ask no plaudits, no eulogies. I am a soldier in greasepaint, serving a free country and freedom-loving men. This service is the actors' imperishable memorial.

In less flowery terms, with the kind of every day meat-and-potatoes language that you found in every letter home from overseas, an unidentified USO trouper described the life of the entertainers "over there" at Thanksgiving. Letters and news dispatches during the war never disclosed the location of the writer. They were always datelined "Somewhere in France" or "Somewhere in the South Pacific." This one was from "a few degrees from the Equator."

The entertainer, whose identity has been lost to history, wrote that the "turkey and all the home fixin's taste just as good or better than usual, as can be attested to by the fact that I'm distributing myself over three Thanksgiving dinners today." She wrote of feelings about serving as a USO trouper: "I have never had less sleep, never felt healthier, certainly never happier, and certainly never so full of respect, admiration, and pride in my fellow Americans that walk this part of the earth. For that jaded faith in human kind, the best thing I could wish anyone is a trip to the Southwest Pacific Theater of War."

The entertainer then listed "a series of unforgettable impressions":

The dense blackout to which you became so accustomed that on a night when someone forgot and lit a cigarette, it took on all the proportions of a burning skyscraper. Playing the show (we did it three times) on the open deck with the wind blowing you about and the deck heaving under your feet; the evening songfests when hundreds of fine, strong men's voices thrilled you more than any concert ever will. The church services in the men's mess . . . closing with a prayer that choked you—not because it was a very good prayer, but because you knew what every man prayed for.

As for the conditions facing the performers, the same letter contains this description of life in New Guinea, with eighty women sharing one barracks, one latrine, one shower and one ironing board:

Since that first day in New Guinea, I've eaten C Rations and I've eaten steak and ice cream—dehydrated potatoes and eggs and the ever-present spam and bullybeef. . . . I've eaten in mess halls far more picturesque than any atmospheric job in New York city.

I've ridden in and driven jeeps, peeps, weapons carriers, command cars, tanks, ducks, M8's and LSTV's. I've flown in an Aussie bomber on a mission over Jap-held territory. I've flown in P-38's, A-20's and Piper Cubs. I've broadcast from a jungle radio station. . . . I've been wakened in the middle of the night by a rat scampering across my face. . . . I've tramped through the jungle, cutting our way with a machete (never understanding how men can fight an enemy through it when I can scarcely walk through it); I've stood in mud up to my ankles with the dust blowing thick around my head.

We've played in 'theaters' that were only a board platform and the rest was left to our stage manager and his detail of GIs. We've dressed in tents in mud to our ankles and we've dressed in dressing rooms graced with the now familiar parachute ceiling and a real, though hastily constructed, dressing table. And often there were flowers in our dressing rooms.

We've played to audiences, many of them, ankle deep in mud, huddled under their ponchos in the pouring rain (it breaks your heart the first two or three times to see men so hungry for entertainment). We've played on uncovered stages, when we, as well as the audience, got rain-soaked. We've played with huge tropical bugs flying in our hair and faces.

She discovered the same thing that LaVerne, Patty, and I did when we went to Italy with the USO—that the men didn't want sex and smut in our shows. She described the typical GI in the USO audiences: "Don't ever underestimate him by thinking all he wants is a leg show and dirty cracks. He talks and listens to 'men talk' day in and day out. Every woman back home wears a halo now and those who represent her had better keep theirs on too. I've heard a girl swear out here and sensed a roomful of men freeze for a second. Give them laughs, but see that they are good laughs."

That determination to "keep it clean" was the subject of an impassioned statement in 1943 by the former national chairman of the Code Committee of the National Association of Broadcasters, Earl J. Glade. His particular concern was the quality of those shows being broadcast on the radio, and the change in that quality when the broadcast ended but the Camp Shows continued.

At a meeting of radio station program directors in Chicago and another in Salt Lake City, he told his colleagues: "There is no necessity to sissify a camp show. After all, an audience of four thousand or more males wants hearty, punchy, he-man entertainment, but that doesn't mean that it must be dirty or nasty. There is frequently an attempt to step up the show after it leaves the air, and therein lies the danger to the industry. The air shows have humor and entertainment at its best. They need no further stepping up to be entertaining to the boys."

Glade pointed out that "most boys coming into camps now

are teen-aged. They are nervous, impressionable, lonely, and (sometimes even hospitalized) for nothing more serious than nostalgia. They are easily shocked and react badly to any sordidness in their entertainment."

This veteran radio executive had a solution. "The overall cure," he said, "is to maintain off-air shows at the same standards as those which are aired. Artists who are unable to ad lib or emcee their extended programs without resorting to double entendre should stick to scripts. Outstanding among those who can go on for hours with acceptable entertainment are Fred Allen and Gracie Fields. There are others who do the same, but there are others who must carefully edit all their material."

Then, apparently with pride in his industry, Glade told reporters: "It would be a fine thing for radio if mothers and fathers knew that the entertainment provided for their sons at camps is the same as that which comes out of the radio in their own homes."

That same unidentified USO performer made another finding similar to ours. "A very important part of the work and fun is trying to be with the enlisted men as much as possible," she wrote to the folks back home. "And the hospitals . . . every visit to a hospital ward just to talk is maybe the finest thing you can do."

Every one of us who traveled overseas had the same experience she did in talking with the troops. "The conversation begins with an invariable pattern. 'Where are you from? How long have you been here? How do you like New Guinea?' . . . and then, 'What's it like back in the States? Do they know there's a war out here?' "

Then that entertainer sounded a warning that looked into the peace to come and what the men fighting the war could expect when it was over: "They don't wave flags, they don't talk about the ideals they're fighting for. It has resolved itself into a job to do. They fight because the guy in the next foxhole fights. They kill because they've seen their buddies killed. But the home land to return to—the ultimate goal of all they've been through—had better be worth it when they get back. And they can't be fooled."

CHAPTER TEN

Any Bonds Today?

When *Time* magazine featured Bob Hope on its cover of September 20, 1943, praising him as "first in the hearts of the servicemen," Bob had done plenty to deserve the accolade—and he admits he learned a thing or two in the process.

Bob wrote a special foreword for *Always Home,* the USO's pictorial history of its first fifty years. "Thanks to the USO," he said, "my knowledge of geography has been greatly enhanced. And I have some wonderful memories—like box lunches, yellow fever shots—and I've learned how to say Kaopectate in nine languages."

He spoke for all of us entertainers when he described some of his flying experiences. "I knew the plane was old," he wrote, "when I saw the pilot sitting behind me wearing goggles and a scarf." He said the plane "belonged to a four-star general—Pershing."

Bob led the first show to entertain our troops, seven months before Pearl Harbor. He took the cast of his weekly radio show to March Field, now March Air Force Base, seventy miles from

Los Angeles, in May of 1944. His vocalist Frances Langford, remembers the reaction of the GIs: "I've never heard so much applause in my life."

Bob described his own USO memories in *Always Home*, and his description included a reference to one of the Andrews Sisters' special wartime songs. "The USO show of World War II," he said, "conjures up the image of a comedian and musicians on a makeshift stage surrounded by thousands of GIs and a singer belting out the saga of 'Boogie Woogie Bugle Boy of Company B.'"

Bob has the same enthusiasm for the GI audiences that every one of us who ever performed in front of them does. "The audiences are still the greatest in the world. When they laugh, they mean it; when they applaud, there just isn't any better sound in the world. The audiences truly appreciate the USO and the performers. When they look up on that stage they see home, family . . . . They see America."

On the GIs side, a letter to the USO from a soldier's girl-friend in New York paid a tribute to the entertainers that was just as glowing and convincing:

> "Gentlemen: Just the other day I received a letter from my sweetheart who is, and has been, over in the South Pacific area for the past two years. He mentioned that the USO had a Camp Show there recently and he enjoyed it very much and asked me to write on his behalf and thank you for the splendid work you are doing. I know that it does mean a lot to the boys away from home, and your organization is doing a grand job.
>
> I am enclosing my small contribution and again say Thanks, on behalf of my sweetheart and all the other soldiers whom you have made happy with your many Camp Shows.

Inside was a contribution of two dollars, almost ten percent of her boyfriend's monthly pay.

By mid-1943, the Army, not taking any chances with the morale of its troops, began training its own acts. Captain Hy Gardner, a postwar TV personality and newspaper columnist, came up with the idea of training the troops themselves to be entertainers who could help the morale of the troops in between visits by USO troupes, reducing the length of the wait between shows at their camps. The Army liked Hy's idea so much that it held a three-day "show business" clinic in New York in June for 155 enlisted men, officers, and WAACS of its Second Air Command.

Billboard said the clinic taught the GI performers "show biz tricks and sent them back to camp with materials and ideas." Entertainers for Second Service Command, covering New York, New Jersey, and Delaware, were now ready to tour camps regularly, after receiving tips on how to perform and entertain.

Private Pee Wee Monte, was one of the teachers, along with such singers and entertainers as story-teller Harry Hershfield, comedian Jan Murray—who taught the GIs stunts involving audience participation—Henny Youngman, the king of the one-liners, and Jimmy Durante, who, one paper said, "demonstrated how to imitate Durante."

The Army was anxious to develop a farm system of developing its own performers, so anxious, in fact, that during the conference, Hy Gardner lost eight pounds.

☆

Patty, LaVerne, and I continued our stateside appearances at military camps and hospitals at war bond rallies, the Stage Door Canteen in New York and the Hollywood Canteen. In New York, where we appeared at the Paramount Theater and later the Roxy, we always went over to Times Square between shows and did other shows over there. Most of the performers on Broadway did the same thing.

There was a big stage right there in the middle of the Square, and thousands of people would line up to buy war bonds and listen to us sing while they waited. We'd sing for two and three hours at a time. Then we'd hurry back before we were due in the theater again.

New York seemed to me to be the most alive city in the country during the war. Other cities in other parts of the country were reacting to the war with personalities of their own. In the Midwest, things were more reserved. The West Coast was a happy medium between the energized feeling of New York and the more conservative Midwest.

The atmosphere in New York was electrifying. The pace was fast, even by New York standards, the city crowded as always, and the daily news bulletins wrapping around the facing of the *Times* Building added to the charged-up environment. The songwriters and script writers had the right word for it. New York City was *teeming* with excitement.

When it came time to promote the sale of war bonds and stamps, sometimes you could do it without a scheduled event. That's what Patricia Morrison did.

She was playing the Earl Theater in Philadelphia, singing five shows a day and with only three gowns in her wardrobe. During her engagement, she noticed large numbers of high school-age kids in the audience, many of them down front so they could annoy the performers. "Their parents were working all day in defense plants," Pat said, "so they'd come to the show and heckle us all day."

One group audience noticed that for her fourth show, Pat wore the same gown she'd had on for her first. They let her have it, asking if she didn't have enough money to buy another gown. Then they started throwing pennies, lots of them.

"I stopped the show," she said, "and started picking up pennies. I picked up all of them. It must have taken me ten minutes." Then she returned to center stage and told her hecklers: "Thank you very much. I'm going to use these to buy war stamps."

The audience loved it, gave her a loud round of applause, and never bothered her again.

War bonds were one of the most sacred causes of the war. People promoted them every way they could, the general public as well as the entertainers. Students at the College of Notre Dame in Maryland ironed blouses, polished shoes, and typed term papers in exchange for the stamps that they pasted into their book. When the stamps totaled $18.75, you redeemed the book for a war bond worth twenty-five dollars. Uncle Sam then used your $18.75 toward paying for the war.

In Tyrone, New York, students tapped maple trees and sold the syrup to raise funds to buy the stamps. Major league baseball players and the members of the teams' front offices took ten percent of their pay in war bonds. Genung's, a department store in New York's Westchester County, gave out stamps in exchange for old umbrellas, then turned the umbrellas in during the scrap drives.

A Hereford bull named General Grant fetched $1.8 million in war bonds during auctions in Oklahoma, but the most famous animal war bonds salesman of them all was King Neptune, a pig from Franklin County, Illinois. King Neptune was bought with war bonds, and his new owner turned right around and gave him to the staff of a Navy Recruiting station. The sailors then put him on an auction "circuit" so he could be auctioned off repeatedly, each time for war bonds. The result was that King Neptune was sold several more times, once to the Illinois General Assembly for a million dollars. Neptune was allowed to retire eventually, with a sales performance of $2.35 million in war bonds to his credit.

Everyone was doing his part, including Irving Berlin, who wrote his tune, "Any Bonds Today?" and published it seven months before Pearl Harbor, with vocal renditions by most every popular singer, most notably Bing Crosby on records and, America's newest crooner, Bugs Bunny in the movies.

☆

LaVerne, Patty, and I were asked to sing it all through the war, and so were all the other soloists and groups. It is a sign of those times that the number was a big hit. Americans enjoyed singing it. Nobody regarded it as forced government propaganda or a boring attempt at motivating us. It was popular because Irving Berlin wrote a good song, and because it struck a responsive chord in all Americans.

The Treasury Department produced musical and documentary shows on local radio stations all over the country, with dozens of spot announcements promoting war bonds. Each of the networks produced at least one Radio Bond Days show, where top stars urged listeners to phone in their pledges.

Newspaper carriers signed up as volunteers to sell stamps to their subscribers and took orders for bonds. Then they bought bonds themselves out of their earnings from their monthly collections for the papers they delivered. Department stores promoted sales, too, and blocked off streets and staged war bond rallies of their own.

Volunteers, most of them women, went door-to-door in cities and towns and farm-to-farm in rural areas seeking out more bonds sales. They had a foolproof sales pitch. They told the farmers war bonds were "the crop that never fails."

There was a booth for the purchase of war bonds and stamps in every movie theater in the country. When you took your seat, there was Bugs Bunny up on the screen singing Irving Berlin's song. The selected short subjects at the movies included news-reel messages and cartoons showed how stamps and bonds were helping us to win the war and how much they could do for each of us as investors. Some theaters and baseball teams held special nights where the price of admission was a war bond. One of the most popular radio shows of the forties, *Truth or Consequences* with Ralph Edwards, did the same thing.

The largest war bond promotion of them all was the Hollywood Victory Caravan, a project conducted by the Treasury Department featuring a train visit by the biggest movie stars to almost thirty American cities. Treasury picked the right man for the job. He was John Maschio, the husband of singer Constance Moore and the agent for Hollywood's brightest names—Fred Astaire, Ginger Rogers, Jimmy Stewart, Henry Fonda, Gregory Peck, Gene Kelly, Van Johnson, and more. He represented more stars and brought more performers from New York to Hollywood and made them stars than anyone in the world.

The Treasury Department contacted Maschio and said the government wanted to put a group of stars together to sell a large amount of bonds—millions of dollars worth. It wasn't the first time Maschio had been asked to help with the war effort. That came earlier, before the war, and the official involved was no less than General George Patton, the legendary "blood-and-guts" commander of the armored divisions whose tanks rumbled across Europe in 1944 and '45. Patton was conducting training exercises with ten thousand troops at Indio, California, near Palm Springs, before taking his unit overseas, and he wanted Hollywood's stars to provide occasional entertainment for his men. Once a week, John would travel out to Patton's outfit with the luminaries he represented and put on a show on a stage in the middle of the desert.

"Then," John still remembers, "that son of a gun would make us do what his soldiers had to do, even the girls." The men were required to put on Army fatigue uniforms and crawl on their stomachs under barbed wire while bullets were being fired just over their heads. The women had to put on fatigues, too, and ride in jeeps across obstacle courses and in dust so thick they could barely see.

It was vintage Patton, forcing the entertainers, who were gracious enough to give up their time, to come to his post and entertain his troops without pay to endure what his men were enduring so they could appreciate what they were doing.

Officials from the Treasury Department called John about their idea for the Hollywood Victory Caravan just after the attack on Pearl Harbor. "They said they'd arrange the schedule," John says, and that was all he needed to know. He assembled a glittering cast that included Bing Crosby, Fred Astaire, Lucille Ball, Jimmy Cagney, Greer Garson, Judy Garland, Kathryn Grayson, Paul Henreid, Betty Hutton, Jose Iturbi, Joan Bennett, Harpo Marx, Dick Powell, Mickey Rooney, Claudette Colbert, Cary Grant, Joan Blondell, Groucho Marx, and Bert Lahr, who was the new favorite of millions of Americans after playing the role of the cowardly lion in *The Wizard of Oz*.

The caravan was a smash hit in every city, beginning with its first stop, in Washington. *The Washington Post* told its readers: "They came, they saw, they conquered." *The Detroit Free-Press* ran a front page headline:

HOLLYWOOD VICTORY CARAVAN TO BRING STARS GALORE TO THE CITY

It began in Washington, D.C., in March of 1942, starting with lunch with President Roosevelt at the White House, and followed by a parade and an evening performance before a standing-room-only crowd at Constitution Hall. From there the caravan traveled to Boston, New York, and other East Coast cities, New Orleans and the South, St. Louis and the Midwest, Dallas and the Southwest, and on to the West Coast. It was a different city every night, a series of one-night stands that lasted a month as the stars pitched in to promote the sale of war bonds.

When the stars entered the room for their lunch with the President, instead of the guests coming into the room first and standing when the President made his appearance, the President was already there, sitting at the table. "He never stood up," John remembers, an example of the continuing techniques employed by Roosevelt's staff to avoid calling attention to his paralyzed legs, the result of polio when he was a young man.

"It was supposed to be a secret."

The schedule was the same in every city—a parade through downtown, a VIP lunch, and a star-studded show promoting the sale of war bonds to pay the cost of fighting the war. "They all received rousing receptions," John says.

Between cities, "it was a picnic on board," John remembers. "Bing Crosby and a few musicians from the band would start at one end of the train, and Mickey Rooney and a few other musicians would start at the other end, and they'd work their way toward the middle, entertaining everybody on board, including themselves."

The Treasury Department picked up the tab for the trip and made sure the entertainers got to travel first class. The performers had their own staterooms on the long train, plus their own barber shop, two large dining cars, a tailor shop, and various other conveniences.

Just how successful the Hollywood Victory Caravan was is illustrated by an incident during the show at Constitution Hall, and in the answer to a request after it from Judy Garland.

At Constitution Hall, one of the men in the audience hollered out to Claudette Colbert, "How much for a kiss?"

She hollered back, "A thousand dollars."

Half a dozen men from various parts of the audience stood up and pledged the thousand each, and Claudette went right down into the audience and closed the deals.

As the caravan rumbled along the tracks from Washington to Boston, Judy told one of the Treasury Department officials on board that she had relatives in Boston. "Could we get some tickets down front for them to see the show?" she asked.

Tickets to the show were sold on the basis of pledges to buy war bonds. One of the government representatives told Judy, "The tickets down front are going for a million apiece."

In 1943 alone, the sale of war bonds and stamps to America's students paid for the manufacture of ninety thousand jeeps. By the end of the war, these efforts and all the others resulted in the sale of $59 billion in war bonds.

Kate Smith seemed to be selling more bonds than the rest of the entertainment industry combined. She stood with a commanding presence in the middle of stages everywhere, weighing 235 pounds and sometimes more, her hands clasped at her waist, usually wearing a long black dress topped by a white collar. She sang the most requested numbers of the war, including "God Bless America," "The Last Time I Saw Paris," and "The White Cliffs of Dover," and she always reminded her audiences to write to "our boys in uniform." She told them: "If you don't write, you're wrong."

With the volume of a Wagnerian soprano, she sang joyously, in Berlin's words, about "the land I love," and her fans knew she meant every word. She is credited with selling six hundred million dollars in war bonds, more than anyone else in history. In one seventeen-hour radio marathon, she accounted for the sale of thirty million dollars in bonds. During the war, she traveled 520,000 miles, equal to crossing the country 173 times.

The New York Times called her the "All-American singer." The *Washington Post* said she was "America's songstress . . . a symbol of patriotism to millions of Americans and one of the nation's all-time popular singers." When President Reagan awarded her a medal for her service to the nation, he called her "a patriot in every sense of the word."

But her wartime ally, President Roosevelt, may have paid her the highest tribute of all. When King George VI and Queen Elizabeth visited Washington during the war, FDR hosted a reception and dinner in their honor. As Kate came to the front of the receiving line, the President of the United States told the King and Queen of England:

"This is Kate Smith—This is *America.*"

Not all the news about the war was coming from overseas. There were plenty of war-related developments on the home front, too.

The "black market" was a problem, with some people obtaining scarce items through underhanded means and private sources, then selling them illegally and at inflated prices to people who were suckers enough to pay the outrageous prices.

Every once in a while the news included a story about someone who got caught. One incident happened near Dover, Delaware, the state capital, where Army officials seized a whole truck load of black market chickens on Route 13. Government inspectors turned the chickens over to the Army, and another black marketeer was foiled in his attempt to make a profit at the expense of the American public while we were at war. By that time, in the summer of 1943, the government estimated that the black market controlled ninety percent of the poultry industry on the East Coast.

Life magazine reflected the views of almost every American, criticizing not only those who operated in the black market but those who were its customers: "The man or woman who patronizes a black market in wartime is not only breaking the law but depriving others of their just share of a limited supply. U.S.

civilians are all on one raft together now; there is not enough to go around, and will not be until the war is over."

In Los Angeles, three thousand transit employees staged a streetcar operators strike at the end of July, after the War Labor Board denied their request for a pay raise of ten cents an hour. The streetcars carried a million fares a day in L.A. Some of the biggest war plants in the country were located there. But a strange thing happened: Those plants reported an *increase* in attendance. The strike was called off after the first day.

In Burbank, just outside L.A., there was a breath of good news. Finley's Credit Jewelers took out full-page newspaper ads to alert customers that a shipment of one of the home front's scarcest items had arrived—alarm clocks. Almost everyone was working six and seven days a week, and many people worked split shifts and double shifts and all kinds of crazy schedules, so alarm clocks became one of the war's necessities. Absenteeism and tardiness were frowned upon, to say the least, and you were considered a slacker if your attendance at work wasn't close to perfect.

The store announced it would open its doors at nine-thirty the next morning with a shipment of five hundred prewar clocks, but a seventy-four-year-old man wasn't taking any chances. He made sure he would be first in line by getting there the day before. Others joined him as the afternoon and night wore on. When the store opened its doors the next morning, the workers bought up the clocks as quickly as the store's clerks could sell them.

On the subject of getting up in the morning, Irving Berlin became our national expert. The man who was born in Russia but had a gift for expressing the feelings of Americans dug out a song he had written during World War I, when he was a soldier at Camp Upton at Yaphank, Long Island. "Every morning when the bugle blew," Irving said, "I'd jump right out of bed. The other soldiers thought I was a little too eager about it, and they hated me. That's why I finally wrote a song about it."

The song appeared first in Irving's show about World War I life, "Yip, Yip Yaphank," and became a big hit of that war. In World War II, when he wrote "This Is the Army," Irving reintroduced what has now become a classic song about life in the Army, "Oh, How I Hate to Get Up in the Morning." He performed it himself, singing it on stage in his World War I doughboy uniform, with the leggings and the three-cornered hat and his whispery tenor voice, threatening to murder the bugler and then to "get that other pup, the guy who wakes the bugler up . . ."

Some of the advertising offered us a glimpse of what the world would look like after the war. One ad showed a futuristic drawing of "a super service station of tomorrow. Automobiles will be serviced on the ground floor—helicopters on the roof."

That prediction might have missed its mark, but an ad by Worthington Air Conditioning and Refrigeration was right on the mark with its own bold prediction. When we read it, we could only dream that someday such a life would be possible:

> Air conditioning of shops—small and large alike—is coming as surely as popular preference for air travel. Only the circumstance of war delays it . . . . Better, more adaptable and economic air conditioner units will be one of the beneficial byproducts of war."

But the war was still a long way from being over. Even as the news included some exhilarating victories across both oceans, people both in government and out were warning us against premature optimism.

On May 17, 1943, ten days after the allies captured Bizerte in Tunisia, *Life* magazine published an editorial cautioning against premature optimism and expressing displeasure against a strike threatened by the nation's coal miners under their flamboyant leader, bushy-browed John L. Lewis.

There was cause for rejoicing in the capture of Bizerte. It marked the end of the North African campaign. The losses in German and Italian troops totaled 349,206 killed or captured. Still, *Life* reminded its readers that "the spring of 1943 is a sort of turning point in the war. Bizerte has fallen. Our Army in Africa has learned to fight. Many shrewd observers think they can see the end of the war. U.S. arms production keeps hitting new highs. The Treasury's Second War Loan was oversubscribed. In some ways, everything seems to be clicking. Then, abruptly, 530,000 coal miners down their tools, and may do so again."

Life offered this assessment of the war: "We stand just about where Churchill said Britain stood after the battle of El Alamein—at 'the end of the beginning.' "

The magazine quoted three members of the Air Corps, one of them a member of the miners' union, on the possibility of a coal strike. A pilot in our 14th Air Force in the Pacific commented: "I'd just as soon shoot one of those strikers as shoot down Japs—they're doing just as much to lose the war for us."

Another airman, described as "a union man," said, "I wonder what the hell John Lewis and his gang would do if we went on strike out here."

Lieutenant William Colantoni, a veteran of twenty-four bombing missions, was a Pennsylvania coal miner and a member of the United Mine Workers before the war. He told *Life* he wished he could take Lewis on his next mission.

Production, our ability simply to manufacture more vehicles, weapons, and ammunition than our enemies, was a national priority to meet our highest priority of all—winning the war. In World War I, it took an average of eleven months to manufacture a warship. In 1942, we were building one in forty-six days.

The movie newsreels, the source for us to see our news in those last years before the postwar mass production of television, never mentioned the locations of the plants, but they were filled with stories of production miracles, partly to stimulate workers everywhere to produce more.

One newsreel story reported that a giant synthetic rubber factory "somewhere in the U.S." was turning out ninety thousand tons of "man-made" rubber a year, leading to the manufacture of sixteen million tires, one of the scarcest items both at home and overseas. President Roosevelt, wearing a black arm band on his left sleeve, made a two-week tour across the country, covering nine thousand miles by car and train, to visit factory workers in twenty-four states.

The First Lady, Eleanor Roosevelt, was a special hero. She seemed to be everywhere, traveling as her husband's eyes and ears and reporting to him on her return to the White House. She wrote a syndicated newspaper column, *My Day*, and she was already a familiar sight in the newsreels from her prewar involvement in various civil rights causes and seeking social change. With the start of the fighting, she was seen launching ships in shipyards on both coasts. When she smashed the traditional bottle of champagne on the bow of the carrier *Yorktown*, she had to hurry. Someone had started the mighty carrier sliding down its keel several minutes ahead of the time shown on the schedule.

In the newsreels we also saw Mrs. Roosevelt at a torpedo assembly line more than a half-mile long, a former tin can factory that was now making "tin fish," the narrator told the movie audiences. She appeared with "America's miracle ship builder," Henry Kaiser, at his shipyards as Kaiser pledged to build six carriers a month. But we weren't told where his shipyards were, only that they were on "the Pacific coast."

With sons in the war herself, Mrs. Roosevelt flew to an Army base in the Caribbean and visited our troops there. She wore a Red Cross field uniform and traveled to hospitals in the South

Pacific, Australia, and New Zealand. The newsreel announcer told us her visit "serves as a tonic and inspiration to wounded American soldiers convalescing thousands of miles from home."

Commentator Eric Sevareid, in narrating the video series, *V For Victory* for Atlas Video Inc. in Washington, said: "Perhaps the best known American woman to contribute to the fight was not an actress but a social reformer, Eleanor Roosevelt . . . . During the war, she pressed officials of her husband's administration to seek the advice of women leaders and to more fully include women in wartime planning. Both at home and abroad, Eleanor Roosevelt was a prominent figure during the war years."

The production achievements continued. More than six million Americans, one-third of our labor force, worked in war plants. Two million were women, but for them, Edwin Newman, the co-host of *V For Victory*, said: "Conditions were far from ideal. Even though the official government policy stipulated equal pay for women, the overwhelming majority did not receive it. In one federally owned shipyard, men received up to twenty-two dollars a day, while the highest paid woman earned less than seven. And yet, their jobs could be as demanding and dangerous as any man's."

Detroit became known as America's "Arsenal for Democracy," turning out four million cars and trucks in its rapid conversion from peacetime and wartime footing. Factories that manufactured automobile fenders before the war were producing propellers. Typewriter plants were now turning out machine guns. The list of different items needed seemed endless. In every B-17 "Flying Fortress" bomber, for example, there were a hundred thousand parts.

A farm family in the Midwest turned its house into a factory, with family members making tools for larger plants. The newsreel announcer told us: "This farm family's innovative genius is typical of Americans from coast to coast."

In the Pacific Northwest, a young woman owned and operated a chrome mine, producing the metal essential for war production but no longer available from the Philippines because of the Japanese occupation there. She ran the mine herself, producing twenty tons of the metal every day. The newsreel announcer said the mine operator was "a typical young American woman." Then he told us proudly: "Again, this is America, all out for war."

In Maine, volunteer "college co-eds" planted potatoes, beans, and tomatoes to be sent to freezing plants for preserving. The newsreel announcer called them "America's army of civilian volunteers, helping to replenish the nation's food larders depleted by the demands of war." Other co-eds made dolls by hand "for little ones" at Christmastime. "Now that manufacturers have converted their plants to war," the announcer reported, "the nation's doll industry is strictly homemade."

Summarizing both our production achievements and the role of America's women in them, Newman concluded in *V For Victory:* "In the end, the miracles of production were miracles indeed. To the absolute disbelief of Germany and Japan, Americans at home enlisted in the war effort with tremendous energy and dedication, constructing a massive arsenal of war. American women were at the forefront of this effort."

Despite the glowing reports in the newsreels and the subtle propaganda in them, government officials, including the Under Secretary of War, Robert Patterson, warned that the Army would not be fully equipped until late in 1944.

Some of our leaders were cautioning us about what a long haul still lay ahead for all of us. One of the blunt messages came from the Vice Chief of Naval Operations, Vice Admiral Frederick J. Horne, who said in the last week of July that "we are planning material and ships for a war that will last at least until 1949. And that is not pessimistic."

The Secretary of the Navy, Frank Knox—one of the Republicans recruited by President Roosevelt at the beginning of the war to show that he was taking a bipartisan approach to the international crisis—said at the same time in mid-summer: "All talk about an early ending of the war is wishful thinking. It has caused a letup in production, and we're already feeling the effects . . . . It's just criminal."

Army officials were voicing the same warning. Lieutenant General Brehan Somervell cautioned American workers: "It is easy to say that the fifty trucks or the two hundred engines which could not be produced against schedule this month can be made up next month, but a battlefield lost on Tuesday is difficult to regain on Wednesday."

Because of this concern, the military researchers were working overtime to invent new weapons and new ways of delivering them. Their research ran all the way from the hush-hush Project Manhattan formed to develop an atomic bomb to an equally secret effort to see if we could use bats—the ones that fly, not the baseball kind—to start fires in Japan. Lytle S. Adams, a dental surgeon from Pennsylvania, sent a proposal to the White House in December of 1941 to attach incendiary bombs to bats and drop them out of airplanes by parachute over Japan in large canisters. His logic was that the bats would fly into buildings, then the bombs they were carrying would explode, and so would the building.

The White House forwarded the brainchild of Dr. Adams to the Army, which worked on the idea until 1943, concluding that the "free-tailed bat" was the best candidate of all the different kinds of bats. The Army decided it could carry a one-ounce bomb in flight and pinpointed the city of Osaka as a prime target. The logic was that eighty percent of the buildings in central Osaka were made of highly combustible materials like paper, wood, and bamboo. Dr. Adams reasoned that the parachute attack could do serious damage and create serious morale problems for the Japanese.

In a program called "Project X-Ray," the Army collected

thousands of bats and put them in ice cube trays and refrigerated them so the bats would hibernate long enough for the tiny bombs to be attached to their little bodies. The Army tested five groups of bats carrying "dummy" bombs, dropping them from a B-25 bomber at an altitude of five thousand feet.

The historic test took place on May 23, 1943. An article by C. V. Glines in the October 1990 issue of *Air Force* magazine describes the result: "Most of the bats, not fully recovered from hibernation, did not fly and died on impact."

The Army officials then gave the plan over to the Navy. Five months later, the Navy stored the bats in four caves in Texas, protected by Marine guards, and conducted some research of its own. The project was canceled in 1944 after running up a cost of two million dollars—and after "drafting" millions of bats.

Jack Couffer documents the whole story in his 1992 book, *Bat Bomb: World War II's Other Secret Weapon.* It is also recorded that Dr. Adams raised serious questions about the American military order of priorities:

> We got a sure thing like the bat bomb going, something that could really win the war, and they're [experimenting] with tiny little atoms. It makes me want to cry.

CHAPTER ELEVEN

Manpower, Womanpower, Kidpower

All day long, whether rain or shine,
She's a part of the assembly line.
She's making history, working for victory,
Rosie, br-r-r, the riveter.

That was always one of the most popular tunes of the war, from the time Redd Evans and John Jacob Loeb wrote it in 1942 until the end of the war. By '43, with all the emphasis on producing planes, tanks, ships and those new, odd-looking open cars called jeeps in numbers that seemed unreachable, "Rosie, The Riveter" was a big hit for a quartet, The Four Vagabonds. It shot to the top of the charts not just because of its bouncy beat but also because of its patriotic, motivational lyrics and its special salute to the six million women who by then were working in our defense plants as riveters, welders, mechanics—and in all the other mechanical trades that had been considered men-only occupations before the war. They were on shift work, and you could see them leaving their homes at all hours of the day and night, dressed in overalls and carrying lunch boxes. They worked not only in factories but climbed telephone poles and lowered themselves underground to install and repair utilities.

Beginning in 1943 they played professional baseball as members of the only women's professional league in baseball history, the All-American Girls Professional Baseball League. The league was founded by a man, Phil Wrigley of the Chicago chewing gum company and owner of the Chicago Cubs. He became so concerned that the manpower shortage would rob us of all the major league baseball players that he decided the best stand-by would be an all-*girls* league. It lasted until 1954 and became the subject of a hit movie in 1992, *A League of Their Own*.

The women in the factories became the target of new fashion campaigns. In 1943, a new line of clothing was introduced for women working in the Boeing aircraft manufacturing plants on the West Coast. It was a case of necessity, because when the women flocked to the factories in 1942, they—and their safety-conscious supervisors—discovered that dressing in what appeared to be appropriate clothing could cause serious problems. Most slacks of the day were baggy or had cuffs at the bottom of the legs or flaps on back pockets. Some of the women's sweaters were made of wide mesh. Too many of their blouses had frills, and thousands of the workers liked to retain their femininity by wearing their hair in the loose, flowing styles movie stars such as Rita Hayworth and Veronica Lake—whose over-the-eye look became her trademark.

Experts began analyzing accident reports in the defense plants and discovered that many of the accidents were attributable to clothing and hairstyles. Safety engineers-turned-fashion-designers began to draw up what they thought their women workers should wear on the job. They held "safety" fashion shows. Although they encouraged their female employees to wear the new lines, most women continued to dress as before.

Then the *safety* experts realized what *clothing* experts knew all along: You had to make the clothes attractive. Enter Muriel King, a successful designer of her day, who created the Flying Fortress line at Boeing's request. Her new fashions became an instant hit not only at Boeing but at the Douglass and Lockheed plants in California, too.

Life's fashion writers described the clothes as having "snug, slimming waistlines, flattering high-cut bosom lines, sleek, tapered trousers." Gone were the prewar cuffs, flaps, and the full look. Instead, the trim, snug fit—in dustproof and lint-resistant materials—was in vogue. The favored color was gray-blue, "flattering but light enough to show grease and dirt which should be easily detected for hygienic reasons."

Designer King didn't limit her new fashions to the women in the factories. She remembered that women still worked in offices, too, more of them than ever and in jobs just as important as their colleagues in overalls. She designed a wardrobe for office workers that featured the "wing motif." A curved wing appeared on waistlines and pockets of office dresses, just as it did on the factory clothing. The new styles displayed insignia that could indicate the employee's division and chevrons to show her length of service. Identification badges could be attached to the tabs and heavy lapels on the dresses.

A typical office dress was described in the magazine as "figure-flattering . . . simple, buttoned-down-front dress . . . cut to fit without sacrificing comfort. Neckline is adjustable. The pockets are roomy and well placed."

The manufacturers did not make wearing of the new overalls and dresses mandatory, but they didn't have to. They immediately became hot items in women's shops.

The large number of women in defense plants wasn't the only sign of the worsening "manpower shortage." Kids were working there, too. Almost three million boys and girls under the age of eighteen were working in factories and on our farms. One Lockheed plant in southern California hired fifteen hundred boys for riveting, as junior draftsmen and for assembly electrical and sheet metal work. Beginners earned sixty cents an hour.

Other, more enterprising high school students started their own war-related businesses. Almost two hundred companies, owned and operated by kids, were in business in fifty cities, producing packing blocks, jewelry, furniture, and toys. Eighteen states passed laws by mid-1943 allowing school students between sixteen and eighteen to work in war industries.

One firm, the Chicago Midget Manufacturing Company, had a contract with the Army to turn out 150,000 pants hangers. Its president and its production manager were both fourteen years old.

Their grown-up counterparts were proving resourceful, too, by adjusting their product lines and advertising to the new way of life in which we all, of any age, now found ourselves. In one case, LaVerne, Patty, and I were having the same wartime experiences as every other woman in America: We had trouble finding nylon stockings. They were scarce from the beginning of the war, and with each passing year they became harder to find.

Mojud Hosiery took out a magazine ad to tell us to make sure we bought the right foot size and weight—"sheer for dress, heavier for business or sports," and to be sure to "handle tenderly."

Columbia Bicycles said bikes were rationed "so that persons who need them for essential jobs—in war production or Civilian Defense—can obtain them. If you need a bicycle, see your local rationing board or dealer who will show you how to get one. If you do not need a bicycle for wartime service, buy War Bonds!"

Other advertisers introduced new products spawned by our wartime needs. Saks Fifth Avenue offered the "bunk bag" for officers at $22.50. It held two uniforms or one overcoat and a uniform, available from its "Army and Navy outfitters at Rockefeller Center." The ad made no mention of any such items for enlisted personnel.

B.F. Goodrich came up with something called a "speed warden." It was a sensitive device for attachment to a car's gas pedal. When the pedal was pressed down to a set speed, the speed warden would be reaching the floor. The resistance was felt in the driver's foot. The product "reminds you when you reach 35 mph. . . . saves rubber, gives you more miles from your gas." You just put the warden on your accelerator and set it for your desired speed, but you wouldn't be locked into that speed the way you are with a conventional speed "governor" on your car. You'd still have extra power for hills and fast acceleration. Goodrich said its new product was "to help you obey the 35 mph. law." The price was right: one dollar, plus installation.

A box inside the ad contained a subtle message that the Office of Defense Transportation had ordered the thirty-five-mile-an-hour limit and the states were passing supplemental laws to ensure its enforcement. Violators, the ad said, could lose their gasoline ration books and face heavy fines and "severe prison sentences."

Gruen Watches appealed to our sentimental side at Christmas, saying the holidays in 1943 would "call for the reassurance of human faith and understanding, for the remembrance of the sympathy and affection human hearts can hold for each other." As an expression of such feelings, Gruen had the perfect gift, from $24.75.

The airline industry, like the air-conditioning business, offered a glimpse into our postwar future. United Airlines said in its ad: "There is really only one business today, and that is to win the war." But after we accomplish that, United said, we would travel by air to an extent no one had experienced before. "The war has advanced the progress of aviation fifteen years," United said. "You and your business belong to the first generation freed from the grip of earth."

Pepsodent, Bob Hope's radio sponsor, offered helpful hints on how to conserve our toothpaste, another item that was hard to get. We were told to use our tooth paste sparingly. "If you save enough for others . . . there will be enough for you."

Pepsodent's basic course in conservation suggested: "Don't let it run down the drain . . . don't use more than necessary . . . don't squeeze the tube carelessly . . ." Those using tooth powder instead of paste were reminded not to pour powder on the brush but to form the palms of their hands into a cup shape and pour the powder that way. And all of us, whether our preference was paste or powder, were told, "Don't blame your druggist if he's out."

Dr Pepper soft drinks took out a full-page magazine ad in December that captured the attitude in America at that point of the war. Its headline said:

NOT JANUARY 1ST . . . BUT DECEMBER 7—
AMERICA'S NEW DATE FOR RESOLUTIONS

The soft drink people urged us to "buy your full quota of U.S. war bonds and stamps—at least ten percent of each day's pay." Dr Pepper's ad writers, borrowing Jefferson's words from the conclusion of the Declaration of Independence, made another appeal:

Let us consecrate our lives, our fortunes and our sacred honor
to avenging the crimes of dictators and to reclaiming this world
for humanity and peace.

We were singing all sorts of songs about winning the war. "We've Just Begun to Fight," whose message was self-explanatory; "A Slip of the Lip," reminding us of the need to keep secret information secret, and a song about the times called "Censored Mail" because the government read every letter that every GI wrote home from overseas.

We sang other numbers that were equally upbeat, such as "Rise Up and Shine, America," "Say a Pray'r for the Boys Over There," "He's 1-A in the Army And He's A-1 in My Heart," and "Dear Mom." Real people were remembered in song, too— "Thank You, Mr. President" and "Fightin' Doug MacArthur." People who served in various capacities were saluted, in numbers like "Waves of the Navy" and "Cooperate with Your Air Raid Warden."

As if that list weren't complete, we even sang about junk. No less than the government itself, in the form of the War Production Board, "approved" a song written by Austen Croom-Johnson and Allan Kent as the theme song for an animated cartoon character named Sammy Salvage.

Sammy appeared in seventeen thousand theaters across the country, singing his song and playing that historic American musical instrument, the fife like the Pied Piper, encouraging all Americans to turn in our pots and pans as scrap material to be used in manufacturing war equipment.

One of the music magazines told its readers: "We cannot win this war with music, but we can lose it for want of scrap metal, rubber, and all the things that are mentioned in the official junk song . . . . Follow its advice and back the boys at the front with 'junk' that can be turned into tools for victory."

With that kind of sendoff from the media and the government, Sammy Salvage began singing on movie screens all over America:

> *Junk ain't junk no more*
> *'Cause junk can win the war.*
> *What's junk to you has a job to do*
> *'Cause junk ain't junk no more.*
>
> *Pots and pans and garbage cans,*
> *The kettle that doesn't pour,*
> *Collect today for the U.S.A.,*
> *'Cause junk can win the war!*

The musicians' year-long strike was in full force at this time, and we couldn't record any songs, even one about junk. But the strike didn't mean any leisure time for the Andrews Sisters. We continued our heavy schedule of personal appearances in theaters, and in every city we continued to visit the GIs at their bases and in their hospitals.

We also found time to make four more movies. Two of them, *Swingtime Johnny* and *Moonlight and Cactus*, were with Mitch Ayres and his orchestra. We were seeing a lot of Mitch and his band at this point. In addition to appearing in those movies with him, his fifteen-piece orchestra toured with us on several long trips across the country.

Even though most people remember that our songs during the war years were upbeat and patriotic, we tried to perform a variety of numbers to avoid being type-cast. We sang such different kinds of songs in our movies as "Ta Ra Ra Boom De Ay," "Down in the Valley," "Boogie Woogie Choo Choo," and "When You and I were Young, Maggie." In *Swingtime Johnny* we sang "Boogie Woogie Bugle Boy" again.

In those four movies we also sang some numbers that you could win a trivia contest with today because nobody else would know them—"Poor Nell," "Wa-Hoo," "Ride On," and "Thanks for the Buggy Ride." But we also had one of our biggest hits in one of those 1943 movies, when we sang "Shoo-Shoo Baby" in *Follow The Boys*, with a cast of thousands. It was one of the upbeat numbers associated with the Andrews Sisters.

Our other movie that year was *Always a Bridesmaid* with Grace McDonald, in which we sang five songs including a popular wartime ballad, "As Long As I Have You."

We didn't make any records at all during the musicians' strike. But as soon as it was over in September 1943, we got right back into the swing of things. In Hollywood on September 20, we cut records with Bing Crosby that became two of the year's biggest hits, "Victory Polka" and "Pistol Packin' Mama," and two more that became popular that Christmas and are still heard every year during the holidays, "Jingle Bells" and "Santa Claus Is Coming to Town."

We enjoyed tremendous success with Bing. At the beginning of our relationship he didn't want to record with us because he didn't like our driving, almost pushy, singing style, but our friend Jack Kapp, the president of Decca, talked him into it.

Our first song with him was "Ciribiribin," which we recorded in 1942. It became our first gold record, and Bing's, too. After that, Bing told Jack: "I'll be glad to record with those gals anytime. They can pick their own songs, their own arrangements, anything they want. I want to record more with them."

We sang with Bing many more times through the rest of the war. Most of the records became big hits. He immediately became our favorite performer to sing with. He was the complete pro. He was always prepared, a fantastic artist. His main concern was to make the record a good one, and he didn't do it by demanding perfection. Sometimes perfection can ruin a performance, so he made sure everybody got it right, but had a good time while doing it.

The Andrews Sisters didn't record the typical war songs. We sang happy songs and novelty tunes, which were selected for us by Jack Kapp, the president of Decca Records, and Lou Levy, our manager. They felt that our songs should provide the public with an escape from the worries of war. Patty, LaVerne, and I felt the same way, emphatically.

Most of the war ballads were recorded by male and female vocalists rather than groups. Some of the fighting songs, such as "Remember Pearl Harbor," "Praise The Lord and Pass The Ammunition," "Comin' In On a Wing and a Prayer," and "We Did It Before And We Can Do It Again" were sung by larger groups to create the sound of a choir or glee club. But the songs of the Andrews Sisters were intended—and arranged—to give the American people the fun and upbeat feelings they needed during this awful war, to help America smile.

Lou remained the guiding genius behind these successes. He couldn't read music any better than we could—meaning he couldn't read it at all—but he had a unique talent, an instinct, for what was good and would be commercially successful. He especially had a gift for knowing exactly what would be a perfect fit for the Andrews Sisters' style of music.

By this time in World War II, we had recorded boogie-woogie songs, waltzes stepped up to a jazz tempo, polkas, folk tunes, and Big Band numbers. He always emphasized the importance of singing songs with clear, strong melodies and avoiding those that featured a heavy beat and not much else.

Lou used to point to Guy Lombardo and Bing as two highly successful members of our profession who always stuck to the melody of anything they were performing. He told a reporter: "We don't want to go over the people's heads. The public buys this kind of music because they want to sing it. They ought to be able to copy our musical phrases and hot licks."

He said he walked in on one of our rehearsals and didn't like what he was hearing because we used a "Wrigley ending."

A "Wrigley ending"?

Lou's explanation was that some old commercials for Wrigley chewing gum had "out-of-this-world arrangements," and he heard us trying to improvise one of their endings for a song we were rehearsing. He told us we had a beautiful arrangement of a wonderful tune already—and what we were doing was useless, "gilding the lily at the end."

Then he gave us one of the oldest pieces of advice in show business—and one of the best: "Sing the song and get off."

We always took his advice, but we always made sure to argue first. Patty was what they called a "hep cat" in those years. Anything with a beat appealed to her. LaVerne would sing anything anybody asked her to, and my preference has always been for symphonic music. Lou was like Patty in his affection for jazz. "I love hot, out-of-the-world jazz," he said. But he had a reason for not recommending it to us to record: "It isn't commercial."

We rehearsed every day. A reporter for the paper, *PM*, Mary

Morris, interviewed us after a rehearsal and described the scene when she walked in: "I found the girls hunched around an upright piano, singing. They made faces, beat their feet while their bodies jumped and swayed. Even the arranger's derriere wiggled madly on the piano seat. The whole room jumped, and I sat on the desk, chin in hand, catching the wail in their voices, the contagious rhythm and excitement."

We were making a new kind of record for "the boys and girls in uniform", oversized "V Disks" played exclusively by the Armed Forces Radio at American Service military bases all over the world. Each one was about three times the size of a standard 33⅓ record. V Disks were never made available to the disk jockeys on commercial radio stations. AFRS disk jockeys spun these extra-long-playing records for the GIs, who were able to listen to some good ol' stateside music with a minimum number of interruptions.

☆

By the end of 1943, some people were saying we had turned the corner in our fight, that victory was becoming inevitable. The news from both overseas battle fronts seemed to confirm that feeling. The allies made an amphibious landing at Anzio, south of Rome, on January 22, 1944, to accelerate the Italian campaign. On the other side of the world one week later, an American task force began attacking Japanese strongholds in the Marshall Islands. On the same day, January 29, Stalin announced that the Moscow-Leningrad area had been cleared of German fighting forces.

In the same month, on the twenty-first, General Eisenhower arrived in England to begin planning Operation Overlord, the invasion that followed on June 6. As a prelude, our Air Corps combined with England's Royal Air Force to form an aerial armada of six thousand bombers and thousands of fighter planes in repeated attacks during "Big Week," February 19–25. Their

unrelenting attacks virtually destroyed Hitler's air force, the
Luftwaffe that had been so feared under the command of Reich
Marshal Hermann Göring.

The aerial bombardment of Germany continued, which
caused enthusiastic cheering from us on the home front. Our
B-17's, the Flying Fortresses, dropped two thousand tons of
bombs on Berlin on March 6. On April 12, thousands of planes
unleashed their heaviest attacks yet on German cities.

On April 18, the Allies staged a thunderous assault against
German airfields, railroads, and factories in Germany and occupied France. Our American planes were from the U.S. Eighth
Air Force, now under the command of General Jimmy Doolittle,
the pilot who led sixteen B-25's over Tokyo two years before, to
the day.

Four days later, on April 22, General Douglas MacArthur
waded ashore at Hollandia in New Guinea as his men advanced
from their beachhead positions. A month later, on May 23,
another general and another beachhead were the subject of still
more good news to Americans everywhere. General Mark Clark's
Fifth Army at long last broke out of its beachhead position at
Anzio, four months after the invasion there. Ten days later, on
June 4, the Allies entered Rome, which had been abandoned by
the Germans. The Eternal City was largely spared, except for
damage to railroad yards, which had been the target of bombing
raids.

As these events unfolded in rapid succession, a popular
singer named Ann Moray was walking through the wards of a
field hospital near Anzio as a member of a USO troupe. She was
cheering up the wounded victims of that battle, one of the most
ferocious engagements of the entire war. She had no musicians
to accompany her, so she sang to the troops by herself—"Ave
Maria," "I Love You Truly," and other selections that she knew
were traditional favorites, even among combat-hardened men.

One of the bedridden veterans motioned for her to come over

to his side. "Will you sing a song for me?" the GI asked her. "I'm going to die. Will you sing *Abide With Me* at my funeral?"

Ann went out of her way to assure him that she would have to wait many years to honor his request, but he insisted he was going to die. He asked her again. "Promise. Please."

Ann said softly, "I promise."

That night, the young soldier died. Two days later, Ann Moray stood in the rain next to his freshly dug grave on the beachhead at Anzio and sang:

> *Abide with me.*
> *Fast falls the eventide.*
> *The darkness deepens.*
> *Lord, with me abide.*
>
> *When other helpers fail*
> *And comforts flee,*
> *Help of the helpless,*
> *Oh, abide with me.*

On June 6, came the biggest news of the war since Pearl Harbor. The Allies, under Eisenhower, had invaded Europe along the Normandy coast of France, where the Germans were dug in with heavy artillery and thousands of troops. Paratroopers dropped behind enemy lines at 2:00 A.M. Six hundred warships and four thousand other ships of various sizes and shapes carried 155,000 men in landing waves at Utah Beach and Omaha Beach. With the British soldiers on the left and the Americans on the right, the Allies swarmed ashore at 6:30 A.M. into barbed wire, mine fields, and heavy enemy fire.

During the unending anxiety before the invasion, USO troupers toured the tent cities in the fields of the English countryside and along the winding beaches of the English Channel and entertained the invaders as they waited.

The wait lasted one day longer than expected. Overlord was set for June 5—"D-Day"—but two days before, General Dwight Eisenhower postponed the invasion one day because of bad weather and rough seas predicted for that day. On the fifth, he gave the order to invade the next day. On the other side of the choppy Channel, German forces were dug in under the command of Field Marshal Gerd von Rundstedt. His assistant was the "Desert Fox" of two years before, Field Marshal Rommel.

While the Allied armada sailed across the English Channel toward the European coast on June 6, the USO performers waited on the English shore for the Allies to establish a beachhead. As soon as the Allies declared the beaches secure, the troupers staged their own invasion on July 28.

CHAPTER TWELVE

Seven Hundred Curtains Going Up

Forty-three men and women landed on Utah Beach on July 28 in eight USO-Camp Show units. Two hours later they were putting on a show. Plywood had been put down on a thirty-ton ammunition carrier to use as a stage, a public address system was set up, and the show was on for the men who had been living in foxholes for fifty-two days. Some of them had walked for miles through the sand to see the performance. Each entertainer gave a shortened version of his or her act in a show that lasted almost two hours. As soon as it ended, the soldiers went back to their positions.

The performers boarded trucks to take their units to the outfits that had already moved forward as the invasion inched its way inland. Their entertainment equipment was supplemented with two other items—cots and tents. They were a traveling road show right on the edge of the fighting.

Radio Reporter Gordon Fraser broadcast a description of the USO shows as the Allies began moving across Europe, and so did the troupers who entertained them:

There were cheers and whistles and loud laughter coming from a building, and that was a mighty good thing to hear in the section of the front, just east of Aachen. I investigated and saw a sign reading, Girls' Dressing Room. This then was the real thing—a show with girls in it. Standing guard by the door was a soldier I recognized. The last time I had seen him he was shooting Germans. He told me how his boys had been given a few days' rest and this show was part of the treatment.

I watched from the wings as a girl in a ballet costume did cartwheels and flips, and every turn brought applause and cheers. Then the magician performed, and his assistant was another pretty girl, thinly clad in an evening dress. . . . Then a girl singer came on stage . . .

As the performers went through their acts, the happy sparkle in the soldiers' eyes eased into crinkles around their eyes and then the crinkles broke into broad grins and the grins into howling guffaws of enjoyment, and for an hour and fifteen minutes that little old building just rocked with fun and hilarity as this USO show called *At Your Service* played to American soldiers taking a rest in the shadow of the Siegfried line.

Fraser reported that the troupers had been performing for five weeks in Germany, "right in the front-line area," living in trucks and tents and applying their makeup "under an apple tree." At other times they lived in abandoned broken houses without windows—"and sometimes the house next to them gets hit by enemy shell fire."

Then Fraser made an important point about many of the USO performers, because not all of them were headline acts with famous names. "They may not be the biggest names in show business back home," he said, "but they're headliners here, and if you could see the faces of GIs watching their performance you would see why."

Fraser was right. Not all of the entertainers were the big names, and some of the most heroic performers were unknowns who hadn't yet seen their names on marquees. But the headliners were there, too, and in the European Theater of Operations—the "E.T.O."—in 1944, the men were seeing an All-Star lineup: Jimmy Cagney, Dinah Shore, Allen Jenkins, Bing Crosby, Marlene Dietrich, Fred Astaire, Spike Jones and his City Slickers, and Morton Downey.

Spike and Dinah put on a show for sixteen thousand GIs in France, and their box-office appeal was demonstrated in convincing terms. Five merchant marines jumped ship and swam to shore to see the show.

☆

Jimmie Baker, the Oklahoma boy, and the Army dance band he'd formed in Florida two years before, were in Europe shortly after D-Day, too, and by the time they got there they were glad to be anywhere.

They shipped out from Fort Dix, New Jersey, aboard a troop ship with escort ships ahead of them to guide them through the still-dangerous seas of the Atlantic Ocean. The musicians played the hit songs every day on board ship during the trip overseas.

As they neared France, large explosions began popping in the sea ahead of them, and they began to fear for their lives. They were sure their ship was the target of torpedoes being fired from German submarines. "Every night," Jimmie says, "I was sure we'd had it."

Jimmie and his boys later learned that the explosions were caused by their own escort ships. They were detecting enemy mines in the waters and were detonating them with depth charges before Jimmie's ship might accidentally run into one and blow up. If only somebody had thought to tell the troops on board that those explosions were intentional and not being caused by the enemy, it would have done wonders for their ability to sleep at night.

The ship pulled into Le Havre, a port city in northwest France on the English Channel. "When we arrived," Jimmie recalls, "I didn't know how we ever made it through to the dock. There were all these sunken ships sticking up out of the water," mute testimony to the furious fighting during the Allied invasion and the days that followed.

If Jimmie thought travel by troop ship in mine-infested waters was less luxurious than the accommodations he would have preferred, he couldn't possibly have been prepared for the next mode of transportation that the Army provided for his band. They were sent across France into Germany in railroad freight cars. The sliding side doors opened during the day to allow ventilation but closed at night to ensure darkness throughout the train for security. The musicians traveled for two long days and two longer nights in those box cars.

The only time they were liberated temporarily from their cattle conditions was to stop, always in the middle of nowhere, far removed from any sign of civilization, to eat in a mammoth mess tent and use the portable toilets standing in the middle of remote farmland. On the morning of the third day, the train rolled to a stop and the box car doors opened they saw that they were in the middle of a city. It turned out to be Bonn, which would become the postwar capital of West Germany.

Their living accommodations were upgraded immediately. They slept in a large German factory—a *flag* factory. "There were all these Nazi swastika flags piled around the factory," Jimmie says. "And Japanese flags, too—the Rising Sun. They had been making flags for both countries."

With the war still in full fury and the sounds of the shooting along the Rhine River clearly audible in their captured flag factory, the GIs decided on their own that those flags were war surplus materials now, so they confiscated them and put them to good use. They slept on them. "We piled them all up," Jimmie remembers, "and used them for mattresses."

While they were guests of the government in Bonn, Jimmie and his musicians ran into a familiar American—Mickey

Rooney. Private First Class Rooney. The two became lifelong friends.

Mickey was one of Hollywood's biggest stars by that time, after making a series of popular Andy Hardy movies with Judy Garland and appearing in other hit films, but there he was as a PFC, and he was performing one of the most unusual services of any of us during the war.

Mickey was making a tour of the troops on the front lines in a jeep, accompanied by an accordion player and a well-known pop singer, Bobby Breen. "Mickey would get as close to the lines as possible," Jimmie says. "They'd get out of their jeep and the accordion player would play a couple of songs and Bobby would sing some numbers and then Mickey would do a stand-up comedy routine, right there in the midst of the fighting."

Later in the war, Mickey starred in a big production that entertained the troops, *OK, USA,* with Bobby Breen, Red Buttons, and a comic actor named Billy Halop, one of the "tough guys" in a series of comedy movies starring a lovable group of characters called the Dead End Kids.

As popular as he was with the GIs overseas and with the folks on the home front, the word got around among some of the musicians and USO entertainers that Mickey was occasionally a source of irritation to the musicians in his own show. The reason was his well-known versatility. Mickey was a graduate of the old school, who could stand up on a stage and do a first-class vaudeville routine, play a character role in a dramatic movie, sing a song—anything, including playing different musical instruments. During *OK, USA,* he would do his own comedy routine, then join the guys in the band, taking over for the drummer, then the piano player, and into the other sections of the orchestra.

He was good and obviously he was unusually versatile, but he wasn't as good on the different instruments as the professionals who played them, so while the GIs in the audience loved it, his own musicians didn't always share their enthusiasm.

A general saw *OK, USA* and took a liking to Mickey, so he assigned a staff car to him. PFC Rooney spent the rest of the war riding in a general's car, complete with the stars on the outside, relaxed in the backseat behind his driver and always making sure to return the many salutes from the GIs as he traveled.

It was every PFC's dream. "He went all over Germany that way," Jimmie says. "When they drove through the different towns, all these guys would throw him a salute because they didn't know who the hell was in that backseat."

Jimmie formed his own big show, *Yankee Jubilee,* and he and Rooney found themselves playing at the same time in Wiesbaden, a large tourist city in Germany. The Rooney and Baker troupes put on their shows in the city's large opera house, and managed to confiscate one of its most comfortable rooms as their living quarters.

From Wiesbaden, Jimmie took his show on the road to play for the troops in other cities, including Rome, Brussels, and Paris, always doing double duty for the USO shows when they came through. USO troupes frequently traveled only with a piano player or an accordionist, so Jimmie provided the band.

In Paris, he was recruited for a new entertainment assignment, as a tap dancer, one of his other prewar experiences, for a new and larger GI show, *Could Be,* and traveled all across Europe entertaining American servicemen and women. His band stayed together, playing under another leader, until Jimmie rejoined his group after the war.

The end of the war didn't mean they would be going home. In the middle of all the rejoicing about the end of the fighting and the return of peace to the world, Jimmie told his musicians they wouldn't be going home—not right away.

"We're going to stay over here," he told them, "and play for the guys who can't go home yet."

☆

The troops in North Africa, having chased Rommel's Afrika Corps off the desert and back to Germany, were being remembered, too. George Raft, John Garfield, Jascha Heifetz, Jack Haley and Ella Logan, among other entertainers, performed there.

In the Pacific and the China-Burma-India Theater of Operations—the "C-B-I"—our troops saw Ray Milland, Paulette Goddard and Andre Kostelanetz, plus Jack Benny, Carole Landis, Larry Adler, Martha Tilton, Ann Sheridan, Judith Anderson, Bob Hope, Jerry Colonna, Frances Langford, Betty Hutton, and Olivia de Havilland. Other groups with other names—famous and not-so-famous—toured other parts of the globe, wherever they could reach an American GI and his buddies, in such far-off places as Alaska, Panama, Bermuda, Labrador, Iceland, Greenland, and Brazil.

The whole USO-Camp Shows operation was expanding dramatically, just as our victories were coming in quick succession. Abe Lastfogel and his staff masterminded the day-to-day details of what was becoming the largest operation in the history of show business, with the curtain going up on USO shows all over the world seven hundred times every day. They added concert artists, ballet, legitimate stage plays, Broadway musicals, and even the Radio City Music Hall Revue. The newest musical sensation, *Oklahoma!*, which opened on Broadway in 1943, was playing to GI raves in the Pacific in '44.

Abe and his staff discovered early in the war that GI audiences wanted and appreciated all kinds of music, classical as well as popular. Even those who had never been exposed to certain kinds of music and art could appreciate it. After Jascha Heifetz gave a two-hour concert on his violin in a bombed-out German theater, a soldier came backstage to tell him: "Sir, I have never been to one of these things before, but if that's good music you just played, I am for it."

Another violinist, Isaac Stern, was one of the stars in a unit that landed in New Guinea in amphibious vehicles called "ducks." On a stretch of coral rock on a beach, they entertained ten thousand silent, appreciative GIs. Concert singers such as Nelson Eddy and Lily Pons enjoyed the same success. Dancer Grant Muradoff formed a company that entertained our fighting men in the ETO over an exhausting tour of their *Foxhole Ballet*.

Judith Anderson performed as Shakespeare's Lady Macbeth in the Pacific. Katharine Cornell and Brian Aherne starred in *The Barrets of Wimpole Street* in the ETO. Peggy Wood, one of the stars of *The Sound of Music* twenty years later, appeared in *Blithe Spirit*, and other luminaries brought our GIs such popular plays as *Kiss and Tell*, *What A Life*, and *Dear Ruth*.

Packing up the props, scenery, and costumes needed for stage plays and Broadway musicals could have presented a problem, but the same ingenuity that produced the wartime products and strategies that won the war for us also solved the problems of logistics. A popular Broadway show, *Mexican Hayride*, cut its cast from 107 to sixteen. Moss Hart took his comedy classic, *The Man Who Came to Dinner*, to the Pacific in two suitcases. *Over 21* was produced on Cape Gloucester on a twelve-by-twelve stage lighted entirely by flashlights.

As grateful as the audiences were, there had to be an occasional setback in any operation of such magnitude. A few stars ran right smack into one in 1944 in the China-Burma-India Theater of Operations.

Roundup, the weekly newspaper for GIs in the C-B-I, published a scorching editorial in October of 1944 reporting that some of the stars in the USO troupes were disappointing our fighting men by canceling their appearances and going back to the States early. The article criticized actor Joel McCrea for allegedly canceling a sixty-day tour in Cairo when he was told the

C-B-I was a difficult area because of the weather and the military conditions.

Paulette Goddard was singled out for leaving six days early because she reportedly was taken ill. And Joe E. Brown was mentioned because he reportedly changed his schedule and appeared instead in North Africa. Similar criticism was aimed at Al Jolson.

The article also mentioned that Ann Sheridan came home from a curtailed trip saying she'd never go back because "it's too rough." The *Roundup*'s editorial said:

> These selfless patriots who, incidentally, are well fed, clothed, housed, transported, and paid by the Army and the USO, discovered in a couple of weeks that C-B-I is hot, wet, full, of mosquitoes and they suddenly develop prior commitments, serious ailments. . . . [They] spend, in the case of Sheridan and Company, a total of thirty-five days out of a promised minimum of sixty, pick up a little money and a lot of publicity, and sneak back to the United States to recuperate from the whole horrible ordeal.

The actors were quick to answer such serious charges. Paulette Goddard said she played all but three days "when I was ordered back to bed by the Army physician." Joe E. Brown, with an outstanding record already and whose son was killed in the war, said he "did all a fifty-three-year-old man could do." He told *Newsweek* magazine: "I played every spot that was humanly possible to play." Al Jolson's spokesman said Jolie had planned to tour the C-B-I, but the Army changed its mind and sent him elsewhere.

The Hollywood Victory Committee, which coordinated requests for actors to tour overseas, said both Ann Sheridan and Joel McCrea had been delayed by a lack of transportation, a problem for everybody at one time or another during the war, especially overseas. McCrea contradicted the charge, saying he was never asked to visit the C-B-I.

The editor of the *Roundup* made at least one mistake—taking on Ann Sheridan. She lashed back at him with one of the most stinging letters ever opened by any editor anywhere. She offered to "fight boy fashion, no holds barred," anyone who said she dogged it. She told him she had made a considerable financial sacrifice in taking time out of her schedule to tour with the USO. All of us were glad to do it, even at the expense of losing income. We knew our GIs were losing income, too, and sometimes even their lives, so nobody was complaining. But that didn't change the fact that Ann Sheridan was right.

She straightened the editor out:

> I'm wondering if your wife, sweetheart, or sister has bucket-seated her way sixty thousand miles . . . at better than a thousand miles a day, playing even two shows, eating C or K rations more often than hot groceries, much of it standing up, and then when it's little girls'-room time, go down to the men's toilet and wait till it's cleared so that the girl troupers may use it.

Then Ann delivered her zinger, mentioning the difficult and dangerous feat accomplished every day of the war by our pilots and our troops and entertainers in flying over what we were calling The Hump—the Himalaya Mountains:

> And by the way, how long has it been since you left that swivel editor's chair of yours to ride The Hump?

Stars from the sports world went overseas, too. Big baseball names like Mel Ott, Lefty Gomez, Leo Durocher, Carl Hubbell, and Frankie Frisch traveled around the world to tell the soldiers, sailors, and Marines how their favorite teams were doing. Dixie Walker, Paul Waner, and Luke Sewell did the same thing on a series of one-night stands in New Guinea. Boxing champions such as Jack Sharkey and Mickey Walker toured the ETO. Alice Marble and Dorothy Bundy played tennis for the GIs in the Caribbean. A champion bowler, Frank Benkovic, and a badminton star, Hugh Forgie, entertained in the fog and snow of Alaska and the Aleutian Islands. Two big names in fishing, Mike and Helen Lerner, toured the Italian front. Nick Munday, a wrestler with forty years experience in the sport, appeared in France and Belgium, and Ruth Aarons played table tennis in the fields of Normandy.

Maybe the most unheralded of all were the artists who drew sketches of our wounded men in hospitals all over the world. The USO program included a hundred and seventy illustrators and portrait painters who drew portraits of thirty thousand wounded men.

The chaplain at the Brooklyn Naval Hospital told the USO about an experience that typified the work of these artists. A GI there became a problem when he refused to cooperate with the doctors after they had repaired the damage to his hands caused by severe burns. They encouraged the young man to use his hands to develop strength and coordination, but he refused. He said the doctors couldn't fool him—he knew his hands were useless. He wouldn't shave. He wouldn't comb his hair. Worst of all, he wouldn't talk. He lay in his bed, silent, staring at the bandages.

A woman artist appeared in his ward, stopped at his bed, and asked if he'd like a sketch of himself. He turned his head away from her and didn't answer. Thirty minutes later, as she finished a sketch of another soldier, one of the patients nudged her and pointed toward the problem patient.

He was sitting up in his bed, shaved and combed, waiting for her to come back. He had slipped out to the men's room and shaved with his "useless" hands.

The chaplain said the GIs recovery began with the arrival of the artist.

☆

Back home, the biggest story in the second half of 1944 was the presidential campaign between President Roosevelt and Thomas Dewey, the governor of New York. There was a story within a story, because the subject of the campaign included debate about FDR's health.

Kathryn Grayson appeared at birthday parties for Roosevelt in Washington every January 30, when funds were raised to combat infantile paralysis, the disease that had left FDR confined to a wheelchair for most of his adult years. The program was called The March of Dimes, with donors contributing dimes that added up to dollars.

FDR was the first presidential candidate Kathryn was able to vote for, and she did, as a loyal Democratic daughter of what in politics was the Solid South. She appeared at several Roosevelt birthday parties, somewhat to the consternation of her two superiors at MGM, Louis B. Mayer and his executive secretary, Ida Koverman. Both were staunch Republicans. Ida's reason was especially understandable, since she had been an executive secretary before—to Republican President Herbert Hoover.

Over the war years, Kathryn noticed a deterioration in President Roosevelt's health. "It was slow at first," she told us, "but then it kind of accelerated."

By 1944, the combined burdens of his health, the war, and his age—sixty-two—were visible to all of us, even those who never saw him except in the newsreels at the movies in those days before television. He began to look haggard, with dark circles under his eyes.

In its issue of April 10, 1944, *Newsweek* reported that the President had suffered through a winter of the flu, head colds, intestinal trouble, and bronchitis. Aubrey Williams, the former head of the National Youth Administration and by 1944 an organizer for the National Farmers Union, dined with Roosevelt at the White House in 1944 and said later that FDR was "so tired and worn that I was shocked."

The President's personal physician, Rear Admiral Ross T. McIntire, assured the White House reporters that the President was "basically okay." He added that "a good rest in the spring sunshine soon would right matters."

Roosevelt was aware of the public concern, so the political war horse summoned new strength and mounted a final campaign drive in late October that would have floored a younger, healthier man. He knew, too, what the polls were showing—that this was going to be a close election, with Dewey running even with him since midsummer. Only the bookmakers seemed to disagree. As October ended, they were giving three-to-one odds that FDR would be elected for the fourth time, and there weren't many takers.

Roosevelt invited the colorful mayor of New York, Fiorello La Guardia, to lunch at the White House during the last week of October. Later that afternoon, the chairman of the Democratic National Committee, Bob Hannegan, announced that the President would make a campaign trip to New York. Then Hannegan revealed the fundamental purpose of the trip: "After the people have seen him, they can make up their own minds about his vigor and health."

As luck would have it, a long and heavy rain poured on New York that day, long before Roosevelt climbed out of his private railroad car at the Brooklyn Army base at 9:50 A.M. As it continued, FDR, always the fighter, ordered the canvas top on his black Packard drawn back. He threw his familiar navy-blue cape around his shoulders.

He was cheered by forty thousand workers at the Army base, and by more at the Brooklyn Navy Yard. Then he went to Ebbets Field. Before nine thousand cheering supporters, he took off his gray fedora, let his cape drop from his shoulders, and spoke for five minutes in the heaviest rains so far.

Then his Packard drove through the streets at twenty-five miles an hour with four Secret Service agents on the running boards, the top down but the bulletproof glass sides up. The presidential limousine snaked its way through Queens to the Bronx, to Harlem, and then to Manhattan and down Broadway. Fifty-one miles of crowds were soaked by the continuing downpour and chilled by the late-October temperatures.

The rain rolled down Roosevelt's trademark pince-nez glasses and down his face. His hair was slicked down by the rain. The indoor crowds on Broadway and the garment district leaned out of their skyscraper windows and did something New Yorkers do best. They showered ticker tape, confetti, and ripped-up telephone books down on the presidential motorcade.

The parade went on for four hours. The New York police estimated the crowd at anywhere from a million and a half to three million people. But Roosevelt's New York triumph wasn't over. There was still a dinner, in the grand ballroom of the Waldorf-Astoria Hotel. His audience was the Foreign Policy Association, two thousand members and guests. "In the unflattering light of the little reading lamp, his weary face looked seamed and haggard," *Time* reported. But the old pro mustered enough of his old dynamic qualities to put on a vintage FDR performance. As he spoke on wartime and postwar issues and spelled out his differences with his Republican opponent, he was interrupted by applause forty-two times. *Time* said, "The diners went off to argue the question only Election Day would answer: Was the speech as good as it had to be?"

The magazine, and all the rest of us, got our answer in the returns on November 7. In those days, people would sit up all night by their radios and listen to the election returns from all over the country. With no computers and exit interviews, it frequently was after midnight—sometimes long after—before we knew the outcome. It was usually an evening of excitement, and people would have election night parties and enjoy the drama together in a festive atmosphere, but Roosevelt took all the suspense out of that evening in a hurry. He and his running mate, Senator Harry Truman of Missouri, carried thirty-six of the forty-eight states, and Roosevelt was elected President for the fourth time. In electoral votes, the margin was 432–99.

CHAPTER THIRTEEN

Victory's Price

By now there were over fifteen million Americans in the armed forces, including two hundred thousand women. Well over eleven million of our loved ones were serving overseas. As a manpower reserve, another fifty million young men were registered in the draft and available to be called up without notice.

While the men and women in uniform, especially those overseas, bore heavy burdens and paid heavy prices in the service of their country, the men registered for the draft at home paid a continuing price of their own. They never knew when the famous "Greetings from the President"—which actually came from the local draft board—might arrive in the mail. Career plans, college, and marriage proposals were put on hold for the duration. Millions of dreams simply had to wait as the young men debated whether to take matters into their own hands and enlist or wait for word on their fate in the draft.

Those who were declared exempt from the draft for physical reasons—in category 4-F—paid a price of their own. The fever of patriotism ran so high all over the country that any young man not in the service carried a stigma of sorts. Military personnel did not wear civilian clothes during their off-duty hours, so any draft-age man spotted on the street in "civvies" was viewed with suspicion by some people. There were whispers behind his back, people wondering why he wasn't in uniform.

Our military might, supported by production miracles back home, continued to roll up victories as the combined force of the Allied fighting machine pushed the enemy back toward the final defeat that moved closer with each passing month. As impressive and exciting as the victories in Europe were, they were being matched by our men in the Pacific.

Some of the most thrilling news of the war in the Pacific came on October 20, 1944, when an overpowering American invasion force entered Leyte Gulf in the Philippine Islands and established a beachhead twenty miles long. It led to what historians call the greatest naval engagement in military history. Our Third Fleet and Seventh Fleet threw everything they had at the enemy in four major battles that began on October 23 and lasted into the twenty-sixth. We lost six ships, the Japanese, twenty-six.

General Douglas MacArthur, directing our western Pacific strategy from Australia since Roosevelt ordered him there just before the fall of Bataan and Corregidor in April 1942, was able to keep the dramatic vow he made in those dark days, when he promised the frightened people of the Philippines: "I shall return."

Now, two and a half years later, he did return, wading ashore on October 20 in khakis in water above his ankles, wearing his trademark cap with all the trimmings, sunglasses, and with his familiar corncob pipe stuck between his teeth. Later he announced into a microphone on the sand:

People of the Philippines—I have returned.

MacArthur was more than just one of the great generals of World War II. He was also one of its dominating personalities, unlike his more reserved Army counterpart in Europe, General Dwight Eisenhower, and more like Eisenhower's armored commander, General George Patton. That wasn't necessarily bad. We needed someone whose bold confidence could keep our chins up in 1942, and who could convince us that he could lead us out of our disasters in the Pacific fighting. MacArthur did that, with a confidence that became even arrogant at times. But whether people liked his personality or not, and many didn't, he was one of the men who masterminded us back to victory.

His boldness inspired Buck Ram to write a song during that string of severe losses in the Pacific in 1942, "Fightin' Doug MacArthur," calling him "a tough old guy." When he wrote that MacArthur "slapped the Japs right down to their size" he was predicting, whether he knew it or not, MacArthur's victories that were to follow two years after Ram's song was published.

His strong personality prompted two GI wisecracks about "Mac's" triumphant return as he once again occupied center stage. The word went around that MacArthur actually planned to walk *on* the water, but President Roosevelt said absolutely not. The other, obviously emanating from one particular branch of the service, was a rhyme:

> With the help of God and a few Marines,
> MacArthur has taken the Philippines.

One of the main reasons that we were winning the war on the battlefields and the high seas was because we were winning the war in the factories. American production was setting records, and the totals by the end of the war still dazzle even the experts. Here's what we produced:

> 71,000 ships for the Navy
> 296,000 planes

86,000 tanks
2,700,000 machine guns

The "Rosies" could take credit for a large part of those production miracles. The women factory workers who inspired us to sing about "Rosie, The Riveter" were helping to turn out all those ships and planes and weapons for their sons, brothers, husbands, and boyfriends who marched off to war.

LaVerne, Patty, and I continued to appear at war plants all over the country because they were so important to our country's success. The plants were a sight to see—or not see—and to hear. Some of them, especially the ones on the West Coast, were hard to spot because they were camouflaged. Many of them in the San Diego area were draped with camouflage material. As we circled before landing and looked down at the ground, we knew those factories were there somewhere, but everything looked like an open field.

When you entered the war plants, you knew they meant business. Women were up on scaffolding and other kinds of stands, shooting bolts and rivets into the frames of the ships and tanks and planes and jeeps, and the rat-a-tat-tat from thousands of riveting guns was deafening in those big, hollow hangar-type buildings. Then you saw the welders, the women with metal shields over their faces and blue flames coming out of their blow torches as they welded together the weapons of war.

While we were on the road in the war years, it was easy to fit into our gowns and costumes. That was the result of the food shortages and the rigors of our schedule. Fast foods restaurants didn't exist then, so we always looked for the closest restaurant. Usually it was a "greasy spoon," and it didn't always resemble a restaurant, either. We tried to be careful with what we ordered, so we lived mostly on sandwiches—egg salad and tuna salad. And the coffee was more like colored water.

People often ask if there was one particular appearance

before our GI audiences that stands out. The answer is that all of them were exciting. We were in our twenties and still growing up, and America was growing up, too. We were maturing together, and the Andrews Sisters were thrilled to be a part of what was going on, so any time we got a chance to entertain our people in the service, that became another big moment for us.

As we matured during the war years, we became more aware of the effect the war had on the servicemen and women, how it was turning their lives upside down and uprooting them from home and family and job. We learned in our visits to the camps and hospitals that many of them were our age but had never been to another city before entering the service—which was just the opposite of what we had been doing for half of our lives.

One of our constant fears was illness. Our tours were long, and fatigue often set in. We wanted to say yes to every request, but we always had to remain aware of our health. We couldn't afford to get run down and then catch a cold or the flu. If one of the three of us got sick, it would be disaster. People didn't want to see two of the Andrews Sisters. They wanted to see all three.

Our fears were real because the threat was real. Our bronchial tubes were sensitive to infection when we became tired and run down from our tours, something we forced ourselves to guard against constantly. But it still happened from time to time. Patty once strained her vocal chords so badly you couldn't hear anything she said for a week. She had to write everything on a piece of paper.

This scared all three of us, so we sought advice and took a series of exercises in breathing and "voice placement," which helps to get the voice out of the throat without straining it. The exercises were not easy, and they weren't fun, either. We'd get dizzy and see black spots in front of our eyes and almost pass out. At times I wondered if the cure was worse than the cause, but the exercises were ultimately helpful and we were able to hold lost time by any of us to a minimum.

Another time we almost had to carry on with only two of us also involved another cruel blow by fate against Patty. In 1942, Patty had to be taken from our train at Rockford, Illinois, late one Friday night and rushed to St. Anthony Hospital. We were on tour and traveling from Milwaukee to Davenport, Iowa, for a weekend engagement when Patty was stricken with appendicitis. She underwent an emergency appendectomy. LaVerne and I canceled the Davenport date and gave Patty as much encouragement as we could so she would be able to get out of the hospital as fast as possible.

We were playing St. Louis when an Army officer who had been a script writer in Hollywood called and asked if we could visit Fort Jefferson. He said the boys there were homesick and trying to adjust to a new life. Many of them had left the family farm for the first time. I hesitated, I said, "Gee, I don't know. It's been a long tour. I don't know if we can make it. We're exhausted." But while I was saying it, I was remembering a popular saying of the day: "Don't you know there's a war on?"

While I was in the process of changing my answer from no to yes, the officer told me how important his request was. "You've *got* to come, Maxene," he said. "We have boys out there who have never seen a pair of shoes or taken a bath in a tub." Then he added, "Besides, it will be a whole new kind of audience for you."

From what he was saying, I was sure of that. Besides, I knew that it wouldn't be a long trip out to Fort Jefferson, and one more show wasn't going to kill us. So we went.

I can't say our responses were always a cheerful, "Sure, let's go get 'em." There were times when we were dog-tired and wanted to beg off, so we growled when we shouldn't have. Doing six shows a day was grueling, and when someone asked us to get in a car and drive out of town to some remote location and do a seventh show that day, it was not always easy to smile and say okay.

But LaVerne, Patty, and I knew what all the entertainers knew. If being tired was going to be the worst that happened to us, when others were losing arms, legs, and their very lives, then we should say yes every time. And we did, even if our yes was sometimes preceded by a growl.

☆

We were staying on the road as much as ever. Our popularity remained strong. *Time* magazine called us "the queens of the juke box," we had sold over thirty million Decca records, and we had two new hits with Bing, "Is You Is Or Is You Ain't My Baby?" and "Don't Fence Me In," the song Cole Porter wrote in 1934 after paying a Montana cowboy two hundred dollars for the rights to use his poem. We cut the record with Bing in July, a few days after we sang it in our thirteenth movie, *Hollywood Canteen*, the first film we made for a studio other than Universal. We finished the Warner Brothers film and literally walked across the street to Decca's recording studios and cut "Don't Fence Me In." It went all the way to the Number One spot on *Your Hit Parade*. It was such a good tune that every other artist wanted to record it, too, and many of them did—Sammy Kaye, Horace Heidt and his Musical Knights, and Kate Smith.

Hollywood Canteen was one of those only-in-Hollywood experiences. The movie was about all the famous entertainers performing for the GIs at the Hollywood Canteen, but the stars never saw each other and the movie wasn't filmed at the Hollywood Canteen.

The movie was shot in sequence, meaning that the performers never appeared together. We sang three songs in it: "Don't Fence Me In," "At the Hollywood Canteen," and a cute novelty number about getting sore feet from dancing with the GIs at the canteen, called "Corns For My Country." The producers had Patty playing the guitar as we sang "Don't Fence Me In," but in truth, Patty never played a note on a guitar in her life.

We never saw any other star from the movie, but Bette Davis and the other stars never did, either. And the producers re-created a set that looked like the Hollywood Canteen instead of filming at the Canteen itself.

This was pretty heady stuff for three sisters who still couldn't read music. We were mobbed in every city on our tours, but another visit back to our hometown produced mixed emotions for us.

We were returning to the Orpheum Theater, where we won our first contest, a kiddie revue that started our careers. In 1944, we went back with Mitch Ayres and his orchestra for a one-week stand and some rest and relaxation at Lake Minnetonka. It was a sentimental journey back to the town of our girlhood, with memories of our old neighborhood and Franklin Junior High and North High School.

During our week back home, thieves broke into our car while it was parked outside the Musicians Club on Glenwood Avenue and stole $1,250 worth of clothing and other items, including two theatrical makeup kits.

June Allyson was becoming a regular at the Hollywood Canteen. She was a newcomer to the movie colony after moving there from her hometown of Pelham Bay, New York, just above the Bronx, where her family was, in her words, "very poor." She made her first movie, *Best Foot Forward,* during the war after appearing in it on Broadway. Then came her first big movie role, in a wartime musical, *Two Girls and a Sailor,* with two co-stars who have remained her lifelong friends, Gloria DeHaven and Van Johnson.

In the last year of the war, she made regular appearances at the Hollywood Canteen with the man she'd just married, Rich-ard Powell, the popular actor and singer. They sang at the Canteen together, choosing mostly "Richard's songs," June remembers2—"I Only Have Eyes for You," "42nd Street"—

which he starred in—and "Shadow Waltz," plus the Glenn Miller favorites.

When we ran into each other in Hawaii at Christmas of 1992, after both of us appeared on cruise ships, we got to spend some time together. It was flattering to hear June say something I'd never known—she always wanted to be one of the Andrews Sisters.

"I didn't think I could sing well enough," she said—although her millions of fans would disagree with her—"but I *really* wanted to sing with them."

In guest appearances?

"No. I wanted to be an Andrews Sister myself. My wish was that they could become a quartet and I'd be the fourth singer."

Like the rest of us, June also spent time visiting the wounded in the military and veterans hospitals. All of us received at least a few real jolts on some of those visits. On one trip, June received a double shock. It happened on a visit to Mare Island, an amputee center near San Francisco.

The first came after she sang a few songs in a ward. "They used to wheel in a piano and somebody to play it, and I'd sing some of the popular songs for these wounded men in their hospital beds. After my performance of the day at Mare Island, there was no clapping. They just whistled. I thought to myself, 'Oh, they didn't like me.' Then I saw the explanation. Most of them had lost at least one hand, and many of them didn't have either hand. So they weren't able to clap. That's why they whistled."

In another ward later that day, June was asked to visit a paralyzed GI who was in a private room. They gave some "don'ts" before she went in: don't cry, don't say you're tired or that your feet hurt, and don't complain about anything else.

The soldier hadn't spoken a word in months, since being admitted to the hospital. June went in and sat with him for a few minutes, trying to say whatever she could think of and avoiding anything negative.

Then, in what sounds like a scene from one of her movies, she began to cry. The fatigue that came over all of us from time to time during those long days and weeks of countless visits caught up with her. The fatigue was never just physical. There was great emotional stress as you spent days and weeks visiting seriously wounded men, young men, with their whole lives still in front of them but lying there in front of you shattered in body and spirit. Sooner or later, it had to affect you. It just had to.

The strain caught up with June as she sat there next to this man—this kid, really—who was paralyzed from his neck down. She started to cry, despite her best efforts not to. She was honest about it with the young man in the bed and said to him, "They told me not to cry and not to say I'm tired or that my feet hurt. But I *am* tired, and my feet *do hurt*, and I'm just going to sit here and cry. I can't help it."

At that moment, the man who had not spoken a word in three months, said to June, "And they told you not to do that."

He continued to talk, never returning to his mysterious silence. June's theory is that he saw that she was being completely honest with him, that she felt sorry for him, but she felt sorry for herself, too. "Maybe he resented all that sympathy and appreciated my honesty," she said.

The hospital sent flowers to June later as a thank-you for getting the man to come out of his shell. From that flowered a friendship by mail that lasted more than ten years. The two wrote to each other regularly. June sent him pictures of Richard and the kids. And he always responded from his home in Pennsylvania, with his mother taking dictation and putting his words on paper for him. His paralysis was permanent.

☆

By now many American couples had been separated for two or three years. In our shows on tour, LaVerne, Patty, and I began getting requests for a new song that described the growing longing of so many husbands and wives and sweethearts to see each other again. It wasn't really written because of the war. In fact, it wasn't written during the war at all, but in 1938 for a Broadway musical that flopped, called *Right This Way.* Tamara, the Russian singer who was killed in the 1943 crash of the USO entertainers in Lisbon, sang it on Broadway. Hildegarde sang it several years later, but it never became a big hit until 1944 when Frank Sinatra recorded it with Tommy Dorsey's orchestra and Tommy's velvet smooth trombone. "I'll Be Seeing You" hit the top spot on *Your Hit Parade.* The music was written by Sammy Fain. Irving Kahal's words told the story of the way so many American couples felt in 1944:

> *I'll be seeing you in all the old familiar places*
> *That this heart of mine embraces all day through:*
> *In that small cafe, the park across the way,*
> *The children's carousel, the chestnut trees,*
> *The wishing well.*
>
> *I'll be seeing you in every lovely summer's day,*
> *In everything that's light and gay.*
> *I'll always think of you that way.*
> *I'll find you in the morning sun,*
> *And when the night is new,*
> *I'll be looking at the moon,*
> *But I'll be seeing you.*

CHAPTER FOURTEEN

Victories and Rumors

Bing Crosby and the Andrews Sisters were a busy combination in 1944, with Decca recordings of additional hits like "Accentuate the Positive," a novelty tune that everyone had fun with called "One Meat Ball," and several big songs like "Lullabye of Broadway," "Don't Blame Me," "Great Day," "Down In The Valley," and "Red River Valley." "Shoo-Shoo, Baby," was one of our tunes whose title wound up on the noses of American war planes as they flew into battle. That was also the year when we recorded one of our biggest hits ever, a song that the GIs got a special kick out of, especially when they made up their own words, "Rum and Coca-Cola."

We sang for the troops over the radio again, via Armed Forces Radio and its worldwide broadcasts. We appeared on its popular show, *Command Performance*, singing three numbers including a tune popular with the GIs, "K-K-K-K P." We sang on another AFRS show, *Lower Basin Street,* and in November we appeared with Bing on still another AFRS program, *Mail Call.*

For the Andrews Sisters, the ending of 1944 was a beginning. On December 31, we started our own radio show, *Eight-To-The-Bar Ranch*, co-starring the cowboy character actor, George "Gabby" Hayes. We were backed, as usual, by Vic Schoen and his orchestra, and our announcer was Marvin Miller. It was a half-hour show, broadcast Sunday afternoons at four-thirty on what was then called the Blue Network, which later became ABC Radio.

Our sponsor was Nash-Kelvinator, makers of refrigerators and other kitchen appliances—all of them hard to get in wartime. To the surprise of absolutely no one, our first guest was our old friend and recording partner, Bing Crosby.

It was a banner year for Bing, too. In addition to the phenomenal success of his records and his soaring popularity as a singer, he won the Academy Award for his performance with Barry Fitzgerald and Ingrid Bergman in *Going My Way*.

For Bing, it was typecasting. He was an Irish Catholic and an enthusiastic baseball fan, and in the film he was cast in the role of Father Chuck O'Malley, a baseball-loving priest. In the film, when he was teaching music to his parish kids and otherwise giving them his time, affection, and good example, Bing wore a St. Louis Browns baseball cap and warm-up jacket.

Barry Fitzgerald almost stole the show from both Bing and Ingrid Bergman, one of the premier acting beauties of those years. He played the role of Father Fitzgibbon, the pastor of debt-ridden St. Dominic's parish.

Going My Way established Bing as a legitimate actor, and LaVerne, Patty, and I couldn't have been happier for our friend. *Life* magazine said the movie "launches him on a career as an actor who is only incidentally a crooner."

Another singer who traveled overseas for the USO, Nelson Eddy, one of the most popular tenors of the era, began a radio show of his own on CBS every Wednesday night at 10:30 P.M., Eastern war time. The show was sponsored by a hundred and sixty electric light and power companies and was called, to no one's surprise, *The Electric Hour.* The show was another sign of the times. Eighty-five percent of its fan mail came from girls and women.

The USO's Foxhole Circuit was one of the busiest parts of the Camp Shows operation by 1944, composed of three other circuits, each bringing specialized forms of entertainment to the troops in the States and overseas. The Victory Circuit produced full-size plays and full-dress musicals. The Blue Circuit was composed of Tabloid Troupes—small, mobile units of variety acts. The Hospital Circuit consisted of various kinds of performers who toured eighty general hospitals in the United States.

Like the rest of the USO Camp Shows, the Foxhole Circuit was an enormous undertaking. In its first three years, the circuit presented 40,000 performances for our GIs, totaling 3,818 weeks of entertainment.

One of those people who brought so much joy to all of us, GIs and civilians alike, met a tragic end as 1944 was coming to a close.

Glenn Miller, Major Miller by now, disappeared on a flight across the English Channel. Our colleague on the *Chesterfield Hour* had been headed for Paris to begin preparations for a Christmas show for the troops there. We quickly sent our sympathy, and it was heartfelt, to his wife, Helen. But there just didn't seem to be anything else we could do. We felt helpless, and so sad. Glenn was our friend, a man we genuinely liked and admired, and now he was gone, another wartime casualty. It was an enormous loss to all of us, and to the music of America.

His disappearance, on December 15, 1944, one day before the start of the historic Battle of the Bulge, has never been explained. Neither his body nor his plane has ever been found. All we ever learned was that Glenn climbed aboard a small, single-engine liaison plane that evening at an air base west of Cambridge, England, with Flight Officer John R. S. Morgan as his pilot. He was headed across the Channel ahead of his orchestra, the famous Glenn Miller Army Air Forces Band, to supervise arrangements personally for their Christmas show. That was Glenn's demand for perfection reflecting itself again. Another, less demanding conductor might not have gone there ahead of his band, and Glenn might still be with us today. But that wasn't the Glenn Miller way. He wanted to get there early and make sure everything was precisely the way he wanted it to be.

Glenn's plane took off in a thick fog over the English Midlands. Today, almost fifty years later, the public can only assume the plane was either shot down or it crashed because of mechanical problems.

However, a new explanation has been making the rounds in the last few years. The word is that maybe somebody took the plane without authorization to fly Glenn to Paris. There was a lot of that done in those years, with people just taking planes for themselves so they could fly various entertainers and other VIPs wherever they needed—or wanted—to go. The speculation is that somebody helped himself to a plane to get Glenn across the Channel, and our own aircraft spotters, thinking it was a stolen plane involving some kind of sabotage or spy activities—or maybe even an enemy plane—shot it down.

In other words, Glenn could have been shot down by our own Allies. If that happened, then it also possible that the government covered up the story to prevent embarrassment to the Army, or whoever was involved. With so many other entertainers killed in plane crashes, the latest theory about Glenn's disappearance begins to take on some degree of credibility.

Jimmie Baker remembers the night and the fog. "He really had no business taking off in fog like that," Jimmie says—and he doesn't argue with the new speculation about what might have happened to Glenn.

☆

Some of the women who were writing fan letters to Nelson
Eddy about his new radio show were pounding away on their
typewriters as secretaries six days a week. The folks at Smith-
Corona, one of the best known manufacturers of typewriters,
bought a full page in the October 30, 1944, issue of *Time* magazine to offer them this hope:

> For women who want careers, typing is the opening wedge to the
> world's most fascinating professions. For women who plan mar-
> riage, typing brings contacts with the world outside . . . keeps
> distant friends in touch, leads to club, business, and social
> activities that less accomplished women miss.
>
> The War Production Board has included our fourth quarter
> allotment of new typewriters to be made for *necessary* civilian
> use. If you can qualify under W.P.B. 1319, we may be able to
> supply you . . .

Certain items were slowly becoming available again. Electric
irons were showing up in a few places for the first time since
1942, coming off the assembly line at the Westinghouse Appli-
ance Division at Mansfield, Ohio. Price: $8.75.

The War Production Board was trying to start the manufacture of more civilian goods, holding out hope that soon Americans would once again be able to buy bedsprings, vacuum clean-
ers, and aluminum pots and pans, all scarce items since 1941.
But officials cautioned against unrestrained joy, reminding us
that production would be at low levels until the war ended. The
U.S. would produce $45 million worth of these consumer goods
in the fourth quarter of 1944. That was equal to what we spent
on war production in three days.

The continuing scarcity of everything, going back, in the
case of some products, to before America's entry into the war,
had lasted up to four years by the end of 1944. Not all of us were

holding up well under the prolonged strain of such shortages, especially those whose living depended on the availability of these items. The owner of a cigar store in Cincinnati locked his door for the last time in 1944 and posted a sign in his window saying:

> Out of cigars. Out of cigarettes. Out of gum. Out of film. Out
> of stamps. Out of patience. Out of town.

We kept hoping to go overseas on a USO tour, and near the end of 1944, we received word that we were to take physical examinations as a preliminary step toward being assigned to the next overseas tour. We did, and flunked.

To our shock, we were told that our urine contained albumin, which the dictionary defines as "any of a class of complex proteins found in milk, egg, muscle, blood, and in many vegetable tissues and fluids." Like almost anything else, too much of it can be a bad thing, so we were "red-lined" and told we could not be sent overseas.

When we mentioned this to our family doctor, he was as shocked as we were, and his reaction was refreshing: He burst into laughter. Then he said, "I can't believe this."

When we assured him it was true, he said, "Look—don't eat any fried foods for two days. Then come back and see me."

We did. Two days later everything was normal. But it took six more months before we made it across the Atlantic.

In the meantime, there was another way of reaching our men and women overseas and in the States, too—Armed Forces Radio Service. We began appearing on its shows more frequently, knowing that they were beamed to our troops all over the world.

We performed on AFRS shows seven times in 1945 alone, beginning with three appearances in February on *Command Performance*. We teamed up with Bing and Bob Hope on the first two shows. In the first, we sang "Rum and Coca-Cola" and "Don't Fence Me In." On the second, we appeared with Bing again on the big hit we had with him on the juke boxes and the radio broadcasts of that time, "Accentuate The Positive," a Johnny Mercer tune that told us we should "accentuate the positive, eliminate the negative."

Less than a week later we were singing for our troops around the world again and having a lot of laughs, too, with an All-Star cast in a *Command Performance* special called *Dick Tracy in B Flat, Or: Isn't He Ever Going to Marry Tess Trueheart?* We played the roles of the "Summer Sisters" and sang "Apple Blossom Time" with new words to fit the story line.

We appeared with Bob Hope again, this time joined by Louella Parsons, the Hollywood gossip columnist, on another AFRS show, *GI Journal*. In March we played on another *Command Performance* show, this one with Frank Morgan, the character actor who played the role of the Wizard of Oz, and the young sensation who was causing all the "bobby-soxers" to "swoon" when he crooned, the skinny kid from Hoboken, Frank Sinatra.

AFRS had another popular weekly show, *Mail Call*. We were happy to sing three songs for the troops on that show: "Saturday Night Is the Loneliest Night of the Week," "Good-Good-Good," and "Frankie and Johnny." We appeared with Nelson Eddy and the comic singer, Cass Daley.

We were back on *GI Journal* in May, this time with Groucho Marx. We sang something called "Go West, Young Man" with Groucho, and two other numbers by ourselves, "My Baby Said Yes" and "Sing a Tropical Song."

By now we hoped we were getting closer to going overseas as part of a USO troupe. But something else was happening, too. The war in Europe was approaching its end. The question was whether we were going to get there before that happened. We didn't anticipate, and no one else did either except the military brass themselves, of course, that even when the war did end, our troops would immediately be facing another strong enemy: boredom. The USO would be called into that battle, too.

Events were unfolding almost too fast for the public to keep up with as the winter passed and the spring of 1945 approached. Our troops in Belgium and Luxembourg broke through enemy lines on January 3 after being trapped on December 16 in a surprise offensive staged as a last-gasp move by Hitler to pull off a dramatic victory.

It was the Battle of the Bulge, so called because the push caused the Allied lines to bulge during the fiercest days of the offensive, while heavy fog forced our pilots to stay on the ground. More than a million men were involved, with the veteran Allied forces fighting under the command of America's General Omar Bradley and England's Field Marshal Bernard Montgomery. The key road center was at Bastogne. Those who survived—tens of thousands didn't—proudly called themselves "The Battered Bastards of Bastogne."

Hitler, who ordered the attack against the advice of his generals, lost 120,000 men, many of them only teenagers, at a time when he was running out of manpower. Another fifty thousand Germans were captured. Once the weather cleared and the American and British planes could take to the sky, the offensive that pitted Hitler's grassy-green teenagers against the experienced, combat-hardened Allied troops became a mismatch.

On New Year's Eve, the destructive force of our planes and General George Patton's tanks restored the Allied lines and eliminated the bulge. By January 21, Hitler's troops were in full retreat. Thus began the final one hundred days of the German empire, and of Adolf Hitler.

☆

The day before the German retreat, President Franklin Roosevelt was inaugurated for his fourth term, two more times than any other President before or since. FDR stood on the south portico of the White House with his son, Jimmy, a colonel in the Marines, and recited the oath of office as administered by the Chief Justice, Harlan Stone.

The weather and the brevity and austerity of the ceremonies were appropriate in view of the wartime atmosphere and also reflected what we learned later was a concession to Roosevelt's failing health.

It was a cold, gray January day, with snow on the ground. A crowd of 7,800 watched as FDR, defying the rumors about his health, stood bareheaded and delivered one of the shortest inaugural addresses in presidential history. It was 551 words and lasted only six minutes. The entire inaugural ceremony was over in fifteen minutes.

Afterward, Dr. McIntyre told reporters who were asking about President Roosevelt's health that everything was fine. "He's carrying a thunder of a lot of work and getting away with it in grand style." In fewer than three months, we learned different. Ten days after his fourth inauguration, Roosevelt turned sixty-three. It was his last birthday.

In the Pacific, our newest enemies were the "kamikaze" attacks by suicidal Japanese pilots who deliberately crashed their planes, loaded with bombs, on American warships. They were calculated, coordinated missions flown by hundreds of pilots in the final year of the war. The Japanese airmen were proud to bear the title *kamikaze*, the Japanese word for "divine wind," and were honored in enthusiastic ceremonies on board ship or at their air field before takeoff. They wore white scarfs. Some applied perfume. Some had their teeth fixed so they could die in perfect condition. Their raids were fanatical attacks, but the pilots became heroes in the Japanese lore because of their willingness to die for their empire and its emperor. Their reward, they were told, was that they would be able to join their "honorable ancestors."

Their families were expected to find pride and comfort in an ancient Japanese poem, broadcast repeatedly over Japan's radio stations:

> We shall die by the side of our Lord
> We shall never look back.

Back home, LaVerne, Patty, and I were taking a breather from making movies in 1945 and concentrating on our tours and records, so we got the opportunity to see the films that others were making. One of them was *Winged Victory*, based on a highly successful stage play by Moss Hart. The movie ads by 20th Century-Fox said it was presented "in association with the Army Air Forces." The title came from the name of a B-24 Liberator bomber in the Moss Hart production. The movie was produced by one of the giants of his time, Darryl F. Zanuck.

Gracie Fields and the bearded Monty Woolley starred in *Molly and Me,* and Katharine Hepburn and Spencer Tracy were united again in *Without Love.* Dick Powell was getting away from his role as a popular singer and going into the movies as a heavy. In 1945, he appeared with Claire Trevor in *Murder, My Sweet.*

The continuation of the war was having its effect on the logistics of moviemaking. *State Fair,* a musical by Richard Rodgers and Oscar Hammerstein II starring Dick Haymes, Jeanne Crain, Vivian Blaine, and Dana Andrews (no relation), was released in 1945 after some innovative techniques by its producers. It was a 20th Century-Fox film, in Technicolor, which won a strong review in *Life* as a "highly ingratiating musical."

The magazine said its "winsome music, homely comedy, and youthful stars make it first-class entertainment."

The production ran into complications caused by the war. The story is set in Iowa, but by 1945, with the growing restrictions on unnecessary travel, shooting a film on location became almost impossible. This was especially true in the case of a major musical production, with all the equipment and scenery required. For *State Fair,* every scene possible was filmed on indoor sets in Hollywood "with a massive array of props . . . made by propmen out of discarded rubber." *Life* said the result looked "more like a combination of Coney Island, the Saratoga race track, and rich New Yorkers' Connecticut farms than it does like Iowa."

Rodgers and Hammerstein were drawing rave reviews in the Pacific, too. Their 1943 classic, *Oklahoma!,* was packed up and shipped overseas by the USO as a stage play that toured the Pacific for seven months in 1945, starring Robert Lynn as Curley and Gloria Hamilton as Laurie. Few shows and few performers ever received more lavish reviews.

One GI wrote to the USO from his post in New Guinea: "I've seen it four times and have hitchhiked almost two hundred miles for it and would like to do it again and again."

Thirty-four singers and dancers were in costumes. The hit musical attracted twenty thousand GIs at one show and seven thousand at another, the second in tropical rains. The shows were performed at night. During the day the cast did extra duty by touring hospitals and visiting their wards to sing the songs from the show. One patient said their visit was "probably the best medication the men have received since penicillin was discovered."

By 1945, the USO performers were coming into contact with the German prisoners of war at the bases they were touring. One USO singer, Betty Heather, found that out. She also discovered that some of those POWs were hecklers.

While she was touring France, Belgium, and Holland, a German POW told her about Hitler's new weapon of terror, the V-2 buzz bomb that was striking London and other parts of England in a last-ditch attempt to prolong the war.

"Just wait," the POW said, "we have a secret weapon—the V-2. That's going to win the war for Hitler."

Betty gave a convincing—and confusing—answer: "Not so fast, brother. We have V-8."

☆

MacArthur's ground forces continued to advance in the Pacific, reopening the strategically important Burma Road and capturing key locations such as Luzon and Manila in the Philippines, retaking the island of Corregidor and defeating the Japanese in massive invasions of Iwo Jima and Okinawa.

In Europe, the Allies rolled on. After the Battle of the Bulge, our Russian allies captured Warsaw, and the Americans took over the vital Remagen Bridge over the Rhine River, barely before a team of German demolition experts could blow it up. Many military experts and historians agree that capturing the bridge shortened the war by several months.

On April 23, Churchill and Eisenhower watched as American troops crossed the Rhine. Hitler, in what would have been one of the most inhumane acts in the history of the world, ordered the German people to leave their homes and move into the center of Germany to discourage the Allies from continuing their devastating bombing raids. But his own munitions minister, Albert Speer, countermanded the order so he could prevent "an unimaginable catastrophe."

Three days later, the entire Allied front was east of the Rhine, and German defenses were falling apart. The American and English air forces were leading the way, softening up the enemy with massive air raids of hundreds—and even thousands—of planes at a time. American GIs told us later that at times the sky was dark at mid-day, with the sun blocked by so many bombers and fighter escorts in the air at the same time, droning on toward their targets in Germany or returning in triumph.

By now optimism on the home front was running high. Nobody could stop our country, especially in Europe, where the end was in clear view. Americans everywhere agreed about the inevitability of our victory in Europe and the coming day of celebration, "V-E Day." In the midst of all this optimism, a song we recorded for Decca with Bing and Vic Schoen in July 1944, "There'll Be a Hot Time in the Town of Berlin," became more popular than ever.

It was a happy song, an upbeat number that said we were about to win this war, that there was no stopping us now. Despite the enthusiasm, Bing's conduct during the recording session was the same as always—thoroughly professional—so we could produce the best record possible.

Cutting a record with Bing wasn't at all like the recording sessions we had with Al Jolson and Danny Kaye. They broke up the joint any time we recorded with them. There was a touch of irony where Jolson was concerned. Bing idolized Al and wanted to be just like him as a performer. He tried to sing in a deeper voice, and even insisted that we record in the morning so his voice would be deeper, but he wasn't the clown in the studio that Jolson was.

Jolie was always on stage—center stage—and if he could get some laughs by clowning around right up until the recording light went on in the studio, he'd go for them. Bing wasn't worried about getting laughs from the band and the crew in a recording studio at ten o'clock in the morning. That wasn't why he was there. It was strictly business with Bing again that morning when we sang our predictions about that happy time just ahead:

There'll be a hot time in the town of Berlin
When the Yanks go marching in.
I want to be there, boy, to spread some joy
When they take ol' Berlin.

There'll be a hot time in the town of Berlin
When the Brooklyn boys begin
To take the joint apart and tear it down
When they take ol' Berlin.

They're going to start a row and show 'em how
We paint the town back in Michigan.
They're going to take a hike through Hitler's Reich
And change that "Heil" to "Gimme some skin."

There'll be a hot time in the town of Berlin
When the Yanks go marching in.
You could never keep 'em happy down on the farm
After they take Berlin.

In the midst of the growing national euphoria, President Roosevelt's new press secretary, Jonathan Daniels, who had just succeeded Stephen Early after Early's twelve years in the job, told reporters at the White House on March 27 that the President had prohibited unnecessary travel by top government officials to the United Nations Conference on international organization at San Francisco beginning on April 25. FDR said the size of the U.S. delegation should be held to a minimum because of the scarcity of housing and transportation caused by the war. Daniels told reporters that FDR had issued the orders on March 16.

The announcement prompted a rash of another wartime enemy—rumors—with reporters apparently overlooking the information that FDR had issued his orders eleven days earlier. One of the first rumors came from Leon Pearson of International

News Service, the younger brother of Washington columnist Drew Pearson. Leon reported that FDR had ordered all of his cabinet members and other top aides, plus "all diplomatic representatives, to stand by on the alert for a possible immediate victory in Europe."

The *Detroit Times* quickly published an extra edition, with a black-and-red headline proclaiming the great news. The *Chicago Herald-American* did the same thing. The Blue Network's Gil Martyn radio broadcast from Hollywood, proclaimed that a victory announcement "hasn't come yet, but official Washington thinks it will, momentarily."

Fifty-five minutes later, the network retracted the report.

The New York Times was flooded with 2,913 calls in six hours. The War Manpower Commission was also deluged, with calls from citizens who wanted to know if they could quit their essential jobs now and go back to their old ones.

The report proved to be premature, but they were a distinct improvement over the atmosphere four years before. In 1941, we were hearing rumors of war. Now we were hearing rumors of peace.

CHAPTER FIFTEEN

Tears Before the Cheers

By mid-afternoon, April 12 had already been an eventful day. Abe Lastfogel's office in New York issued a press release that began:

> Henry Armstrong, famous boxing champion, has arrived in the China-Burma-India war theater with a special Negro sports unit sponsored by USO-Camp Shows.

The Secretary of War, Henry Stimson, announced that American combat casualties—the total of U.S. men killed in action, missing, wounded, or captured—had reached 899,390 since December 7, 1941. At Yankee Stadium, the Brooklyn Dodgers, after losing to a college team the week before during the worst effects of the manpower shortage on major-league baseball, defeated the New York Yankees in a game that raised twenty-two thousand dollars for the Red Cross.

Overseas, Hitler's Minister of Propaganda, Joseph Goebbels, admitted: "The war cannot last much longer, in my opinion."

Writing in his weekly column *Das Reich,* Goebbels said; "We have sunk very low." He showed the desperation of the Nazi machine by proposing that the Germans resort to guerilla warfare to slow down the onrushing Allied forces. "To gain time in this phase of the war," he wrote, "means to gain everything. Only in this way can the enemy be held. He must be engaged in guerilla warfare and must be made to suffer great loss of blood."

Hitler was revealing the same attitude of desperation, according to the United Press. UP said it had an "unconfirmed" report that a newspaper in Stockholm said it had learned Hitler "and his henchmen personally would lead the Nazis in their Armageddon at Leipzig, throwing all their secret weapons, and possibly poison gas, into a climactic battle to the death."

UP quoted the paper as reporting that the "final, decisive battle of Germany would be fought on the historic Napoleonic battlefield at Leipzig." Its report said, "Hitler, high party members and Nazi *gauleiters* or district leaders intend to die with Germany on the last battlefield."

"Berlin itself," UP said in its dispatch from London, "indicated that the Nazis believe their doom to be at hand." Reporters in London who were monitoring Nazi broadcasts from Berlin heard announcers appeal to Germany's civilians to become spies for the Army, thus indicating that the German Army's intelligence operations were becoming disorganized and useless.

One Nazi broadcaster warned: "Tomorrow your home village may be in the front line without your knowing how this came about." Another broadcaster appealed desperately: "People! To grips with the enemy!"

☆

In Washington on the same day, ranking officers of the U.S. Army were giving the Senate Military Committee the same assessment about the inevitable collapse of the German forces. The Associated Press reported that "high Army officials," testifying behind closed doors, "told senators today the end of organized fighting in Germany probably will come within a few days."

The former dean of agriculture at UCLA, Professor W. H. Chandler, predicted that "the end of hostilities in Germany will not relieve the food situation at all. Actually, the demand for food will be far greater this year than in any previous war year."

Professor Chandler, who was chairman of the County Farm Advisors Home Food Production and Preservation Advisory Committee, urged all Americans to plan "Victory Gardens." He based his concerns on a variety of factors: "The armed forces are farther from their home base . . . . Our armed forces are taking over Germany just at a time when it will totally demoralize their spring planting . . . . Because of the manpower, machinery, fertilizer, and insecticide shortages, a definite shortage in food production is indicated this year."

Senator Burton K. Wheeler, a Democrat from Montana, warned that the black market for meat "is breaking down the confidence of the people in their country." He told a committee investigating food prices: "When you have wholesale black markets and wholesale violations of the law, people lose respect for their government."

On the other side of Capitol Hill, Representative Gordon McDonough, a California Republican, said the recent announcement that child movie star Shirley Temple was engaged to be married was "democracy in action."

Congressman McDonough saw all sorts of wonderful things in her announcement. "We may rest assured," he said, "that democracy is vigorously alive after reading the announcement recently made by Shirley Temple [five days before her seventeenth birthday] that she is engaged to an ordinary American soldier, GI John G. Agar of Beverly Hills, California."

On the other side of the world, the Japanese were showing desperation, too. On the island of Okinawa in the Ryukyu Island chain just south of Japan, the enemy began to open the gates to hospitals "for the insane and lepers," AP reported, "permitting thousands of crazy and diseased inmates to roam through the Okinawa hills." AP said its source for the information was Major Charles Sweet, who said, according to AP, that "more than fourteen hundred insane people and an undetermined number of lepers were turned loose."

On the same day, in Warm Springs, Georgia, a place he visited frequently for the therapeutic effects of its waters on his stricken legs, President Roosevelt, his health the subject of continuing whispers around Washington, died of a massive cerebral hemorrhage at 3:35 P.M., central war time. He had been posing for a portrait by artist Elizabeth Shoumatoff.

The reports about the President's health had been more than just rumors to the insiders in Washington. Secret Service agents were told in January that he was in poor health. The Service took prudent action, telling those protecting the new Vice President, Harry Truman, that they might be guarding a new President on a moment's notice. At the beginning of March, the agents on the vice-presidential detail were notified that Roosevelt might die at any time.

Meanwhile, even the general public was becoming concerned, despite denials from the White House. After his death, *Time* magazine reported: "Months ago, persistent rumors were circulating in Washington the President was in grave physical condition. But because there were official assurances that his health was sound, the people had refused to believe the visible evidence."

But we could see for ourselves, even in those days before television. Americans saw their celebrities in newsreels at the movies, where the news and personalities of the week were the subjects of stories in the same way they are today on the nightly TV news.

"In newsreels," *Time* reported, "the well-fleshed, strong face had begun to look wasted and faintly wistful, and sometimes the firm jaw quivered unaccountably. The ringing radio voice seemed now and then to drag with weariness. These were bad signs, people felt uneasily, but they also felt that the doctors and the White House insiders must know."

The new presidential Press Secretary, Jonathan Daniels, was described as "shaking and white-faced with shock," so Steve Early moved back into his old job temporarily to announce the tragic news to the world. He set up a three-way call to the three press associations—Associated Press, United Press, and International News Service—and told them simultaneously: "Here is a flash. The President died suddenly early this afternoon."

Moments later, the entire White House press corps jammed into the Press Secretary's office. Then Early climbed up on a leather chair and recited the chronology of the last hours in the life of Franklin Roosevelt.

"Extras,"—special editions still being published by newspapers at a time of a major national development even though radio was now a much faster source of news—hit the streets of America within hours. The circulation manager of the *New York Daily News* said: "In all my years of newspapering, I've never seen papers sold so fast."

The *Daily News* and another New York paper, *PM*, devoted their entire front pages to enlarged photographs of FDR. *The New York Times* was on the streets before midnight with five pages on Roosevelt's career, prepared in advance. Other papers had done the same thing ahead of time. The *New York Herald Tribune* dropped all display ads from its pages so it would have enough paper to print an extra hundred thousand copies.

Even one of Roosevelt's arch political enemies, the *Chicago Tribune*, whose editors opposed Roosevelt and his policies with acid bitterness on their pages every day, paid him a tribute. The paper was printed with its front page framed in black.

Readers of the *New York Post* saw the first name at the top of that day's list of those killed in action:

ROOSEVELT, Franklin D., Commander in Chief . . .

Radio moved just as quickly. The news was announced from the White House at 5:48 P.M. Two networks were on the air with the story one minute later. Two minutes after Early's announcement, H. V. Kaltenborn, one of the most prominent radio commentators of the war years, was broadcasting his commentary on NBC.

We got the awful news just before going on the air with Abbott and Costello on their radio show. It was an overwhelming tragedy to all of us in that radio studio. I felt that the whole world had stopped and started to weep. Even Papa cried later that evening, one of only two times in my life that I ever saw him cry. The only other time was when Mama died.

I wept, too. Most Americans did. Our wartime leader, who also was the one who led us out of that terrible Depression in the 1930's, was gone. All of us except FDR's bitterest political enemies felt we had lost a true friend.

One of those enemies was our own Gabby Hayes. He despised President Roosevelt and never made any secret of it, but—wouldn't you know it?—after the writers of our show came up with a beautiful eulogy of FDR, our producers gave it to Gabby, of all people, to read on the air. That struck me as the height of hypocrisy. The producers clearly should have given it to someone else, even a staff announcer, but not someone who absolutely hated the man and was so vocal and public about it. And Gabby should have turned it down and suggested that someone else read it instead. But he didn't.

He did a convincing job of acting. He even got all choked up. It was a long time before I was able to forgive the producers and Gabby for that.

☆

Two hours after the first radio flash, overseas correspondents were reporting the reaction from other countries. Don Pryor of CBS, broadcasting off the coast of Okinawa, where that battle was raging, said he heard a sailor remark: "It's like somebody dying in your own family." Another CBS correspondent, Douglas Edwards, reported from London: "Everyone here wonders if there couldn't be some mistake."

In Rome, reporter Clete Roberts of the Blue Network hadn't heard the news when an American GI walked up to him and said, "The President is dead. I feel so funny. I've got to talk somebody."

At four o'clock the next afternoon, all U.S. radio stations went silent for one minute.

The combination of national shock and grief was almost overwhelming. Almost instantly, our records weren't being played on the radio, and neither were anyone else's. Instead, America's radio stations played only somber chamber music for the next eighty-five hours, until after FDR's burial on the family estate at Hyde Park, New York. Movie theaters shut down for the same period. Thousands and thousands of store owners all over America immediately closed their doors and posted handmade signs in the window:

CLOSED OUT OF RESPECT FOR FDR

Roosevelt was the dominant personality in the entire world in the 1930's and the first half of the '40s. When he died, the shock was felt around the globe. In London, Churchill was interrupted from wartime paperwork at midnight by a secretary who gave him the grim news. His face grew pale, then he lifted his head and said in a soft voice, "Get me the palace."

In Moscow, our ambassador, W. Averell Harriman, was hosting a party when he received the news. He immediately telephoned Stalin's Foreign Minister, V. M. Molotov. In Chungking, China's wartime leader, Generalissimo Chiang Kai-shek, was given the news just as he sat down for his usual 6:00 A.M. breakfast. He left his food untouched and withdrew for meditation.

Roosevelt and Charles de Gaulle of France were never members of a mutual admiration society, but when de Gaulle was informed of the President's death, he immediately went to the U.S. embassy in Paris and signed his name in the register of bereavement.

The intensity of the reaction worldwide may have been expressed most convincingly by the voice of England's BBC—the British Broadcasting Corporation. In that nation that had felt the war's devastation so extensively, with enormous suffering and loss of life over five years, the BBC said the news made the evening "the most tragic night of the war . . ."

Even our military enemies reacted in ways that testified to the domination of the Roosevelt personality and policies on the course of history. Joseph Goebbels told Adolf Hitler with great excitement in his voice that Roosevelt's death was an unmistakable sign that Germany would win the war. Goebbels said he was sure of it, because it was in the stars that things would start turning their way in April.

Japan's premier, Admiral Kantaro Suzuki, broadcast a message in English that surprised many Americans. After all, we were still fighting the Japanese as well as the Germans. But Suzuki said:

I must admit that Roosevelt's leadership has been very effective and has been responsible for the Americans' advantageous position today. For that reason, I can easily understand the great loss his passing means to the American people and my profound sympathy goes to them.

When the train carrying Roosevelt's flag-draped coffin wound its way slowly up the East Coast toward Washington, D.C., one of those on board was FDR's faithful companion, his five-year-old Scotty, Fala. He also attended the funeral service at Hyde Park and barked when the riflemen fired their final salute. During one of the hymns, Fala rolled over in the grass, almost as his own final salute to his master. It was FDR's favorite trick.

☆

Like the death of President Kennedy eighteen years later, the nation was both stunned and sad, but, unlike JFK's, the death of FDR came while we were still deep in a world war, and he was the only leader we had ever had in that war. People were worried that Truman, smaller in inches, might not measure up to Roosevelt as a leader, either.

Truman moved out of his five-room apartment at 4701 Connecticut Avenue in the Northwest section of Washington and into the White House. Four days after Roosevelt's death, President Truman told an anxious nation that "with the faith of our fathers in our hearts, we do not fear the future."

Truman, a Baptist, then read from the Book of Kings in the Bible:

Give therefore thy servant an understanding heart to judge thy people, that I may discern between good and bad . . . I ask only to be a good and faithful servant of my Lord and my people.

CHAPTER SIXTEEN

And Then the Cheers

Not long after leading the nation in prayer, President Truman was entertained at the White House by the Olsen and Johnson troupe, flown there by a young pilot named Bill Lear, who was flying his own twin-engine Fairchild plane. Later Bill would fly his own planes—Lear Jets.

With the war still going on, the troupe staged its madcap comedy for the new President, and Lou Wills, still a teenager, didn't pull any punches. Part of his act was to whip out a pair of scissors and cut off the neckties of several men in the audience. He didn't play any favorites. Doing what he always did—almost automatically—he walked up to the President of the United States right there in the White House and cut off Truman's tie halfway up his shirt, before realizing just whose tie he was destroying in front of everyone. He began to apologize, immediately and frantically, saying in a rush of words, "Excuse me, Mr. President. Oh, I'm sorry, sir. Please excuse me."

Lou's embarrassment and desperation only made the incident funnier. Truman threw his head back and howled, laughing louder than anyone else. Then he had the last laugh.

A short while after getting his tie clipped, the President escorted the group on a tour of the second-floor living quarters. When the elevator came to take them up the one flight, Truman jokingly refused to let Lou get on. He made him walk upstairs while the rest of the troupe rode with Truman on the elevator.

"He had an incredible sense of humor," Lou says today. "He got even with me."

Twenty-six days after President Roosevelt died, Germany surrendered. Hitler wasn't around for the occasion. He shot himself on April 30 in his personal underground bunker, after ordering his staff members to cremate his body in the Reichs-chancellery gardens above, along with the body of his mistress, Eva Braun, who poisoned herself. The two were married in the final forty-eight hours of their lives.

Our long-awaited V-E Day came on May 8, President Truman's sixty-first birthday and the twenty-sixth day of his presidency. Churchill and Truman made the announcement in simultaneous broadcasts. Crowds formed immediately to whoop it up in London, New York, Moscow, and Washington. President Truman addressed the nation by radio from the White House. In a dark suit and dark tie and holding his text in his hands in those days before teleprompters, he looked into the newsreel cameras and spoke into a single microphone on a clean desk:

> This is a solemn but glorious hour. I wish that Franklin D. Roosevelt had lived to see this day. General Eisenhower informs me that the forces of Germany have surrendered to the United Nations. The flags of freedom fly all over Europe. For this victory, we join in offering our thanks to the Providence which has guided and sustained us through the dark days of adversity and into light.
>
> Much remains to be done. The victory which was won in the West must now be won in the East. The whole world must be cleansed of the evil from which half the world has been freed. United, the peace-loving nations have demonstrated in the West

that their arms are stronger, by far, than the might of dictators or the tyranny of military cliques that once called us soft and weak.

The power of our peoples to defend themselves against all enemies will be proved in the Pacific war as it was proved in Europe.

Our joy was almost unrestrained. And winning the war in Europe was only one reason for our elation. All of us knew that there was a second reason: With V-E Day already here, could V-J Day be far behind?

Laverne, Patty, and I were working harder than ever, while waiting for the USO to send us overseas. Bing and the Andrews Sisters were the top selling recording artists in the country.

Immediately after we recorded "Rum and Coca-Cola," Decca sold almost two million copies. In the first six months of 1945, we topped our sales for all of '44. And our weekly radio show with Gabby Hayes and the Riders of the Purple Sage was becoming established as a Sunday afternoon favorite.

Not long after the great news about V-E Day, we got other great news: The USO wanted us to go overseas. We were going to be soldiers in greasepaint at last.

We were thrilled beyond words. We had done so much entertaining of the troops in the states, but we wanted to get overseas, too. We wanted to reach every GI we could. We felt that going overseas was a part of that commitment and was something we should do. Now we were getting that chance.

When the word finally came, it was swift and sure. We received a phone call to get to New York as fast as possible. When we asked exactly where we were being sent, the USO told us not to ask.

The war in Europe had just ended, but things were still hot

and heavy in the Pacific. Maybe we'd be going to Okinawa or Iwo Jima, or the Philippines, we thought.

We were met in New York, taken to a hotel, and then told to go to Saks Fifth Avenue and pick up our USO uniforms. After that, we were asked to report to an address on New York's West Side to audition. They said every act had to audition before it was accepted for a USO tour.

Patty had a quick response to that. She told the USO representative: "The Andrews Sisters don't audition for *anybody*," and that was that. The subject never came up again. We were driven immediately to Fort Dix, New Jersey. There, in the middle of the night, we were routed out of bed and driven under cover of darkness to LaGuardia Airport, where we boarded an Air Corps plane with its windows covered.

We had been issued winter uniforms, so we knew we were headed north. Then we were handed an envelope of papers finally telling us where we were going.

Italy. Italy? Wearing winter uniforms in July? Then we began to feel like Jinx Falkenburg when she arrived in the Caribbean in her winter uniform and carrying a fur coat three years before. Besides, the war in Europe was over. Why did they need us in Italy?

We were told that the Army was more concerned than ever about boredom, afraid that it would become a serious problem with our troops in Europe now that they didn't have a war to occupy their time and attention. Immediately after V-E Day, the Army asked USO Camp Shows to provide one hundred units for duty in the European Theater of Operations by July 15.

Eleven Broadway musicals, twenty legitimate plays, ten concert units, and fifty-nine variety troupes were airlifted overseas in a hurry, adding to the twenty-six troupes that were already there touring hospitals. At the same time that LaVerne, Patty, and I were headed overseas, others were, too—ice skater Sonja Henie, Amos and Andy, Jack Benny, Ingrid Bergman, Bob

Hope, Allan Jones, and the host of one of the first radio quiz shows, John Kieran of *Information Please*.

Camp Shows met the Army request on time. We were going to be part of something big.

We got another hint that things might be, well, unusual, in this experience. We landed in Newfoundland for refueling, and I was excited at the opportunity to see and tour some of the countries I had learned about in geography classes. Except it didn't happen in Newfoundland. We weren't allowed off the plane, and the windows remained covered.

We were told many hours later—it seemed like days—that we had to make another refueling stop. As we made our final approach on that leg of our journey, the windows were uncovered and we looked at the scene below. We were told that the beautiful city down there was Casablanca. Casablanca? Casablanca, Italy?

We were sitting in stifling temperatures inside our plane, in Morocco, not Italy, already dripping wet in our winter uniforms in the July North African temperatures, the only three women, with thirty young second lieutenants who looked as if they were fresh out of Officers' Candidate School and our accompaniment—a pianist and an accordionist. A young-looking major leaned in from the plane's steps and asked, "Which of youse guys are the Andrews Sisters?"

After we identified ourselves, in response to the major's question, he said, "Are youse guys ready?"

"Ready for what?" we answered.

The major said, "In thirty minutes you're supposed to be . . ." and he mentioned some town we'd never heard of. But we were in the Army now, and we knew to do what we were told and not ask any questions, so we didn't. We had waited too long and wished too hard for this tour. We weren't going to do anything that might get us in trouble or cut it short and give somebody the idea to send us home.

We hopped into the major's jeep and were whisked out into the desert, sweating even more now in temperatures of 120 degrees. We ended up in some desolate-looking location with seven thousand American soldiers screaming and yelling at the sight of us. We put on a show right there, with no notice or rehearsal, and were greeted with the same GI enthusiasm that all USO performers received.

We did another show later and put on ten shows over two and a half days in Casablanca, wondering the whole time why we weren't in Naples, which was the destination shown in our papers. We were treated to a tour of the city by the major, including parts of the city which were forbidden to women.

When he took us back to our hotel after our tenth show for GIs all around Casablanca, the major found a cablegram waiting for him. That's when we finally were able to piece things together and find out for ourselves why we were in Morocco instead of Italy. Suddenly our young major became flustered, then very official, in his best Army behavior. I thought he was going to salute us right then and there.

He quickly grabbed the nearest telephone and said to the party on the other end in a snappish way, "Book this troupe on the next plane to Naples. We have to get them out of here in an hour."

Then he told us to get packed and get ready to leave right away. Packing wasn't much of a problem. We didn't have much clothing, except for our professional wardrobes, which we still hadn't worn yet. We made all those appearances in our winter uniforms, still never saying a word to anyone because we didn't want to get shot at sunrise.

The major hurried us in his jeep from our hotel to a waiting plane, without a word during the whole ride. After we arrived in Naples, we found out the reason for the sudden change in his behavior: We had been kidnapped.

The major in Casablanca had intercepted us while our plane

was being refueled and grabbed us so we could entertain his troops instead of letting us continue on to Naples, where we were supposed to be. And he got caught. We were AWOL—Absent Without Leave—and we got chewed out for it when we landed in Naples, but that major back in Casablanca was in a whole lot worse trouble than we were.

What the officers in Naples might not have known was that we gave two other unscheduled shows before we ever got to Naples. The troops were hungering for entertainers, and everyone was grabbing whatever performers came through their post. Our first unscheduled stop on the way from Casablanca to Naples was in Oran, and a million-to-one shot came through when we landed. The first GI to greet us was Harold Wrightson. All of us recognized him right away. He was the boy next door, literally. He lived next to us in Minneapolis when we were growing up. When he greeted us, I asked him whatever happened to that little boy I used to play with? But I knew the answer—he had just finished fighting a war for us.

☆

The USO tour was one of the highlights of our career, but that didn't mean everything went flawlessly, or that we had a fun time seeing the world on our own terms. Just the opposite was the case. The USO sent their entertainers overseas with a long list of strict "rules and regulations," as they say in the Army. And as if the USO requirements weren't enough, we were also placed under Army discipline. The briefing materials they gave us and the laws they laid down made us feel as if we had enlisted in the Army itself instead of volunteering to serve in the USO.

One Briefing Memorandum prepared for USO representatives carried a clear message. The memorandum, prepared by N. W. Dreschler, one of Abe Lastfogel's associates, said, "I can assure you that the reputation of your unit will be fixed within thirty days after your departure from New York, and if you are a bad or difficult unit, you surely will not get, nor could you expect to get, any of the best of the breaks. If, on the other hand, you people will behave yourselves properly, you will have enhanced your chances of making the better tours and you certainly will improve your living and feeding conditions throughout the tour. Your reputation will precede you throughout the area."

Dreschler's memo continued: "You must remember that you are in the hands of the Army and/or Navy, that you are not officers, but that you are in fact civilians attached to the Army." This meant, "that while you have no privileges of rank, you are under obligation to obey Army regulations and are under the provisions of the Articles of War."

We were told to travel only in Army transportation "without question" and to travel as a unit at all times from our living quarters to our performances and right back to our quarters, with no side trips. "You will not be permitted to have guests with you in this transportation," the memo said, "and there will be no stage door Johnnies or visitors backstage."

We were not allowed to take civilian clothes on our tour and could not be seen outside our quarters "in anything other than the official uniform as given to you here in New York by Camp Shows." Within the privacy of our quarters, we could "dress as you please, but not in civilian clothes, so long as you are decently clothed."

Women members of the USO troupes were allowed to wear scarves on our hair, "but these scarves must be the regulation Army drab. No other colors will be permitted." On these and all other matters, the memo said flatly, "the decision of the Army is final and not subject to explanations."

On the positive side, we were "required" to visit the enlisted men's rec halls and mess halls after our performances, and that was just fine with the Andrews Sisters. That's exactly what we had been doing the whole war anyhow.

On the other hand, visits to officers' clubs were not obligatory. The memo went beyond that, saying that even on such visits, no performances were allowed. "You will under no circumstances ever perform at an officers' party, dance, or club," it said. "If you are urged to do this, your manager must point to the Army directive which specifically prohibits such use of our entertainment."

We were given a booklet before going overseas, *A Guide to the Foxhole Circuit,* published by USO Camp Shows. The booklet was a compilation of suggestions based on the experiences of those performers who had gone overseas before us. Its introduction stressed that the booklet "does not emanate from a swivel chair in an air-conditioned office with the sound of battle far away. It is based on the sweat and blood of fourteen hundred entertainers who have gone overseas before you, over the hot, grinding circuit of the foxholes. What they discovered is put down to guide you. What the War Department asks you to do is also put down, so that you will not unknowingly play into the hands of the enemy."

By now USO Camp Shows had grown to include offices in New York, Chicago, and Beverly Hills. The stars worked as unpaid volunteers, with many of them recruited through the Hollywood Victory Committee. Other, lesser known performers, who were either beginners or had not reached star status, were paid salaries, but in every case much lower ones than they were making in their show business careers.

Some of the most basic things in life had to be spelled out in preparing to go on a USO tour. Women, for example, were given a specific list of what they could take or buy from the Army's Quartermaster Depot at their Port of Embarkation. Some of the items on the approved list, in typical GI lingo, were:

Anklets, wool
Stockings, beige cotton, rayon

Stockings, knee length, wool
Pajamas, winter (WAC)
Slip (WAC)
Panties, winter, summer (WAC)
Vest, winter (khaki)
Shoes, service, low; field
Overshoes, low; arctic 4-buckle
Gloves (dress leather, olive-drab wool, WAC work cotton)
Shirt, HBT, Special
Trousers
Sweater, WAC, Nurses' coat style
Cap, wool, knit

To this day I don't know what a "shirt, HBT, special" is.

We were given some helpful tips about what to take and what not to, what to do and what not to. The restriction against civilian clothes did not apply when we were on stage. On the contrary we were told: "The most important baggage is your stage wardrobe. A GI doesn't want to see you in slacks, and he's not interested in your uniform. He wants to see you look like the girls back home on an important Saturday night date. Remember that, and take your best clothes with you."

We were encouraged to take artificial flowers for our hair because "they make wonderful souvenirs." We were told that a tap dancer, Edith Delaney, "always got a big hand when she finished her act by tossing out the red poppies she always wears in her hair."

Bobby pins were an essential item, and we were encouraged to pick up an extra bottle of nail polish and a reserve supply of cosmetics. "You'll need cold cream," the booklet said, "as you've never needed it before."

Then there was this practical hint for those women who believed that gentlemen prefer blondes: "One thing you definitely won't find in a PX is a bleaching agent. The GIs are not trying to be blondes. So either take along your own peroxide or make up your mind to stay brunette until you get back home."

Strict censorship was imposed on us for the duration of our tours. We weren't even allowed to keep a diary. Everyone was forbidden from showing up for their departure with any family members or friends. Our mother was strongly opposed to our trip because there was always an element of danger, and when we told her we didn't know where we were going or how long we'd be gone, that only made her more worried, and more opposed.

We weren't allowed to take a camera, but I did. Nor were we allowed to sit in the cockpit of the plane. That, in fact, is where I spent most of my time. I took my cameras—three of them— and sat up there across from the pilot and clicked away to my heart's content.

The pilots went out of their way to accommodate my photography and would ask me if I'd like to fly here to get a picture of this spot, or there for another interesting shot. My photography wasn't always as good as their flying. As a result, I took what may be the only photograph ever made of the Leaning Tower of Pisa standing straight up.

We were treated to the inevitable inoculations before departure: smallpox, typhoid fever, tetanus, and the rest. I told a reporter during the weeks before we were notified to report to New York that my arms felt like a couple of toothaches.

We were also given a long list of "don'ts." We were told not to complain, which should have been obvious to anyone who remembered what the members of our audiences were putting up with, and I never heard anyone do it. One "don't" that surprised some of us was the suggestion that we "don't wave the flag." But the reason made sense: "The men you're playing to don't need pep talks. They'll do the fighting. You do the entertaining."

For the many hospital visits all of us made, we were told not to sympathize too much. "You can show your sympathy without putting it into words. No soldier likes to be wept over in public."

Another suggestion, and it seemed like a little thing to some people but we were always aware of it anyhow, was to "refrain from using the word 'boys.' " The USO booklet pointed out what all of us should have had no trouble remembering: "The Army has put a great deal of effort into making these 'boys' men."

We were told to "keep it clean," and the booklet included a reprint of an editorial in the GIs own newspaper, *Stars And Stripes*. "Call it sentimental," the editorial said, "but when the doughboy thinks of girls from home, he thinks of his mom, his sister, or his best girl. He's seen enough of the other girls. Girls from home have to be nice."

The USO's booklet emphasized its point: "Here is a good guide: Keep your material as clean as if you were going to deliver it on a radio network. Whatever you do—KEEP IT CLEAN! Use Good Taste!"

There was another matter to be considered: censorship. Every act had to be reviewed before it went overseas, so the Army could approve of the material and then make sure it wasn't deviated from at any point in the tour. "All speaking and singing members of units must submit in writing for approval the material they will use," the USO's booklet for us said. But ours never was reviewed, thanks to Patty's emphatic statement about auditions before we left on our tour.

In *Home Away from Home,* Julia Carson wrote: "The show is reviewed by the Army's Special Service Division (Entertainment Branch). Vulgarisms, double entendres, and references to race, color, and creed are not permitted."

Violators were dealt with swiftly. "When the script has been approved," Carson continued, "it cannot, under the regulations, be altered during the tour. Occasionally, a script has been departed from. When on rare occasions proof of improper behavior in changing a script has been made clear, the guilty performer has been promptly ordered home."

Patriotism was fine, but with the USO and the Army it was not enough. Performers were required to sign an Oath of Secrecy, contained in the Espionage Act. We were cautioned that any performer convicted of violating the oath would be sentenced to one of two fates: a prison term of up to thirty years, or death.

The pledge said:

> I solemnly promise that I will not collect, record, publish, communicate, or divulge to anyone not entitled to receive same any information which may directly or indirectly come into my possession as a result of my entrance upon a military or naval reservation under the sponsorship of USO-Camp Shows Inc. or otherwise—with respect to the movement numbers description, condition, or disposition of any of the armed forces, ship, aircraft, or war materials of the United States, or with respect to the plans or conduct or supposed plans or conduct of any naval or military operations, or with respect to any works or measures undertaken for or connected with, or intended for the fortification or defense of any place—or any other information relating to the public defense which might be useful to the enemy.

That seemed clear enough to us, even if it did sound like something written by a Philadelphia lawyer. But just in case any performer didn't understand it fully, or thought maybe it was just a routine reminder that we could forget as soon as we got overseas, the USO booklet gave us a firm warning: "Remember that oath. This is war, and the Army means what it says."

The USO also appealed to our sense of patriotism, which was why so many performers were volunteering to go overseas as part of a USO troupe. The *Guide to the Foxhole Circuit* told us: "When you sign up for an overseas tour, you are giving yourself an opportunity to serve your country and your fellow Americans. In this great war for freedom, you are putting your name down on the list of those who have fought to win." Then the booklet mentioned the thought that has stayed with every one of us USO entertainers in the fifty years since: "When peace comes again to the world, it will be good to know that you found your place in the struggle."

CHAPTER SEVENTEEN

Over There

From the minute we arrived in Casablanca and then Naples, we remembered some excellent advice from Bing. During a recording session with him the afternoon before we left for New York, recording "Along the Navajo Trail" and several other songs, he gave us several helpful tips based on his own USO overseas tours. Bing was never one to give out a lot of advice, so when he did, we listened.

"Don't ask for *anything*," he said. "Sing for the guys because that's what they want, but don't ask for anything special." We agreed with Bing's advice wholeheartedly. We knew what we were overseas for, and it wasn't special privileges. We were there to sing for the guys. Period.

Our first show in Italy was at Caserta, in the same opera house where Enrico Caruso, the world-famous operatic tenor, made his major debut. Our stop there was uneventful except for our enthusiasm over singing in the same concert hall as The Great Caruso.

We went from the sublime to something else at our next stop. We were quartered at the Pink Palace, a real-life palace—

alone. It may have been the nurses' quarters, but there wasn't a nurse in sight. They were living in another location, so LaVerne, Patty, and I had the whole palace to ourselves; among rows and rows of cots, all of them empty.

LaVerne made sure to pick the cot between Patty and me. LaVerne was always afraid of being alone. As the oldest child, she had the fringe benefit that every kid yearns for—her own room. Patty and I shared a room, but it was not unusual for us to wake up in the middle of the night and find LaVerne between us.

For most of our tour, we were based in Caserta, a town north of Naples. In addition to our surplus of cots, we discovered we had another surplus—toilets. A building designed to house that many women had a corresponding number of toilets, a situation that we were able to convert quickly into a major bonus for our GI buddies. All performers were given a weekly allotment of nine bottles of beer. LaVerne, Patty, and I didn't drink anything alcoholic back then, not even beer, but we came up with an idea that the soldiers thought was a stroke of genius.

We were allowed twenty-seven bottles of beer for the three of us every Friday. We put them in all those toilet bowls to keep them cool in the water. The GIs would visit us every day, but they were not allowed in our quarters, so we'd pull a few beers out of the toilets and sit on the steps of our building and enjoy bringing the guys up to date about things back home—while they drank our beer.

We were enjoying the luxury of having our own beds. For most of our tour, we had only one bed, with never more than two pillows, sometimes only one. We frequently had the impression that the Army and the USO thought the Andrews Sisters were either one woman or Siamese triplets. And we were sure that those pillows were really rocks with pillowcases over them. We never complained, though, not even to each other. We were well aware that we weren't living any better than most of the GIs, and we never forgot the hell that most of them had gone through during the war in Italy. Crowded conditions for sleeping and two hard pillows for the three of us weren't enough to make us gripe.

Most of our shows were in Naples. We were scheduled for only one show a day, but, as always, we did three or four, sometimes more. After our last show, some of the guys would invite us to visit the Orange Club, a private room above a restaurant, where the waiters were Italian prisoners of war from our American prison camps.

We put on impromptu shows at the Orange Club, for the three or four GIs in our group, and they would sing along. It was never work to us. We wanted to sing as long as even one soldier wanted us to. We were as happy when we were singing for them, or with them, as they were listening or joining in.

It was clear to us that the GIs never wanted us to stop. We could see it in the looks on their faces. Many of them were unshaven and wore grimy fatigues, still looking like what they were—soldiers, mostly kids, who had just fought a bloody war and had seen a lot of their friends get killed around them.

They were tired. They wanted to go home. And they faced another danger: There was a strong possibility that they would be shipped out to the Pacific to fight another war, in our final big push to defeat the Japanese.

When our tour took us to Rome, we discovered that others were singing for *us*. We woke up on our first morning there, and we could hear voices coming from below. We went to the window of our hotel and looked out, and there were forty or fifty people in the street below, singing "Roll Out the Barrel" in Italian. It was their way of welcoming us.

Our afternoon wasn't nearly as pleasant as that morning. We encountered our first experience with military discipline shortly after we started out, innocently enough, on a quiet walk in the mid-day heat of a Roman summer. As required at all times, we were in our USO uniforms, the winter ones we were issued, with our jackets over our shoulders, our neckties loose, and our collars unbuttoned, happily noticing everything we could in downtown Rome. Our walk had lasted only a few minutes when a young officer coming from the opposite direction stopped us and starting snapping questions.

I've always believed he stopped us because we were women. Maybe he recognized us and decided to impress anyone within hearing distance by putting on a show of his own. The Italian campaign had been one of the longest and heaviest of the war, so in those first days after the war, no one was concerned yet with rigid adherence to the proper method of wearing a necktie.

Except for this juvenile General Patton. He blocked the sidewalk so we couldn't walk around him, and barked at us, "Put those jackets on!"

We didn't know whether to salute him or slap him, but we thought the smart thing would be to do what he said. We put our jackets on while he supervised. Then he looked at our lapels and barked again. "Where are your insignia?"

I gave him an honest answer: "Mine are in my pocket."

"Well, they weren't given to you to put in your pocket! Pin them on!"

We started to put them on in a hurry. As we were, he barked, "And button up your collar!"

When we started to do that, it was: "And tighten your tie!"

Then he stepped around us and resumed his walk down the sidewalk, apparently all barked out.

☆

During one scary night, next to Lake Garda, between Milan and Venice, we were missing in action—or was it *inaction?*—but the world never knew it. We had finished our last show at midnight, and a couple of GIs drove us out to an open field next to Lake Garda, where our plane, *The Stars and Stripes*, was due to pick us up. It was a C-47 cargo plane, named after the daily

GI newspaper, which had its own planes to deliver the paper to American forces all over the world every day. It was our transportation throughout our stay in Italy. We had been offered our own private plane for our tour, but we said no thanks. We were happy to make do with one that was already going our way.

After the guys drove us out to the field, they apologized and said they couldn't wait with us because they had to get back to camp, so they took their jeep and left.

In the first hour, we enjoyed the beauty of the night and the tranquil sound of the lake's waters lapping up on the shore. Our appreciation of the sounds that reminded us of the lake country back home in Minnesota gave way to real fear after that first hour. We were all alone in the middle of nowhere, next to a lake, with no car, no protection, no nothing, knowing that plenty of people still had guns and ammunition left over from the war. And we had no idea of when our plane would show up.

We sat close together in the dark and tried to keep calm by talking about our tour, but we were genuinely scared. We reminisced about the folks back home and how sitting there by that lake reminded us of our summer vacations with our uncles Pete and Ed.

I was always supposed to be the brave one, so Patty and LaVerne snuggled up closer to me, Patty on one side and LaVerne on the other. It might have made them feel safer, but it didn't do a thing for me.

As dawn began to break—just before we did—*Stars and Stripes* finally arrived, four hours late. We got no apology or sympathy from the crew, which didn't necessarily surprise us, and no explanation, either, which did. The pilot and co-pilot made it clear to us they were upset that they had to pick us up. It didn't matter to them that we were the ones who should have been upset. But that was only part of the story.

When we reached our next destination, we were immediately called on the carpet by a Major Greenberg because we were four hours late, and he didn't care whose fault it was. Greenberg turned out to be the brother of one of our friends in show business, Mort Green, a comedy writer for radio shows in New York. The major didn't want to hear that we knew his brother and worked with him back in the States. He wanted to chew us out, and he did. I wondered if he might be related to our friend in Rome who had those definite ideas about our uniforms and how we should wear them.

We tried to explain to Greenberg, but it was useless. Then he threw us to the wolves, in the person of a General White. The general threatened to bring us up before a court-martial board on charges of insubordination, even though we had been sitting in that field doing exactly what we had been told to do—waiting for our plane.

The members of the crew of *Stars and Stripes* were the guilty ones, and I started to tell that to General White. "It didn't happen that way," I began.

He cut me off with a sharp, "I'm not interested."

His remark made it obvious to all three of us that these two guys wanted to stand there in front of three young civilian women and play soldier. The smartest thing for us to do was to shut up and let them have their fun. But that didn't make it right. This was sex discrimination, pure and simple, and today they wouldn't get away with it. We knew even in those days that we were being put through their wringer simply because we were women. If we had been three men, that whole incident never would have happened, and we knew it.

When their little game was over, the general and the major graciously allowed us to leave—so we could do more for their troops than they apparently did. Then they could head down to their officers' club, perch on a stool at the bar, and tell their fellow officers how they really let the Andrews Sisters have it.

It made us believe that some of the other tales of horror the GIs had told us must have been true. They had told us on different occasions about women performers in USO troupes who never got the best of it if they didn't cooperate with various suggestions from the Army officers. We heard one story about a troupe that mysteriously had its travel schedule changed and was left to perform at some remote outpost for six months because they refused the not-too-subtle suggestions of the Army officers who controlled their transportation, and even their fate.

The whole episode left us with renewed love and respect for the enlisted men.

☆

In Italy we were scheduled to give a show every night, but we always exceeded that. We wound up doing two, three, or four shows a day on our own. We'd see fifteen or twenty GIs and they'd ask us to sing something for them, and we'd be off and running with another impromptu show. Sometimes we'd find two or three noncommissioned officers—and we'd have a little singalong right there in an NCO club that was almost empty.

Our hearts belonged to the enlisted men. We remembered our orders from the USO briefing materials not to worry about entertaining the officers and to stay out of their clubs. That was fine with us. We weren't there for the officers anyhow. We were there to sing for the troops.

Not every entertainer felt that way. Arthur Treacher, the British actor who later starred in *My Fair Lady*, was one of the exceptions. We had the same impression of him that Anne Jeffreys did when she toured with him in Texas earlier in the war. He seemed very stuffy, somewhat like some of his roles. He obviously didn't enjoy being around the GIs. At various stops on our tour, people would ask us where he was and we'd say we didn't know—but we did. We knew he was at the British Officers' Club.

Arthur even got somebody to fly him back to England for a little private R&R during the middle of our tour. Once he even

said to me, "If you want to go to Greece to look up some of your
relatives, I can get you a plane to take you there."

I told him I didn't know if we had any relatives there.
Besides, I told him, we didn't speak Greek. Those responses
were my way of telling him that I felt we were overseas to work
hard and entertain the guys instead of scheduling some nice
vacations for ourselves and forgetting about our mission.

Despite going without a shower for too long and primitive
living conditions and meals on the run and adventures in the air
with some of the Air Corps' hotshot pilots, we enjoyed our USO
tour as much as our GI audiences.

Every audience lived up to the reputation that USO audiences had—the best any entertainer or singer ever performed
for. The small groups of only three or four that we sang for
obviously couldn't make the noise that a thousand could, but we
could still see and feel their enthusiasm and appreciation.

The guys seemed to sense that we were on the same wave
length as they were. As a result, they went out of their way to
show us every respect and to give us every consideration, such
as the time we arrived at a new stop on our tour and there waiting
for us on the back of a flatbed truck were three combat helmets.
One contained hot water, one held cold water, and the third had
soap chips. These things were rare, almost nonexistent, and the
soldiers were sharing these scarce items with us so we could
enjoy the luxury of washing briefly with warm water and soap.

At another stop, a small group of grateful GIs traded three
cases of pineapple juice to some English soldiers for one case of
White Horse Scotch. We used the Scotch as a way of saying
thank you when somebody did something extra nice for us. Once
we poured some of it out to a few guys who somehow managed
to come up with three fresh eggs for us, something you rarely
saw over there.

The gravest danger we faced wasn't on the ground. It was
when we were on *The Stars and Stripes*. The pilots were kids,

and they always liked to see how fast they could take off or how close they could come to the trees at the end of the runway. They were terrific pilots, even if a little too adventurous for us at times. Still, we could never quite get over how young the men were who were responsible for our traveling safety. We took off on one flight, and I noticed that the pilot was wearing gold maple leaves—a major. We were still only in our twenties ourselves, but I remember looking at him and thinking to myself that he couldn't possibly be twenty years old.

Except for their late arrival at Lake Garda, the pilots were extremely accommodating, sometimes almost too much. They liked to take the boredom out of flying. Once the pilot asked us if we wanted a thrill, and we said sure, so he flew us around the crater of Mount Vesuvius, the active volcano on the Bay of Naples. When we were talking about it at dinner that night, one of the men at our table said we had been lucky. He told us there were terrible downdrafts inside the volcano, and we could have been sucked inside the crater and never been found.

At one of our stops, we played before a combined audience of seventy thousand soldiers at a racetrack in southern Italy that Mussolini built to house the 1940 World's Fair, which never took place. We did five shows there, and each time we looked out at fourteen thousand grateful and cheering GIs.

At another stop, however, some of the soldiers almost didn't get to see the show. In fact, at one point, there was a strong possibility that all of them would miss out, because there almost wasn't a show.

A band of black musicians was on the same bill with us. They were already playing when we arrived, so we jumped into our stage clothes and started putting on our stage makeup, which was a waste of time, of course, because we were in an open field in daylight. That meant there were no lights, and that we didn't need any makeup, but we had it half on before we realized we were wasting our time, so we had to finish the job. As I was applying mine, I looked out from the wing and saw a mass of humanity, a standing-room-only crowd—GIs everywhere, even in some trees off to the side. But then I noticed something strange. Right there in that SRO audience were three vacant rows. Not just any three rows—the front three.

I spotted a second lieutenant near us and asked him why the first three rows were empty.

"They're for the officers," he said.

I gave him a blunt contradiction: "No, they're not."

"What do you mean they're not?"

I told him we wanted the members of the band who were playing to be able to sit in those first three rows and enjoy the rest of the show just like all other GIs.

The lieutenant said: "Oh, they'll find something out there." That was obviously impossible. Even all the trees were taken. It was a clear case of prejudice—and not just one case but two. These professional musicians, who were soldiers like everyone else in the audience, were being discriminated against because they were enlisted men, *and* because they were black.

I talked with LaVerne and Patty. We agreed that we would not go on stage until the musicians were seated in those three front rows. I was elected to give the lieutenant our ultimatum. "My sisters and I agree," I told him. "There will be no show until all of the musicians are seated in the front rows."

"I can't do that."

"Then there will be no show. We're not here to entertain the officers. I'm sorry, but those are our instructions. We're here to entertain the GIs. Are all of these men GIs?"

"Oh, yes."

"And so are these musicians," I reminded him.

The lieutenant was determined. "I'm sorry, but they're not going to get those seats."

I was determined, too. "Well then, *I'm* sorry. We're not going to do a show."

The audience waited for a half-hour, while the lieutenant found his superiors and they held a meeting. Then he came back and said, "Okay, you can do the show."

But I said again, "Not until they're seated."

At long last, the musicians were allowed to take their seats. They filled every one in those first three rows.

☆

I had to be firm on two other occasions, but these episodes were with individual GIs who were making a request we couldn't honor. A cook with a Brooklyn accent pulled me aside after one of our shows, as we were washing up backstage, and asked if I could do him a favor.

"That depends," I told him.

He reached into his pocket and pulled out a wad of money and said, "I've got thirty-five thousand dollars here that I won last night in a crap game. I have to get it to my mother. Can you take it to her?"

"I'm sorry," I said, "but I can't help you."

He persisted: "Look, you take half and give her half. This is more money than she'll ever see in her life. I'm afraid if I keep it I'll lose it tonight."

He told me I could put the money in my shoes, my stockings, and in my clothes. "They'll never know." But with my luck, they'd find it and put me away somewhere for a long time. Besides, we were forbidden from taking anything back to the States for any GI.

Instead, I offered to write the guy's mother a note. I apologized to him backstage and to his mother in the note.

Another GI, also with a Brooklyn accent, made the same request at a later stop. He wanted to get his winnings home so his family could save the money for his education. I had to refuse him, too.

There was another element involved in these requests. You

never knew where the money was coming from, where it was really headed, what it was going to be used for, and who the guy was who was making the business proposition.

The new American intelligence gathering agency, the Office of Strategic Services—OSS—was always giving us reminders to be careful in situations like that. We didn't know whether the money might really be coming from a transaction instead of a typical GI crap game and whether organized crime or some other international group might be involved.

Besides, LaVerne, Patty, and I were always aware that those guys, even if they were telling the truth, were singling us out because they figured we were just three dumb kids from Minneapolis.

Everywhere we went, the ravages of the Italian campaign were all around us. The environment was always the same—bombed-out buildings, craters in the roads, telephone poles and streetlights blown all over the place, and the poor Italian people, the innocent victims, standing in their homes literally without a roof over their heads—in doorways that didn't have doors and at windows that were now just empty holes in the wall.

The numbers told us the story of that long and horrible battle of the two hundred and fifty thousand American soldiers in ten divisions, twenty-five thousand of them killed, eighty thousand wounded. The fiercest fighting had been in Anzio, Florence, Cassino, and Rome. It took our GIs nine months to get halfway up Italy's boot and eleven months before Germany surrendered.

It's hard to determine who remembers our performances with more affection and nostalgia—us or our audiences. I remember how well behaved the GIs were while we were on stage. The boys would come up onto the stage after we were finished and say things like, "Do you mind if I kiss you on the cheek?"

Or they'd give us a big hug. But they never, never would leave their seats while we were performing. After the hell they fought in and survived, they were still respectful and polite.

I'll always remember the last day of our tour, back in Naples. But that's not why I remember it so well. It would be the day the war in the Pacific ended—V-J Day.

By then, everyone knew it was only a matter of months or weeks, maybe only days or hours, before Japan would surrender. We were pounding the Japanese empire into defeat, and there was no letup. One thousand U.S. planes bombed Tokyo in one day. And that was only the bombing from the air. Admiral "Bull" Halsey's Third Fleet commanded a heavy naval bombardment only three thousand yards off the Japanese mainland from his fourteen warships—aircraft carriers, battleships and cruisers. They sat within easy reach of the Japanese shore guns north of Hokaido, yet none returned the American fire. Then we dropped history's first two atomic bombs on Hiroshima and Nagasaki.

We did many of our shows at the depots where all the guys were shipped out after a long, bloody, and hard war in Europe. Our last show was packed with eight thousand GIs, and it was the unhappiest audience you ever saw. Those guys knew they were being shipped out to another long, bloody, and hard war, the one in the Pacific with Japan. Some of them hadn't been home for four years. We were just trying to put them in good spirits.

Patty was doing a scene with Arthur Treacher when a soldier motioned me offstage and said he had a very important message for Patty to read to the audience. I started to laugh. The GIs were always pulling tricks on me, and this probably was another one. But the soldier saw I was still suspicious, so he said, "I'm not kidding. It's from the CO."

I told him I couldn't do it in the middle of the show, but he pleaded with me, saying, "You're going to get me into trouble."

So I took the paper and walked out onto the stage without reading it, thinking that now I was the one who was going to get into trouble—with Patty, Treacher, and the CO, too. When I got out there, Patty was expressing the same kind of objections to me that I had expressed to the GI, but she finally gave in.

Then Patty told the GIs, "Look, there's a big joke going on up here. I have a note *supposedly* from the CO." Without looking at it first, she read it out loud. It announced the end of the war with Japan.

There wasn't a sound in that whole depot. Patty wasn't sure of just what had happened, so she looked at the note again. Then she looked at me. It was beginning to dawn on her that the message really was on the level. This was V-J Day.

She looked out at the audience again and said, "No, fellas— this *is* from the CO. This is an announcement that *the war with Japan is over.* You don't have to go to the Pacific."

With that, she started to cry. So did I. So did LaVerne. Still, there was no reaction from the audience. Patty said it again: "This is the end! This is the end!"

Suddenly all hell broke loose. Those GIs yelled and screamed. We saw a pair of pants and a shirt come down from the rafters where men were crammed together above the stage, followed by a human being. He fell on the guys sitting in the audience, but he didn't care and neither did his human cushions.

Then Patty asked the GIs, "Do you want to go out and get drunk? Or do you want to see the show?"

The audience hollered back, "We want to see the rest of the show!"

So we finished. Aware that this was a moment in history, we kept our act short. After all, this was both our last performance of World War II and our first performance in the new world of peace.

CHAPTER EIGHTEEN

The Lights Went on Again

The surrender document was signed by the American and Japanese officials at 9:08 on Sunday morning, September 2, aboard the battleship *U.S.S. Missouri* in Tokyo Bay. It was a cloudy day, but the sun came out as the last members of the delegations signed the sheaf of documents.

Twenty American generals were on hand as General MacArthur signed for the United States. One of them was General Jonathan Wainwright, the hero of the brave stand by American soldiers and those of the Filipino Army on the peninsula of Bataan and the island of Corregidor in the Philippines three and a half years before. After withdrawing from Bataan on April 9, Wainwright, nicknamed "Skinny," had the humiliating responsibility of surrendering our troops to the Japanese on May 6, 1942, on Corregidor and was their prized prisoner of war for thirty-nine months.

MacArthur ordered his new American staff in Tokyo to "have our country's flag unfurled" atop the U.S. embassy, "and in Tokyo's sun let it wave in its full glory as a symbol of hope

for the oppressed and as a harbinger of victory for the right."
The flag that the staff members raised was the same one that flew
from the dome of the U.S. Capitol in Washington on December
7, 1941.

The peace treaty called for unconditional surrender by
Japan, the release of all prisoners, and the unlimited authority
of MacArthur to govern Japan through its years of recovery. Just
in case the Japanese had an eleventh-hour change of heart, U.S.
war planes stood on alert with eight thousand tons of bombs,
ready to take off for Japan on a moment's notice if such a
command should be radioed from the *Missouri* at the last minute.

The treaty was signed by more than representatives of the
United States and Japan. Officials from Great Britain, France,
Australia, Canada, the Netherlands, New Zealand and Russia,—
which had joined the fight against Japan only twenty-five days
earlier—also signed. The other nations had credentials which
qualified them to be co-signers. Canada had fifty-three thousand
men stationed in the Pacific during the war. New Zealand had
ten thousand members of its Air Force, one-third of whom
became casualties.

☆

When our USO tour was completed, the trip home—and
even the attempt to find someone willing to get us there—was as
exciting as the rest of the tour, but in a different way. The Army
played its favorite game with us again: "R.H.I.P.—Rank Hath
Its Privileges."

When we reminded the colonel in charge of our transportation in Naples that our tour was completed and we had to get
back to the States, he suddenly developed an acute shortage of
airplanes. This was a critical problem for us, because we had
signed a contract to begin a radio show with Bob Crosby, Bing's
brother, for Campbell's Soup. We were to appear on Mondays,

Wednesdays, and Fridays, and Margaret Whiting would be the star on Tuesdays and Thursdays. It was going to be a thirty-minute show, fifteen minutes on the air and another fifteen minutes just for the studio audience.

We had to get to California quickly or we'd lose the contract. The USO knew it, and so did the Army.

When I pleaded with the colonel, he shrugged me off with the greatest of ease. I was getting desperate, so I said, "You can't do this to us."

"Oh yes I can," he said, with a smug smile. "I'm in charge."

After a few seconds, he suddenly developed an inspiration. "However," he said, "some of my boys and I are having dinner together tonight. If you and your sisters would care to join us and sing a few songs, I might be able to find a plane for you."

Patty, LaVerne, and I went into a huddle. We agreed that we *had* to get to California. We also agreed that we had no choice. We were being forced to sing for this guy and his underlings, or else we'd lose our radio series. We performed.

When LaVerne, Patty and I came back home just in time to save our contract, we returned to a United States that was already different. Instead of checking the daily casualty lists in their hometown newspaper, Americans were taking pad and pencil to figure out how many points their loved ones had accumulated to see how soon they would qualify for discharge from the service under the government's newly announced "points system." Instead of reading about more items being rationed, we were reading about those coming off the rationed list. Instead of singing songs of war, we were singing of peace. And instead of fearing the unknown, we looked forward to it.

State Fair was one of the popular movies, despite its prefabricated props that *The New York Times* complained about. *Rhapsody in Blue* was another hit film, with Joan Leslie, Charles

Coburn, Alexis Smith, Al Jolson, Hazel Scott, Oscar Levant, Paul Whiteman, and Robert Alda, the father of Alan Alda, star of the *M*A*S*H* TV series thirty years later. *Guest Wife,* with Don Ameche, always a popular actor, was another popular film as we quickly made the adjustment back to our peacetime routine.

There was a new radio quiz show, *Detect and Collect,* but the Capehart and Farnsworth manufacturing company was telling us that something new called television was on its way, and people began to predict that the new medium, which Americans immediately nicknamed "TV," would kill radio. A large ad by Capehart and Farnsworth in *Life* showed four members of the New York Yankees playing their sport with a bold headline proclaiming:

HOME RUN IN YOUR LIVING ROOM—BY TELEVISION!

Americans were thrilled at the picture painted by this ad and others. Under the headline, the ad excited us by stating flatly, "From the comfort of your living room, you'll watch the runs that win the pennant, the champ's knockout punch, closeups of the great moments of sport, news and entertainment . . ."

As if that weren't enough, the ad also promised that "many of the new models will include full-toned FM." At the bottom of the ad, more than a month after Japan's surrender, was a reminder in italics that the war still had to be paid for:

Keep on Buying War Bonds

Not all the ads were up-to-date. Frigidaire kitchen appliances ran a display ad in the same issue saying, "Frigidaire, now busy in war work, is dedicating its resources to building materials to speed a complete and final victory." The only problem with that ad was it appeared five weeks after our "complete and final victory."

Ford was getting us excited with its ads, which gave us the long-awaited news about new cars: "Production has started but is very limited. More cars soon." We were excited even more by its new slogan, one that was especially appropriate then and remained the theme of Ford's ads and commercials for many years in the postwar period:

THERE'S A FORD IN YOUR FUTURE!

General MacArthur, looking very much in command of everything, looked out from *Life*'s cover, dressed in his trademark khakis, without a tie as usual, his five stars in clear view. He had a stern expression on his face. The first time MacArthur was on *Life*'s cover was the day after Pearl Harbor. The reason his photo was on the cover this time told the story of the outcome in the Pacific: He was the first foreigner to rule Japan.

On the back cover of the same issue, Camels cigarettes ran a full-page ad saying proudly:

Army, Navy, Marines and Coast Guard—wherever they go in their winning of the war, they have first call on Camels.

The ad told us about Camel's "T-Zone," with the "T" standing for both taste and throat. Camels told us: "Only your taste and throat can decide which cigarette tastes best to you . . . and how it affects your throat."

☆

Wars produce heroes of many kinds, many of whom aren't even in the armed forces. In this war, some of the heroes wore a different uniform, the USO's. The 293,000 performances presented by the USO came from 4,484 professionals in every field of the arts.

The sick and wounded weren't forgotten. If they couldn't come to the shows, the shows came to them. In 1944 alone, the Hospital Circuit of USO Camp Shows gave 5,444 performances for 850,537 patients at 79 hospitals. The Victory Circuit entertained another 352,000 patients. By the end of the war, USO performers had entertained 3.3 million patients in 192 hospitals.

There were 702 units entertaining our GIs on tours that lasted from three weeks to six months. In those days of segregation by race and sometimes by gender, the roster of USO troupes included twenty "all-Negro units" and sixteen "all-girl units."

Maybe the most heroic of all was Gertrude Briefer, a tap dancer who performed for our GIs overseas for twenty-three months, traveling one hundred fifty thousand miles on eight trips to different countries. Myles Bell and Nan Bedini were gone for twenty-one months on six trips overseas that covered one hundred thousand miles. And my good friend, Jo Andrews Bernier, logged almost three years over there and many more months over here, extending back to the days before America entered the war.

Not all of the heroes were performers on stages or flatbed trucks. Don Barclay was a hero, too. He was an artist who took his pencil and sketch pad literally around the globe to draw sketches of our GIs for them to send to their folks back home in the States.

When we got a break from our postwar radio show, we returned to one of our favorite spots, the Paramount Theater in New York. Forty-second and Broadway never looked better. The war had changed so many things that it was refreshing to see that the area around New York's famous Times Square remained the same. It wasn't the same, of course. Postwar life is never the same as it was before. We were headed for problems caused by inflation, labor unrest, a lack of housing, the entrance into the labor market by millions of women workers—not all of whom wanted to go back to working in the home—the inevitable "baby boom," more racial strife, and the start of a tense relationship with Stalin and his Russian dictatorship in what Winston Churchill called the Cold War.

None of this was visible to us average Americans in those first heady days after the war ended. As far as most of us could tell, things would be the same. Even our daily routine was the same as before. We were up for breakfast by ten, after getting back to our hotel around midnight after our last performance of the night before. Our first show went on at noon, with LaVerne, Patty, and me on stage for fifty minutes. We were back to doing four shows a day during the week, five on Saturdays and Sundays.

We also rehearsed for an hour and a half every day after our first show, learning new songs and new routines and preparing for our radio show. After our second show, Patty and I would cave in on a massage table or do some shopping. We never had much time between shows, so we had to take care of our errands or shopping in a hurry. We once set a record of our own by buying two dresses and two hats each in twenty-eight minutes.

Coming back to our civilian routine was almost like a rest after our USO tour. We never seemed to be able to slow down in Italy. We were there to work as hard as we could for the guys in our audiences, and when we got back, over here, we figured out that we had been on stage for the equivalent of six months of shows in those six weeks.

When we returned to the Paramount, the theater gave us special treatment by building a ranch scene for our act, to go along with our *Eight-to-the-Bar Ranch* radio show with Gabby Hayes. We appeared in white cowgirl outfits, with fringe on our sleeves and the hems of our skirts, and full-sleeved white chiffon blouses and western boots.

Even with the national feeling of joy and relief that the war was over, the GIs we met and sang for overseas were still on our minds. A soldier we met at our first show in Italy told us the thing he missed most of all was good American Jewish salami. When we got back to New York, it dawned on us that we were in the Jewish salami capital of the nation. We told the story to the Paramount's stagehands, and they immediately went out and bought three salamis for us to send to the GIs still in Italy. We hung them up in our dressing room until we had time to ship them overseas.

In the meantime, Paul Denis, the Broadway columnist for the *New York Post*, interviewed us in our dressing room and saw the three salamis hanging there, so he wrote in his column: "When you visit the Andrews Sisters backstage at the Paramount, bring a salami with you." We picked up several more from that mention in the paper and shipped the salamis to our waiting GIs overseas. If there is one place in the world with more salamis than New York it's Italy, but when it comes to keeping a promise to an American soldier in a foreign land, laughable ironies like that one don't make any difference.

As the excitement, and the challenges, of the "postwar period" came over the horizon in 1945 and '46, Patty, LaVerne, and I began singing the new hits, songs that didn't have anything to do with war.

The Big Band Era was coming to an end, although we didn't realize it. In a sense, the big bands, which did so much to keep our young people, especially couples, emotionally bound together across the miles of their separations during the war, were also a casualty of the war. Many of the musicians were eventually separated by their wartime military service, and their bands simply had to go out of business. At the same time, people couldn't drive to night clubs to dance to their music during the war because of the gasoline shortage.

In 1946, many American young people were beginning families, and counting their pennies, and millions of the returning servicemen were starting college with their tuition paid for by the government under the new GI Bill of Rights. They didn't have any spare change for going to a night club on Saturday night. And the saddest reason of all for the fading of the big bands was that their leader, the most famous leader of all the big bands—Glenn Miller—was gone.

The emphasis now was on a bumper crop of outstanding vocalists instead of on the bands playing behind them: Perry Como, Nat "King" Cole, Dinah Shore, Frank Sinatra, Margaret Whiting, Andy Russell, Lena Horne, Buddy Clark, Vaughn Monroe, Pearl Bailey, and Bing, always Bing. They, and we, were singing "Linda," "I Can't Begin to Tell You," "Rumors Are Flying," "Winter Wonderland," and "You're Nobody 'Til Somebody Loves You."

As we flew back to California, I was aware of a combination of emotions and reactions stirring within me. Soon I would be with Lou and Dutchie, our adopted daughter, again. She was six months old now, so I wondered how much she had changed in the time we'd been gone. Almost two months had passed, and children change so fast, especially when they're infants. I'd be seeing Mama and Papa again too, and Lou, Dutchie, and I would be a family once more.

I looked out the plane's window at the checkered Midwestern farmland ten thousand feet below. The view was one of stark contrast compared to what we had seen from our *Stars and Stripes* plane in Italy. There were no bomb craters on those farms down there, and no bombed out buildings. The cities we flew over were standing and vibrating with activity. The homes were undamaged, and most of the people living in them had not seen the horrors of war or been its victims.

As Americans, we had reason to be thankful, even with 405,000 of our young men killed in action, another 670,000 wounded, and 139,000 more who were imprisoned for months and years as prisoners of war or were missing in action. We had paid a heavy price, and too many families had been called on to make the ultimate sacrifice, but we were still free, and our nation was still whole and healthy.

On the surface, nothing had changed. It had, of course. I knew it. I felt it. Our USO performances, over here and over there, made me grow up, which should not have surprised me. After all, America herself grew up in World War II. I felt aware of my new maturity as a person. I had never seen starving people before, or bombed out buildings, or children playing amid wartime debris in their streets with no clothes on because they didn't have any, and other kids begging for food to give to their parents, who had no home for them.

I didn't know how Patty and LaVerne felt, but experiencing what we did in Italy during our tour jolted me out of the dream world of the Andrews Sisters, just as the war itself jolted Americans out of their dream world of believing we were safe from any overseas nation just because we have an ocean on each side of us.

The war had threatened our freedom and that of many other nations, and we had defended it successfully and sent the evil men who started it to their deaths. No sane American enjoyed fighting the war, but every one of us had reason to rejoice in our victory. That tour, however, and the experience of seeing the results of war with my own eyes made me hate it more than ever and convinced me that it is never the answer to any problem between nations and their leaders.

As our plane continued its westward flight, I hoped World War II had made the earth a better place, but I wasn't sure—and that's what was bothering me. I was afraid too many people might still hate each other. Too many might still judge others by their color or what church they go to or whether they go at all, or where they come from or how much money they make. Too many might still want to take land and other possessions that didn't belong to them.

I was afraid that the war we had just won might not be the war to end all wars any more than the one before it. And I was unsure about what kind of world Dutchie and any other kids we might be blessed with would live in, especially in the new "atomic age."

These fears and uncertainties gnawed at me as the Andrews Sisters flew home. Maybe they had been welling up in me before we went overseas and I just didn't know it. Maybe they would have floated to the surface of my thoughts and emotions even if we hadn't gone overseas. Whatever the reason, I wasn't thinking or worrying about these things before Patty, LaVerne, and I flew to Casablanca and Italy two months before, but now I was. Still, I reminded myself, the war was over and maybe people would work together now to make it a better place for all of us.

Many people were thanking America's entertainers for what we contributed to the war effort both here and overseas. So many had done so much, and all of us had reason to be proud of ourselves and our profession. None of us felt that we deserved a medal. We simply did what millions of other Americans did. We served our country in the best way we could.

That's what made those four years special, and keeps them so today. We worked together, fought together, served together, and in too many cases died together for our country and our freedom. Maybe that sounds corny today to some people, but it is a matter of history—and fifty years ago, nobody called it corny. Instead, it was the only attitude to have, and the only one that was acceptable.

The words of a song from our war seemed to be the best expression of our peace. As Americans sang "When The Lights Go On Again" the first time around, right after its release in

1942, the world was a dark place. We had been thrust into a new, strange, and frightening life of air raid drills and blackouts, of rationing over here and young men dying over there.

Vaughn Monroe sang the song with his orchestra, with the words and music by Eddie Seiler, Sol Marcus, and Benny Benjamin. It was Vaughn's first big hit, and the words described our longings in that first year of the war. Every American yearned for the day when the lights of the world would go on again, especially in the symbolic sense.

Now that great day was here. The victory and peace we fought and died for over almost four years was ours. Throughout those years, maybe more than in any other period of our nation's history, we really *were* the *United* States, a unique blend of American unity and spirit that future generations will be able to admire but may never be able to equal.

And so we sang:

> *When the lights go on again*
> *All over the world,*
> *And the boys are home again*
> *All over the world,*
> *And rain or snow is all*
> *That may fall from the skies above*
> *A kiss won't mean "goodbye,"*
> *But "hello to love."*
>
> *When the lights go on again*
> *All over the world,*
> *And the ships will sail again*
> *All over the world,*
> *Then we'll have time for things like wedding rings*
> *And "free" hearts will sing,*
> *When the lights go on again*
> *All over the world.*